Apostles of Greed

APOSTLES OF GREED

Capitalism and the Myth of the Individual in the Market

Allan Engler

Fernwood Publishing
HALIFAX, NOVA SCOTIA

Pluto  Press
LONDON • BOULDER, COLORADO

First published 1995 by Pluto Press
345 Archway Road, London N6 5AA
and 5500 Central Avenue, Boulder, Colorado 80301, USA

First published 1995 in Canada by Fernwood Publishing
PO Box 9409, Station A, Halifax, Nova Scotia, B3K 5S3

British Library Cataloguing in Publication Data
A catalogue record is available from the British Library

ISBN 0 7453 0950 X hbk

Library of Congress Cataloging in Publication Data
Engler, Allan, 1938–
      Apostles of greed: Capitalism and the myth of the individual
in the market / Allan Engler.
      p.   cm.
Includes bibliographical references and index.
      ISBN 0 7453 0950 X hbk
1. Capitalism. 2. Big business. 3. Liberalism. 4. Conservatism.
5. Supply-side economics. 6. Economic policy. 7. Economics—
History. I. Title.
HB501.E62 1995
330.12'2—dc20   94–49044
                                                                   CIP
Canadian Cataloguing in Publication Data
Engler, Allan, 1938–
      Apostles of Greed
      Includes bibliographical references and index.
   ISBN 1 895686 53 9
      1. Capitalism. I. Title.
HB501.E63 1995   330.12'2   C95–950068–5

99 98 97 96 95   7 6 5 4 3 2 1

Designed, typeset and produced for the publishers by
Chase Production Services, Chipping Norton, OX7 5QR
Printed in the EC by T J Press, Padstow, England

Contents

Preface

I began writing *Apostles of Greed* in 1981 while working as a cook on British Columbia coastal towboats. During two week periods of twelve-hour days cooking for a crew of six, I was left with three or four hours a day to study the books I brought with me. Alternating two-week periods at home gave me time to write.

Why would a towboat cook write a book on capitalist social relations and free market theory?

Class politics, social history, economic theory have interested me all my adult life. I grew up in Saskatchewan in a trade union family and joined the Cooperative Commonwealth Federation (CCF) – the socialist governing party in the province – when I was 15. In 1956, a scholarship from the company that employed my father sent me to the University of Saskatchewan. My intention was to study economics and mathematics but I soon became more interested in Karl Marx. After taking a year off to work as a newspaper reporter on my hometown daily, *The Moose Jaw Times Herald,* I spent a second year at the university and then moved to Ottawa where I worked for two years as a technician in the National Research Council. I also got involved in the formation of the New Democratic Party – which brought official trade union support to what had been the CCF.

In 1962, Jean Rands joined me in Toronto where we were active in the New Democratic Youth and then in the League for Socialist Action, a Trotskyist group. In 1964 we moved to Vancouver. Our political activity revolved around opposition to the war in Vietnam and support for local trade union struggles. By 1968 Jean and I had come to reject the idea of a vanguard party. Jean participated in women's groups. I tried to win new radicals to a traditional anti-capitalist perspective.

By 1970 our home had become a centre for feminist trade unionism. Jean got involved in strikes to win collective bargaining rights for restaurant workers and was active in successful campaigns to organise support staff in British Columbia universities and colleges. Later in the 1970s Jean was a leader of the union that initiated a widely supported but unsuccessful attempt to organise bank workers. My role was to urge other trade unionists to support these efforts and when needed to hand out leaflets and walk picket lines.

Otherwise, my interest turned to early twentieth century revolutionary syndicalism and to the 1917–21 workers' council

viii   *Apostles of Greed*

movements. With Joe Irving, I worked on an often revised and
never published manuscript 'Beyond Leninism'. We argued that
centralised state control remained a system of domination of
majorities by minorities and concluded that anti-capitalist movements would have little appeal to working people until they
advocated democratic management of social labour.

Meanwhile, more of my time was taken up by my own trade
union activity. In 1973, I began working on towboats, first as a
deckhand, then as a cook-deckhand, and finally as a cook.

In 1981, shaken by the election of Margaret Thatcher and
Ronald Reagan, I decided to write a pamphlet exposing the class
roots of the neoconservative reaction. To explain the Keynesian
policies that were being abandoned, I went back to the *laissez
faire* ideas of the nineteenth century – to Marshall, Jevons, Walras
and Mill – and then to Marx, Ricardo, and Smith. To explain
Smith I went back to Locke and Mandeville. By 1983, I had
written 500 pages. These included sections on the historical
origins of free market theory, on the inequities of the present-day
global market, and on the central role of corporate oligarchs in
the neoconservative reaction, as well as material on long-wave
business cycles, on the relevance of Marx's labour theory of value
in a world of great disparities in customary wages, on the need to
restructure unions to combat the wealthowners' offensive, and on
a democratic and pluralist alternative to capitalism.

By the end of 1984, Thatcher and Reagan had been elected to
second terms. Brian Mulroney was prime minister of Canada.

In 1987, I was elected secretary treasurer of the local. This
full-time position included responsibility for the union hiring hall
as well as the general duties of a union representative. I found
negotiations, grievances, and union administration a challenge.
Successes clearly benefited the individuals and groups involved.
Still, it was frustrating to see how constrained the union was by
forces beyond our control.

By 1990, I had become convinced that a major problem was
labour's failure to provide an alternative to capital's vision of the
individual in the market. With the intention of devoting my free
time to writing, I returned to towboat work. The following year,
employers succeeded in forcing the union to accept the elimination of cooks jobs on most towboats. Cooks' duties were
assigned to cook-deckhands. Although I was shaken by the loss
of my employment, the severance package gave me the means and
time needed to complete this book.

Introduction

George Gilder's 1981 best-seller *Wealth & Poverty* captured the spirit of the neoconservative reaction that was sweeping Britain, the US, and Canada. Starting from the premise that 'a successful economy depends on the proliferation of the rich', Gilder urged that governments abandon the welfare state and tax policies designed to redistribute income. [1]

Unregulated capitalism should not be feared because,

> giving is the vital impulse and moral center of capitalism ... The unending offerings of entrepreneurs, investing capital, creating products, building businesses, inventing jobs, accumulating inventories ... constitute a pattern of giving that dwarfs in extent and in essential generosity any primitive rite of exchange ... Successful entrepreneurs ... are the heroes of economic life, and those who begrudge them their rewards demonstrate a failure to understand their role and their promise.

David Stockman, Director of the Office of Management and Budget for Ronald Reagan, said *Wealth & Poverty* 'shatters once and for all the Keynesian and welfare state illusions that burden the failed conventional wisdom of our era'. It is 'the best thing written on economic growth in fifteen years'. President Reagan gave the book to senators.

Gilder had also said that politicians would be more likely to 'comprehend the dynamics of capitalism and the necessity of great rewards for triumph against great odds' if they were 'paid at least four or five times their current salaries'. [2]

Politicians weighed the arguments and voted themselves higher salaries, bigger tax-free expense accounts and generous pension benefits. In return they voluntarily abdicated responsibility for economic wellbeing. This, they agreed, is best left to private individuals in free markets.

As urban centres decayed, social services deteriorated, and chronic unemployment and homelessness worsened, politicians shrugged and said there was nothing they could do. Deficits were already too high. Raising taxes would leave private enterprise with even less money to create jobs. A new global reality had to be faced.

Neoconservatives like Margaret Thatcher, Ronald Reagan and Brian Mulroney insisted that the new reality required a new way of looking at the world. Was neoconservative ideology new? True, for 40 years until the 1970s, most economists and politicians had believed that full employment and aggregate demand were the responsibilities of government. The prolonged depression of the 1930s had convinced economists, politicians, and even business leaders that government had to protect the victims of capitalist markets. Tentative theories of oligopolistic or 'imperfect' competition were elaborated to explain deviations from free market models. Theories of a managerial revolution challenged individualist entrepreneurial assumptions.

Neoconservatives dismissed early twentieth-century experience, but the ideas they turned to were far from new. Friedrich Hayek and Milton Friedman consciously set out to revive nineteenth-century *laissez faire* beliefs. To make the case that governments should not intervene in economic affairs, they appealed to the authority of Adam Smith's theory of the beneficial effects of market forces. Smith's *The Wealth of Nations* was published in 1776. Its propositions were rooted in John Locke's glorification of private wealth and Bernard Mandeville's claim that public prosperity is a product of private vices.

1 The Origins of Competitive Market Theory

From Bernard Mandeville to Adam Smith

Bernard Mandeville was born in Holland in 1670. He moved to London in the 1690s, a few years after his countryman William of Orange became King of England. In London he worked as a physician to the rich and powerful, specialising in the 'hypocondriack and hysteric passions'.[1] He mastered English, wrote a treatise on his medical speciality, and translated fables.

In 1705, Mandeville published a doggerel poem called *The Grumbling Hive: or Knaves Turn'd Honest*. The hive, ruled by a constitutional monarch, was plagued by 'sharpers, parasites, pimps, players, pick-pockets, coiners, quacks, and soothsayers'.[2] Its lawyers encouraged feuds and shared the resulting business among themselves. Its doctors were more concerned with fame and wealth than with the health of their patients. Its priests were known for laziness, avarice and pride. Its soldiers and generals, while able to defeat all the hive's foes, took bribes, conspired with enemies and padded payrolls. Its justice system allowed some to go free and hanged others for the same offences. In short, everyone cheated everyone else.

Despite some grumbling, the hive was generally happy, prosperous and industrious. This good life came to a sudden end when righteous church bees, who had been making a good living deploring vice, had their prayers answered. Sinners were transformed into saints. As the bees gave up their pride and avarice and stopped cheating and stealing, bees producing luxury goods lost their jobs. The price of land and houses fell, employment in the trades dried up. Very soon the virtuous hive could support only a hundredth part of its population.

The *Grumbling Hive* at first generated little interest. When it was reissued with added commentary in 1714 as *The Fable of the Bees: or, Private Vices, Publick Benefits*, it caught the attention of churchmen and was denounced from pulpits. Socially conscious clerics were appalled by the attack on charity schools. Mandeville responded in a tone of disbelief. Why would any of the better sort of people sincerely advocate educating workers? Doesn't studying encourage habits of indolence and make people unruly? Doesn't knowing how to read – even reading the bible – make workers think they can rise above their station. Doesn't prosperity depend on the willingness of the poor to labour long hours with little pay? By organising charity schools for workers, churchmen are undermining the prosperity of their country. More conservative churchmen were scandalised by the claim that vice was beneficial. Mandeville responded with a wink and a nudge, suggesting they look at the bright side. Overcharging by merchants and underpayment by employers can be called evils, but the first increases the funds available for the genteel life; the second adds to the desperation that keeps the poor at work. Judges taking bribes may be an abomination, but a corrupt judiciary, by discouraging the filing of complaints, keeps workers in their place.

Mandeville's defence of the exploitation of labour was cynical, but *The Fable* rang true. In Britain at the time, textiles were the primary source of domestic wealth. To make way for wool from sheep, thousands upon thousands of rural people were being dispossessed and evicted from their ancestral lands. Unemployment and child labour pushed down wages. By Mandeville's time, real wages in Britain had fallen to half the level of 200 years earlier.[3]

When *The Fable* was reissued with additional commentary in 1723 and again in 1724, Mandeville denied that he advocated vice. He was merely ridiculing the self-righteous hypocrisy of his critics. People who enjoy the prosperity that comes from pride and vanity, greed and corruption, trade and warfare are in fact accepting the benefits of vice.

Who could deny that great fortunes were made in colonisation schemes that required the violent dispossession of indigenous people in the Americas, or that fortunes were made in the buying and selling of African slaves and in the employment of slave labour on plantations? Who could deny that victory in a prolonged series of bloody naval wars with Holland, Spain and France had given Britain its leading position in world trade? Mandeville urged people to accept reality. If they truly wished to live in frugal, honest, peaceful societies, they should admit that they were choosing life in small, poor countries away from the main routes of commerce.

A dozen books were published attacking *The Fable*. It was presented as a public nuisance to a Grand Jury in Middlesex. When Mandeville died in 1733, one cleric, perhaps relieved that the source of his spiritualities would no longer be exposed, gloated that the 'Man-devil' will 'prate no more'.[4] In France a translation of *The Fable* was ordered to be burned by the common hangman. Still, *The Fable* circulated widely, if surreptitiously, in England and Europe throughout the eighteenth century. In the

Thirteen Colonies it supplemented the righteousness of Puritan and Calvinist creeds and inspired the rising class of merchant capitalists to pursue wealth regardless of the harm done to others.

Mandeville influenced the theory of the individual in the market far more than Adam Smith cared to admit. Smith's first major work, *The Theory of Moral Sentiments*, a work on psychology published in 1759, was an attack on Mandeville's 'licentious system'.[5] Here Smith denied that vice leads to public good and rejected the claim that virtue is a cover for self-serving hypocrisy. He insisted that people are motivated by sympathy as well as by self-interest. Sympathy, he said, leads to concern for others, to feelings of approbation and shame, to the sense of propriety, and to commitment to duty – to the morality and virtue that give life meaning and worth. However, by the time Smith wrote *The Wealth of Nations*, he had accepted much of Mandeville's position. By claiming that the common good is best achieved through the pursuit of self-interest in competitive markets, Smith had agreed that greed and envy are the driving forces of human wellbeing. He had conceded the field of moral philosophy to Mandeville.

In *Moral Sentiments* Smith relied on observations of human behaviour to develop a theory of human motivation. *The Wealth of Nations* includes numerous detailed economic observations. However, both books were motivated by Smith's spiritual beliefs. Smith, like his friend the philosopher David Hume, was a rational deist.[6] Rational deists did not believe that God performed miracles, intervened in daily life or favoured some and punished others. They saw God as a celestial engineer who had put the world in motion and then left it alone to work according to its own natural laws. They set out to discover such laws. In this they were inspired by the work of Isaac Newton, the mathematician and scientist who had formulated the laws of gravity, added to the understanding of colour and mechanics, and developed differential calculus.

After writing *Moral Sentiments* the role of self-interest in the market had struck Smith with the force of revelation. The market accepts us as the selfish beings we are and guides us, with an invisible hand, to work for the wellbeing of others. The guiding principle is 'give me that which I want, and you shall have this which you want ... It is not from the benevolence of the butcher, the brewer, or the baker, that we expect our dinner, but from their regard to their own interest'.[7]

Smith did not exactly conclude that sinners will save the world by sinning. He was, however, convinced that there was no need for the forces of law and order to intervene in the vain, envious, greedy struggle of each against all. The market itself drove people to fair play. Because exchange is voluntary, only transactions which satisfy both buyers and sellers will be completed.

Smith rejected the argument, put forward by guild members, that regulation of trade is necessary to avoid overproduction and loss of employment. In free markets overproduction and unemployment would not be problems. For every increase in production there is a corresponding increase in consumption. As workers produce more, higher wages increase the markets for consumer goods. As profits rise, capitalist savings and invest-ments rise, increasing the 'wages fund' – the revenues that provide employment and income for workers. People need not fear overproduction. Equilibrium in a free market will be reached only when labour, capital and resources are all fully employed.

The theory is captivating. But how relevant is it? Smith himself recognised that market forces are universally beneficial only where sellers and buyers are so numerous that none can control supply or demand and where people are free to move from one occupation to another in pursuit of the most remun-erative work. When producers are free to shift from one line of work to another, they have little reason to exchange their products for less than their value and little reason to buy goods for more than these would cost them to produce. As producers shift from less profitable to more profitable occupations, returns for equal effort will tend toward equality.

In fact capitalist property rights give wealthowners the right to deny others access to means of livelihood. Domination of indus-tries by monopolies or oligopolies is common. When one or a few companies dominate industries they have the means to regulate output and price to their benefit. They have the legal right to deny others access to these means of livelihood. The claim that market forces bring supply and demand to equilibrium can be reduced to the observation that every purchase is matched by a sale. This is of course true, but goods are produced that cannot be sold. Overproduction and unemployment are recurring prob-lems in capitalist markets. Why?

Fernand Braudel, in his encyclopaedic *Civilisation & Capital-ism*, distinguished three types of exchange: the direct exchange of goods produced for consumption; exchange in competitive mar-kets; and capitalist exchange.[9] In Smith's time, most goods were still produced for direct consumption; households produced their own food, drink, clothing, housing and transportation. This direct economy was neither driven by self-interest nor regulated by the exchange of equivalents. Women – who then as now did most of the work in the direct economy – were expected to subordinate their interests to those of their fathers, husbands and children; they were supposed to work out of love and duty, not self-interest. The distribution of goods was based on custom, dispute and power relations. Those who provided consumption goods did not get, nor were they expected to get, direct equivalence in exchange. Because the direct economy was clearly not regulated by the invisible hand of market forces, Smith ignored it.

Competitive markets were lively in Smith's day and had been ever since people had been able to produce more of some goods than they needed. Competitive markets developed as people became accustomed to exchange the surpluses they produced for goods produced by others. Eventually, people produced with an eye more on the market than on their own consumption. So long as market conditions and production methods were common knowledge and people were free to move from one line of work to others, the exchange of equivalents made such markets self-regulating much as Smith described. But by his time, capitalist exchange was well on the way to overtaking competitive exchange.

Capitalist exchange is based on relations of domination and subordination. Braudel makes the case that the unequal markets of capitalism developed in overseas trade before industrialisation. He cites the sixteenth-century Dutch-controlled European grain trade to illustrate the inequalities inherent in capitalist exchange.[10]

Dutch merchants, having inserted themselves as intermediaries between Polish producers and Mediterranean consumers, were able to profit at the expense of both. As the sole buyers of Polish grain for export, they bought grain after the harvest when prices were low. As the sole suppliers of Polish grain to the Mediterranean, they waited until grain supplies were scarce to sell when prices were high. Their control of credits for both producers and consumers added to their profits. In an age when profits in competitive businesses were usually 6 per cent or less, Dutch grain traders made annual average profits of 30 per cent, rising in some years to as high as 200 per cent. These high profits were a result not of competitive exchange but of control over markets. This control was based on advanced ship-building technology, on exclusive and closely guarded knowledge of market conditions in both Poland and the Mediterranean, and on Dutch domination of banking and international credit. When push came to shove, Dutch merchants were able to call on the formidable fire power of their country's navy.

Adam Smith knew that control of markets undermined the beneficial effects of competitive forces. He said that exclusive

royal monopolies like the British East India Company 'are
nuisances in every respect; always more or less inconvenient to
the countries in which they are established, and destructive to
those which have the misfortune to fall under their government'.[11]

Smith not only called for the abolition of royal monopolies, he
opposed corporations and joint stock companies. Corporations in
Smith's day were combinations of capitalists who got together to
set prices and wages and regulate production methods. Joint
stock companies – more like present-day corporations – pooled
the capital of many investors in one company. Smith said, 'The
pretense that corporations are necessary for the better government of trade is without any foundation.'[12] He proposed that the
law should limit joint stock companies to banking, insurance,
canal building and the supplying of water to cities – businesses
that required the mobilisation of large amounts of capital and
whose 'operations are capable of being reduced to what is called a
routine, or to such a uniformity of method as admits of little or
no variation'.[13]

Smith understood that the exclusive rights granted by royal
charters and the monopolies set up by corporations and joint
stock companies undermined the self-regulating mechanisms of
market forces. He did not see that capitalist property relations
do the same. When land, buildings, materials, tools, machinery,
inventory and marketing networks are owned by some as capital, others do not have the unrestricted access to means of
livelihood assumed by the theory. Capitalists set conditions of
employment for others and command their labour time. Their
economic activity is guided not by the invisible hand of market
forces but by the commands of their capitalist masters.

John Locke and Acquisitive Individualism

Smith's failure to see the difference between competitive individualism and capitalism was not surprising. At the time wage workers,
who did not have the right to vote, were not considered to have
individual rights. Individual rights, according to John Locke, the
most influential English thinker in the seventeenth century, came
from the ownership of capital.

Locke, born in 1632, was the philosopher of the Glorious
Revolution. His insistence that the individual's right to property
is equal to the right of the Crown has been the basis of civil
law in Britain since 1688. His opposition to government interference in the enjoyment of property remains a fundamental
tenet of capitalist ideology everywhere. His assertion that the

majority has the right to defend itself against its legislators, if these should 'be so foolish and wicked as to lay and carry on designs against the liberties and properties of the subject',[14] inspired the merchant classes of the Thirteen Colonies to launch their War of Independence.

Locke was a product of the momentous social upheavals in seventeenth-century Britain. He began his political career – after the Restoration of Charles II (1660–85) – as secretary of the Board of Trade, a position he acquired through his patron and employer, Lord Shaftesbury. Shaftesbury was Chancellor of the Exchequer and leader of the Whigs – the party of merchant and finance capital. When James II came to the throne in 1685, Locke, who like his patron was identified with the Protestant opposition, fled to Holland where he remained until the Glorious Revolution of 1688.

Locke was a leader of a struggle that had been fought throughout the century. In the 1640s, the king's right unilaterally to raise taxes and declare war had been challenged by Parliament. A civil war followed. Charles I lost and in 1649 was beheaded. With the king gone, the parliamentary forces divided into Independents and Levellers. The Independents were led by Oliver Cromwell and represented 'independent' men – merchants and landowners. They believed that all men who owned sufficient capital to free them from the necessity of personal labour had a fundamental right to take part in making laws. They insisted that the right to vote for Parliament should be restricted to such men.

The Levellers – so called because they were accused of supporting the levelling of hedges constructed to enclose what had been communal fields – represented the small-holders and self-employed artisans who had provided the parliamentary army with most of its soldiers. They conceded that any man who worked for another had thereby forfeited his political independence. They demanded voting rights for all men who were self-employed; who owned the products of their own labour. Cromwell, who had the support of the officers and cavalry – including John Locke's father, a captain of horse – settled the issue by arresting and hanging Leveller leaders. Cromwell had himself proclaimed Lord Protector and during the Long Parliament (1640–60) nobody voted.

Cromwell's Protectorate laid the foundation for Britain's imperial power. Ireland was crushed; two-thirds of its lands were seized for British landowners. Scottish armies allied with Charles II were defeated and Scotland, like Ireland, was annexed to England. Navigation Acts encouraged merchant shipping, gave preferential treatment to export industries and strengthened the navy. Victories in wars against Holland and Spain established England's mastery of the seas. Imperial success masked what was an oppressive and unhappy time.

When Cromwell died in 1658, few objected to the restoration of the monarchy. Charles II, who had taken up his father's cause and had been defeated in Scotland, was invited to return. His subsequent 25 year reign was not controversial. The same could not be said for his brother, James II, who became king in 1685. A Catholic and an absolutist in a Protestant and constitutional country, James held the throne for just three years. In 1688 he was overthrown by William of Orange who crossed the Channel from Holland with 15,000 troops. William and Mary (James's daughter) were welcomed as liberators by the merchant classes.

From the perspective of wealthowners, the revolution of 1688 was glorious not only because the king accepted the rights of private wealthowners but also because the revolution had not involved the people. The leaders of the revolution, having come to power on the shoulders of foreign troops, did not have to contend with an armed people clamouring for political rights, as had been the case in Cromwell's time. The new monarchy restricted the right to vote to capital-owning men – much as had been proposed by Cromwell. A parliament of wealthowners shared power with the Crown and the courts, leaving the majority without a voice or vote in public affairs.

John Locke returned home from Holland to work for the new government. He and his friend Isaac Newton – who had quietly opposed James II from within England – were 'the back room boys' of the new government.[15] Locke became Commissioner of Trade and Plantations. Newton, as warden of the Mint, established the gold standard that would make the British pound the leading world currency.

A few years after returning from Holland, Locke took time off to write *An Essay Concerning the True Original Extent and End of Civil Government*. He held that the sole purpose of government is to protect the interests of the individuals who made the compact to form the government. These individuals were the property-owners. When their will was in dispute it could best be expressed by a majority vote. Locke rejected the opinion that property, law and civil society flowed from the monarchy – a view that had gained ascendancy after the rediscovery in the early Renaissance of the *Corpus Juris Civilus*, a law code of late Imperial Rome.[16] Property, Locke said, is not bestowed by the monarch, it is a natural right.

Locke then aimed his conception of a natural right to property against common rights. The ancient belief in common rights had been fortified by the pre-Renaissance view that God had created the land, the sea and all its creatures for the enjoyment and use of all his children. In opposing common rights, Locke wrote,

> Though the earth and all inferior creatures be common to all men, yet every man has a property in his own person; this nobody has any right to but himself. The labour of his body and the work of his hands we may say are properly his. Whatsoever, then, he removes out of the state that nature hath provided and left it in, he hath mixed his labour with and joined to it something that is his own and thereby makes it his property.[17]

Superficially, this seems a defence of the rights of labour. It was not. It was a defence of capitalist rights against common rights. Locke's point is easier to see if 'capitalist' is read where he writes 'man', and 'the labour he has hired' where he writes 'his labour'. Altering his text this way also eliminates what would otherwise be a blatant contradiction in Locke's theory and practice. Although he wrote, 'The supreme power cannot take from any man any part of his property without his own consent',[18] Locke was a leader of a government that was actively involved in driving rural people from land their ancestors had possessed and worked for generations.

Locke did not see a contradiction here because the right to property meant the right to revenue-earning capital. The working classes who were supposed to occupy themselves working for others could hardly expect to have such rights. In this view, he was not alone. R. H. Tawney wrote that for most wealthowners of the time 'the possession of landed property by a poor man seemed in itself a surprising impertinence which it was the duty of Parliament to correct'.[19]

Before capitalism, property meant a right to things – land, waterways, buildings, tools, stocks – which one used and possessed as one's own or shared with designated others. This conception of property was held by common people and by the great thirteenth-century church scholar Thomas Aquinas.[20] Property rights were established by legal documents, memory and custom:

> In spite of the fiction under which feudalism operated – that all land in England belonged to the king, who granted it to his barons, who in turn granted it to lessor lords, who granted it to the peasants – a pervasive sense of hereditary rights prevailed among the peasants, as among the barons.[21]

In *Women in the Middle Ages* Frances and Joseph Gies go on to explain that inheritance rules were precise. A peasant family's holding was normally inherited by the eldest son. If a family had no sons, a daughter inherited. Her husband would act as the landholder during his lifetime. The land would then pass on to a child who would be 'regarded as his wife's heir rather than his own'.[21]

Ancient customary rights were destroyed by capitalism. By making legal title the only claim to property and then creating a market in titles to property, capitalism broke the tie between use and property. People who could not produce title documents were evicted. Property became capital. Rights to it were bought and sold. The right of producers to their means of livelihood was transformed into the right of wealthowners to own others' means of livelihood and to revenue from others' labour. In Locke's time thousands of families were being driven from the land and pushed into the growing urban slums. Locke supported these dispossessions and insisted that rising unemployment was a result of 'nothing else but the relaxation of discipline and corruption of manners'.[22]

Rising unemployment was actually in the interests of wealthowners. It drove down the price of labour. Like Mandeville, Locke believed in the utility of poverty. He argued that wages should be kept low so that Britain would have a competitive edge in international trade. Where money could be made, Locke did not hesitate to urge the exploitation of children. In his treatise on government, he had written that the powers of parents should be limited to what was in the interests of children. However, when speaking for the Commission on Trade, he recommended that the children of the unemployed be taken from them at the age of three and put into workhouses to labour for their own keep and for the profit of their overseers.[23]

Locke, now respected as one of the greatest early modern philosophers, was in daily life a transnational corporate executive. His career began as secretary to Lord Shaftesbury, one of the 19 original investors in the Hudson Bay Company, which had been granted a charter as a royal monopoly by Charles II in 1670. Now the oldest existing corporation, the Hudson Bay Company controlled the fur trade in British North America with a network of fortified trading posts. These were designed more to defend the company's monopoly than to protect its servants from attacks by indigenous people. It fixed the wages of its servants, the prices of furs it purchased from Indians and the prices of trade goods sold. It prohibited its servants and outsiders from engaging in independent trade and protected its monopoly with all the powers of a government. Armed officers roamed the territory to keep the Bay's servants in line and renegade traders out.[24]

During the height of its power in the late eighteenth and nineteenth centuries, this private company relied on military command structures. It maintained a rigid hierarchy between Scottish officers, French-speaking voyageurs and native hunters and trappers. It pioneered the scientific exploitation of labour. Because labour costs were high in water transportation, the tempo of work was strictly regulated. Paddling was set at a rate of more than one stroke per second; fifty minutes of paddling was followed by ten minutes of rest. Each voyageur had to carry two 90 pound sacks in the portages between rivers. Because voyageurs had to work together carrying their canoes, the Bay looked for men of uniform height. Because long legs took up too much cargo space, only short men with strong arms were hired.

Can we assume Locke – the advocate of individual rights – at least opposed slavery? He did say 'every man has a property in his own person; this nobody has any right to but himself'. In fact he was up to his neck in the slave trade.[25] His employer Lord Shaftesbury was a leading investor in the Royal Africa Company as well as Lord Proprietor of the Carolinas. Locke himself had substantial personal investments in slaving and was appointed Commissioner of Trade and Plantations at a time when the British dominated the slave trade.

In accepting the dispossession of common people, poverty for labour, the exploitation of little children and the enslavement of Africans, Locke was representing the interests of his class. He was doing the same when he campaigned for the right of individuals to choose their government by majority vote. His peers would have taken it for granted that individual rights applied only to the heads of capital-owning households. Such households contained domestic servants, labourers, apprentices and journeymen, as well as female relatives. The law of the time presumed that the male head of the household represented all these people; only he had the right to vote; only he had full citizenship.

Capitalism: Dispossession and Control

Capitalist domination of markets, as Braudel pointed out, began in international trade. Within England, capitalist property developed by destroying traditional communal rights to land.

The pre-capitalist rural population was not as oppressed as is sometimes assumed. Each householder in a village had recognised customary rights. A substantial minority were freeholders who had clear title to land. The majority were tenants. Tenants included copyholders whose rights to land were registered in court documents, leaseholders who had rights to land for fixed terms and cottagers who lived on the land at the will of the lord. All householders – usually men but occasionally widows – had the right to participate and vote in the Manor Court, presided over by the lord. When feudal lords acted in an arbitrary or tyrannical manner – as they sometimes did – this was seen as exceptional and unacceptable. Villagers could, and did, meet among themselves in village assemblies to organise against their lord.

In *The Agrarian Problem in the Sixteenth Century*, R. H. Tawney explained that village democracy in late feudalism had evolved from open field agriculture.[26] In this system households had separated strips of land of varying fertility. Crops were sown over areas larger than the individual strips and all the fields were open after harvest to every household's animals. Each household was responsible for work on its own fields, but the village commune, meeting in the Manor Court, decided what crops to grow, when to plant, when to harvest and how many animals each household could graze on the open fields and commons.

The lord's control over daily life was minimal. He had a right to annual payments in money or in kind and a right to collect transfer fees when land passed from one tenant to another. Such payments were usually fixed by custom. Otherwise, tenants owned what they produced. Some tenants had to perform services, but by the sixteenth century customary labour services took up less than a fifth of the typical household's labour time. Most villagers were in command of their own persons most of the time and were free to consume, barter or exchange goods as they chose.

This independence was a direct result of 'the possession by the majority of households of holdings of land'.[27] Land was so widely distributed that households entirely dependent on wage work were exceptions: 'The typical family has a small holding of from two and a half to fifteen acres.'[28] Even cottagers, who were expected to work as artisans or as farm labourers, usually had an acre or two on which to grow food and graze a few animals.

Widespread independence did not please everyone. The rising class of merchants complained 'that men who should work as wage-labourers cling to the soil, and in the naughtiness of their hearts prefer independence as squatters to employment by a master'.[29]

Independence was lost to enclosures. As production for the market replaced local subsistence, acquisitive freeholders began to see communal rules as barriers to the most profitable use of land. To control their own land, they exchanged fields with neighbours, with the aim of assembling adjacent fields which were then enclosed with hedges or ditches. Having removed their fields from the common lands, they could then choose their own crops and graze their own animals, confident in the knowledge that they would themselves get the benefits of any investments made. Communal agriculture was being undermined, but such early enclosures were often accepted by other house-holders. Nobody was displaced and more intensive farming provided poorer members of the manor with increased oppor-tunities for wage work. [30]

A few enclosures were reported in the thirteenth and four-teenth centuries. The number increased in the fifteenth, six-teenth, seventeenth and eighteenth centuries. Whenever political changes loosened restraints on wealthowners, a tide of enclo-sures followed. Great waves of enclosures swept the countryside after the confiscation of Church lands by Henry VII in the 1490s, after the death of Henry VIII 60 years later, after the proclamation of Cromwell's Protectorate in the 1640s, and after the Glorious Revolution of 1688. Opposition to enclosures also grew. Each new wave provoked unrest, riots, mini-insurrections and repression.

In the early seventeenth century, promoters of capitalist agri-culture launched great projects to drain the fens around Peterbor-ough, Ely and Bedford. [31] The fen people responded with protests and riots. They had for generations lived by catching fish, eels and water birds. They grazed their animals in natural meadows and fashioned mats, hassocks, mattresses and other goods used in daily life from the reeds, grasses and other plants found in the marshes. In 1638 Cromwell, then leading the parliamentary oppo-sition to the king, supported the protesters and was for a time called 'Lord of the Fens'. However, after 1646, when the civil war had been won, Cromwell allowed the drainage schemes to go ahead. Large areas of marshes, ponds and meadows connected by natural waterways were drained and diked. The drained lands produced rich cash crops, but 'Improvements in the productivity of the land were shared neither by the poor nor by the original occupants of the marshes – the fish, fowl and marsh plants that over thousands of years had evolved a complex set of ecological interdependencies.' [32]

These and other enclosures took means of livelihood from many people. The new capitalist landowners – 'the graziers, the rich butchers, the men of law, the merchants, the gentlemen, the knights, the lords' [33] – evicted cottagers, terminated leases and raised rents beyond the ability of people to pay. They bribed

courts to ignore customary rights and hired armed gangs to
terrorise tenants and demolish houses. The logic of the capitalist
marketplace required people to make way for sheep. Sheep were
more profitable because traditional self-sufficiency in food crops
had caused the price of wool to rise relative to the price of grain.
Thomas More, writing in 1516 – during the first wave of capitalist enclosures – expressed his horror with a world in which sheep
that were once 'so meek and tame and so small eaters' now 'eat
up and swallow down the very men themselves'.[34]

People driven off ancestral lands swelled the ranks of migrant
day-labourers travelling from place to place looking for work.
Many had no success. Sheep grazing required only a fraction of
the labour of grain growing. Many became beggars, others disappeared into the slums of the growing cities. Governments
responded to the desperation of the dispossessed by hardening
the penalties against vagabondage.[35] The able-bodied unemployed
were sentenced to whipping and to branding with red-hot irons.
Those found guilty of persistent vagrancy could be hanged.

Customary common rights and local self-sufficiency were
finally swept away in the greatest wave of enclosures – from 1760
to 1810 – just as Smith's theory of the independent individual in
the market was becoming popular. Enclosed fields were drained,
irrigated, deep ploughed, manured and mechanically seeded in
grains, legumes, potatoes and turnips for expanding urban markets. Substantial investments were required in horses, machinery
and equipment, but returns were high. Chronic rural unemployment coupled with a loss of land for hunting and gathering and
subsistence agriculture now meant that labour was cheap. Growing industrial centres had created a seller's market for food and
fodder crops.[36]

The dispossessed followed earlier generations to the cities.
To get the means to survive they had to submit to the commands of others and work for their profit. Earlier ruling classes
had demanded a share of the goods people produced. They
sometimes claimed the right to circumscribe religious belief. The
rising class of capitalists went further. They demanded control
over working time, over bodily movements and over the entire
product of wage labour.

Before capitalism, no one – not a conscript, convict or slave –
had to submit to such direct control by others. Looking back at
the origins of capitalism in *Discipline & Punish*, Michel Foucault
argued that freedom for capital was freedom for the few and
discipline for the many. The aim of factory discipline

> was to establish presences and absences, to know where and
> how to locate individuals, to set up useful communications, to

interrupt others, to be able at each moment to supervise the conduct of each individual, to assess it, to judge it, to calculate its qualities or merits. It was a procedure, therefore, aimed at knowing, mastering and using.[37]

The aim was to eliminate all distractions – all self-conscious awareness of surroundings or others – so that the maximum time and attention would be devoted to work. The method was surveillance. Without surveillance, employers could not know that workers were actually expending the maximum effort on capital's behalf.

Since surveillance was itself an expense, it had to be efficient. Jeremy Bentham, writing in England in 1791 – 15 years after *The Wealth of Nations* was first published – believed he had solved the problem. He devised a 'panopticon' which he recommended for jails, barracks and factories. It consisted of a central tower separated by a courtyard from a surrounding main building. The observers in the central tower could view all spaces in the surrounding building, but the design of the windows in the tower and the direction of light blocked any view of the observers from outside. The observed, in the surrounding main building, not knowing if or when they were being watched, would have to act as if they were being watched at all times. Bentham, the founder of utilitarianism – a philosophy that advocated the greatest happiness for the greatest number – had succeeded in devising a structure that would allow the fewest to control the most. [38]

Relations of command and subordination in workplaces preceded industrialisation. In the traditional workshop apprentices and helpers were expected to do what they were told, but journeymen working for a master were supposed to be in charge of their own work. Capitalist master–servant relations began when wealthy merchants established manufactories, gathering dozens of workers under one roof. Work was still done by hand, with only the simplest tools, but each worker was assigned only one or a few repetitive tasks and work was strictly regulated by overseers. According to Adam Smith, manufactories achieved levels of output many times greater than the combined output of the same number of artisans each doing the entire job at his own home workshop.

While manufactories did provide capitalists with experience in managing labour, most goods before industrialisation were produced by artisans. They worked at home, owned their own tools, purchased their own materials, finished and sold the products themselves. They were independent, but their existence was not idyllic. They often lived from hand to mouth; real living standards had been declining since the sixteenth century. Independence had been eroded by the putting-out system in which wealthy merchants supplied the materials and bought the prod-ucts of hundreds and sometimes thousands of cottagers. Still, artisans were in command of their own persons. Most lived in the country, where despite the progress of enclosures, many still had access to land that provided food for their families. Not long before Smith's time, independent artisans, along with free-holders, copyholders and leaseholders had been a majority of British men: the rugged individuals who had given the country its economic strength, its pride in independence and its com-mitment to personal freedom.

Industrialisation and the Loss of Independence

The Industrial Revolution pushed independent production to the fringes of economic life. The Industrial Revolution began in Britain as Adam Smith was writing *The Wealth of Nations*. From 1720 to 1776, the Darby, Smeaton and Wilkinson firms refined a process for making wrought iron using coking coal instead of charcoal. This made it practical to construct large machines and reduced the dependence of industry on shrinking forests. James Watt patented an improved steam engine in 1769. These engines, fuelled with cheap and plentiful supplies of coal, could power the new machines.[39] Plunder from India, after Clive's victory at Plessey in 1757, doubled the funds available for investment in Britain for the next 20 years and substantially increased these for another 30 years. Those who first got their hands on the booty often squandered it on conspicuous consumption. Even so, the increase in money in circ-ulation dramatically increased the funds available for industrial investment.[40]

Machine industry developed first in textiles. The spinning jenny was invented by James Hargreaves in 1764. The spinning mule, a refinement, was produced by Samuel Crompton in 1779. A decade earlier, in 1769, the capitalist Richard Arkwright patented the water frame which allowed him to replace skilled spinners with children. The mechanisation of spinning made large-scale mechanical weaving practical. Arkwright's mechanised textile mill in Derbyshire was initially powered by animals. He shifted to water power in 1771 and to steam engines in 1790.

Once spinning and weaving were mechanised, prices fell so low that independent craftsmen could not earn enough to feed themselves, let alone their families. Mechanisation spread to agri-culture. Mechanical threshing eliminated the off-season hand labour that had allowed many to survive the barren winter months. People resisted the new reality as best they could. Some, known as Luddites, deliberately wrecked machines. Others formed trade unions or joined political reform clubs demanding a People's Charter. Mass demonstrations were denounced as riots. Protesters were beaten and imprisoned. Some were hanged. Others were transported to penal colonies in the far reaches of the British empire.

Britain, once 'a nation of shopkeepers', became an ugly patchwork of 'dark, Satanic mills'. Women and children went into the factories first. The men followed; their pride in independence now a disability, they sold their labour to factory owners. Entire families laboured under the direction of overseers for wages less than a skilled worker had previously earned himself at his own time. Each morning before sunrise, seven days a week, legions of wretched men, women and children marched into factories where they remained until past sunset. The hours of work extended to 12, 14 and to 18 hours. The numerous Holy Days that had given labourers relief from toil in the old days were no longer celebrated. Factory owners, claiming to be fighting superstitions and Papism, had abolished them. [41]

By the time Smith's vision of the individual in the market had become the foundation of economic theory, the rise of machine industry had made economic independence an unattainable dream for most people. How could factory workers freely exchange the products of their own labour in the market when it belonged to others? Few people had access to the capital needed to engage in mechanised production. The new class of wage workers was growing rapidly. They were not the *self-directed* individuals of market theory; they had little choice but to be *other-directed*.

Why did Smith not see that capitalist relations of domination and subordination were rapidly replacing free exchange in the market? He cannot be dismissed as an apologist for capitalism. At its most compelling, *The Wealth of Nations* is an appeal to the rich and to governments to stop interfering and let people arrange their affairs as they themselves choose. Unlike Locke and Mandeville, Smith was not hostile to the interests of working people. He rejected the mercantilist doctrine of the utility of poverty, saying 'Servants, labourers and workmen of different kinds, make up the far greater part of every great political society ... what improves the circumstances of the greater part can never be regarded as an inconvenience to the whole.' [42]

Fernand Braudel suggested that Smith, despite his erudition, was not a particularly astute observer of his own surroundings. In *Civilization & Capitalism*, he wrote that Smith 'understood the American colonies he had never seen in his life better than the industrial revolution taking place under his nose at home'. [43]

Smith is best understood as a myth-maker. In his praise of
self-interest and in his sympathy for people as they are, he
idealises the real. In advocating a free market, dominated neither
by the politically powerful nor by the economically privileged, he
tries to realise the ideal.

This blurring of the ideal and the real led Smith to confuse
the exchange of equivalents in competitive markets with the
unequal exchanges of capitalism. However, Smith did condemn
the concentration of wealth in a few hands. He called the great
merchants and manufacturers of his day

> an order of men, whose interest is never exactly the same with
> that of the public, who have generally an interest to deceive
> and even to oppress the public and who accordingly have,
> upon many occasions, both deceived and oppressed it.[44]

Even though Smith considered the capital–labour relation a form of
free exchange, he knew that capitalists actually imposed conditions
on workers. He said,

> Masters are always and everywhere in a sort of tacit, but
> constant and uniform combination, not to raise the wages of
> labour above their actual rate ...   Masters too sometimes enter
> into particular combinations to sink the wages of labour even
> below this rate ...   It is not difficult to foresee which of the
> two parties must, upon all ordinary occasions ... force the
> other into a compliance with their terms. The masters, being
> fewer in number, can combine much more easily; and the law,
> besides, authorises, or at least does not prohibit their combi-
> nations, while it prohibits those of the workmen ... In all such
> disputes the masters can hold out much longer ... though they
> did not employ a single workman [the masters] could generally
> live a year or two upon the stocks which they have already
> acquired. Many workmen could not subsist a week, few could
> subsist a month, and scarce any a year without employment.[45]

Mechanisation Gives Ricardo Second Thoughts

Adam Smith had believed that expanding markets would lead to
improved wellbeing. The most immediate effect of expanding
capitalist markets was a decline in living conditions. Before the
Industrial Revolution, the prosperity of English common people
had been the envy of Europe. By 1820 the poverty, squalor and
disease of English working-class life would horrify outsiders. In
1826 a French visitor wrote, 'In poor nations the people are

comfortable, in rich nations, they are generally poor.' [46]

Why? Machine industry, by increasing the volume of goods each labourer could produce, should have made goods more plentiful and people more prosperous. Goods produced in the newly mechanised factories were cheaper, but this was of little benefit to the growing numbers of people who suffered from chronic unemployment or were compelled to work for wages that barely sustained human life.

David Ricardo searched for an explanation for the adverse effects of mechanisation. Now virtually forgotten, Ricardo was at least as important as Smith in formulating market theory. Born in 1772, Ricardo joined his father's London banking firm at the age of 14. A few years later he set up his own stockbroker's business and then, at 25 – already one of the wealthiest men in Britain – he retired to a country estate to devote his life to the study of economics. He was soon recognised as the leading expert on currency and banking and in 1819 bought himself a seat in Parliament.

Ricardo and his close friend James Mill were the central figures in the London Political Economy Club. Here Ricardo charmed industrial capitalists by arguing against tax increases and government attempts to alter market forces. He became a leading spokesman of campaigns against the Corn Laws (tariffs that favoured landlords) and the Poor Laws (an early welfare system). [47]

Ricardo's *The Principles of Political Economy and Taxation*, first issued in 1817, founded the discipline of economics as we know it today. [48] Ricardo, like Smith – but with even less justification – began by assuming an economy of small producers, none of whom dominates markets or supplies and all of whom are able to move from one line of work to another in pursuit of higher profits. He then derived the 'laws' of economics from these assumptions. Unlike Smith – who was inspired, moralistic and often inconsistent – Ricardo was logically rigorous. Where Smith expressed optimistic belief in the beneficial effects of self-interest in the market, Ricardo viewed market forces as natural laws which could be defied or ignored only at great peril. With Ricardo, economics becomes the dismal science. All of the major English-language schools of economics from marginalism to Keynesianism, monetarism and supply-side economics owe more to Ricardo than to Smith.

However, Ricardo is distinguished from most who followed him by being as committed to the logic of his system as to the short-term interests of capitalists. This can be seen in his determination to stand by his labour theory of value. In developing the logic of free market forces, Ricardo defined the 'natural price' or 'exchange value' of a commodity as the price at which producers receive the average rate of profit. If producers receive this average rate of profit, and labour of customary skill and intensity is paid the prevailing wage, it can then be concluded that exchange value is a measure of the labour time embodied in a commodity.

In response to the obvious objection that the prices of commodities fluctuate in response to supply and demand, Ricardo said yes, but over time market forces bring these to points at which capitalists receive the average rate of profit and workers the customary wage. To the objection that the selling prices of commodities also include outlays for machinery, equipment, materials and land, Ricardo said that the exchange value of machinery and equipment is a measure of the labour time (plus the average rate of profit) required to produce these things. The exchange value of materials and land represents payments for labour time plus the average rate of profit required on the least productive properties that are brought into service to meet the existing demand. The exchange value of labour, he added, is a measure of the labour time it takes to feed, clothe, house and educate workers in the customary fashion.

His more class-conscious friends, notably the population theorist Thomas Malthus, viewed the labour theory of value with suspicion. Ricardo held to it. Because his labour theory of value explained how movements of supply and demand pushed prices to levels at which manufacturers got the average rate of profit and workers got customary wages, Ricardo was convinced that he had shown how competitive economic activity led to general wellbeing.

Unfortunately, economic development did not correspond to his theory. The progress of mechanisation was accompanied by a decline in real wages. Ricardo therefore concluded that market forces would be generally beneficial only if real wages rose in response to increases in productivity. For Malthus this was totally unacceptable. He argued that it was irresponsible to suggest that the material conditions of the masses should or could be improved. Rising real wages would simply encourage the masses to breed more rapidly. Meanwhile, rising real wages – coming as they must at the expense of profits and savings – would reduce the funds available for the investment needed to provide employment for the expanding population.

Ricardo held to the logic of his position. In 1821, he added a chapter 'On Machinery' to the third edition of *The Principles*. In it he conceded that 'the substitution of machinery for human labour, is often very injurious to the interests of the class of labourers',[49] but he continued to believe in the longer term benefits of market forces. He searched for a conjunctural explanation for declining wages. He speculated that perhaps the migration from agriculture to industry had reduced the labour available for the production of basic necessities. In addition, increasing industrial productivity reduced the demand for factory labour. That would explain a shortage of consumer necessities and an increase in unemployment. But it would also suggest that total production was falling. If that were the case, how could rising profits be explained? If profits rose while production was falling, how could it be said that market forces bring economies to equilibrium at full employment or that they have generally beneficial results?

Ricardo did not have access to the information needed to answer these questions. He died in 1823, long before any comprehensive statistics on production or consumption levels were available. He had, however, stumbled on a basic difference between the free market of economic theory and the controlled markets of capitalism. In developing his theory, Ricardo had assumed that everyone has equal access to means of livelihood. Like Smith, he knew that the exclusive possession gained through royal monopolies denied equal access to means of livelihood. And like Smith he seemed not to see that exclusive possession – the right to deny others access to means of livelihood – is inherent in capitalist ownership. When capitalists control economic activity, the market cannot be said to be self-regulating. Instead of having generally beneficial results, the capitalist market makes the rich get richer and the poor poorer. This is precisely what happened in the first period of industrialisation.

Shortly after Ricardo's time, real wages did begin to rise.[50] Despite recurring depressions, material conditions gradually improved. Does this vindicate Smith and Ricardo's theory? Not really. The turnaround had little to do with the beneficial effects of market forces. It had more to do with political reform within the country and imperialism abroad. The improvements began at the end of the 1820s, after the initial repeal of the anti-combination laws, which had treated trade unions as criminal conspiracies. Once workers were allowed to organise for collective bargaining, real wages began to increase. Meanwhile, Reform Acts, beginning in the 1830s, extended the right to vote to working men, banned the employment of children in factories and mines, limited the length of the working day and provided for government inspection to ensure safe working conditions.

Profits from world trade made it easier for British capitalists to accept rising living standards at home. This flow of funds into the country cannot be ascribed to free exchange in competitive markets. International trade in the nineteenth century was dominated by national monopolies like the British East

India Company that relied on military power to back their exclusive rights. Such companies controlled the exporting of manufactured goods and the importing of raw materials and agricultural products from colonial countries.

European domination of world trade began in the fifteenth century with the Portuguese circumnavigation of Africa and the discovery of a sea route to the East Indies.[51] Despite the inferiority of European trade goods, compared with those produced in the Middle East and South Asia, Portugal's superior naval power allowed that country's merchants to take by force what they could not get by fair trade. The wheels of European commerce were then greased with the gold and silver plundered by Spain from the Americas. Some of this new wealth was invested by the Spanish, Dutch, British and French in the slave trade, in plantation agriculture and in the building of larger and better-armed merchant ships. The British defeat of Indian armies in 1757, the defeat of China during the two Opium Wars (1839–42 and 1856–8) and the carving up of Africa in the late nineteenth century completed European control of global trade. At the height of the imperialist epoch, European capital controlled world trade in all major commodities: coal, coffee, copper, cotton, furs, gold, grain, iron, lumber, opium, silver, spices, sugar, tea and tobacco.

This capitalist trade was not universally beneficial. For Africans and indigenous Americans it was a catastrophe.[52] Africa's ancient subsistence and trading cultures had already been subject to a 350-year assault by European slavers armed with superior weapons and inferior morals. After the slave trade was abolished in the nineteenth century, Africans at home were forced by head taxes, beatings and executions to labour in plantations and mines controlled by Europeans. In America the more populous agricultural and trading cultures had already suffered the ravages of European diseases. They had been victimised by the depredations of *conquistadors* looking for gold and silver and seeking slaves for plantations. In the seventeenth, eighteenth and nineteenth centuries hunters, fishers and gatherers, as well as agriculture cultures, were overrun and driven from their lands by waves of European settlers.[53]

The consequences for Asia were little better. In 1750 the United Kingdom had produced less than 2 per cent of the world's manufactured goods; India produced 25 per cent and China 33 per cent. By 1900 the UK produced nearly 20 per cent; India produced 2 per cent and China 6 per cent. In 1750 per capita goods production in England and Asia had been close to equal. By 1900 per capita production in the UK was 50 times greater than that in China and India.[54]

The decline of Asian manufacturing is usually attributed to the inability of handicraft workers to compete against machine industry. Competition from cheap machine-made goods does explain why Asian handicrafts fell into decline. But it does not explain why Asians did not invest in the new industrial techniques. Both India and China had levels of literacy matching those in Europe; they had large urban populations, wealthy profit-seeking merchants and long histories of producing for market exchange. The problem was not that Asians could not adapt, the problem was that European capitalists controlled trade and much of the investable surplus produced in Asia. This was not a consequence of market competition. It was a result of military defeat. In India the British not only appropriated surplus, they reduced the capacity of the country to generate wealth.[55] In the aftermath of the British victory, the exactions on artisans and peasants were so onerous that fields were abandoned and irrigation works allowed to decay. A similar fate befell China after its defeat in the Opium Wars in the middle of the nineteenth century. Defeat not only denied the Chinese government the right to restrict the opium trade, it gave the British control of China's economy. The Indian opium that British merchants sold in China demoralised artisans and drained silver currency out of the country. The British administrators who regulated China's internal trade and external finances forced the country to accept machine-made goods from Europe. Surpluses that could have been used for industrialisation were taken as profits by overseas traders and manufacturers and were appropriated to pay for the foreign administration and the debts it accumulated.[56]

Smith and Ricardo's theory of free, individual exchange in competitive markets does not explain why Europe became wealthier and other continents poorer. Bernard Mandeville would not have been surprised by the polarisation between rich and poor that followed nineteenth-century globalism. He never claimed that all would benefit from vice. He understood that the prosperity brought to aggressive trading nations by greed, theft and violence must come at the expense of others.

The Marginalist Reaction

In the second half of the nineteenth century, the theory of the individual in the market became the foundation for the highly abstract discipline of economics as we know it today. The new economics profession used the language of differential calculus to explain price as a function of marginal utility. The aim was to get rid of the labour theory of value.

David Ricardo was not alone in ascribing exchange value to labour. In the seventeenth century, John Locke had said,

It is labour indeed that puts the difference of value on everything ... if we rightly estimate things as they come to our use and cast up the several expenses about them – what in them is purely owing to nature and what to labour – we shall find that in most of them ninety-nine hundredths are wholly to be put on the account of labour. [57]

In the eighteenth century, Adam Smith had said, 'Labour ... is alone the ultimate and real standard by which the value of all commodities can at all times and places be estimated and compared. It is their real price; money is their nominal price only.' [58] After Ricardo, in the middle of the nineteenth century, John Stuart Mill said, 'What the production of a thing costs to its producer, or its series of producers, is the labour expended in producing it.' Mill included the costs of natural resources and capital in the value of goods, but explained that natural advantage usually means that less labour is required to bring commodities to markets and that 'capital is itself the product of labour: its instrumentality in production is therefore, in reality, that of labour in an indirect shape'. [59]

Market theorists accepted labour time as the source of exchange value until Karl Marx turned the labour theory of value into the premise of a revolutionary anti-capitalist programme. Marx reasoned that since social labour was the source of value, social means of production should be socially owned. His arguments inspired leaders of the workers' organisations who came together to form the International Working Men's Association in 1864. The International was a coalition of labour organisations in Britain, the US and Europe. It organised international solidarity during labour struggles, encouraged the formation of unions and campaigned for the right to vote for working men. Although its supporters probably never numbered more than 100,000, the Paris Commune of 1871 convinced wealthowners that the International was a serious threat. [60]

The Paris Commune was a response to the sudden and unexpected defeat of the French army in the Franco-Prussian war. Disgusted with the incompetence of the overpaid and lavishly decorated officers of Napoleon III, the common people of Paris decided to take matters into their own hands. Shopkeepers, artisans and wage-workers – men and women – met in their districts, proclaimed Paris to be self-governing and elected delegates to the Commune. French government officials and wealthowners fled from Paris to Versailles.

The first decree of the Commune was to abolish the standing

army and to put defence in the hands of the armed people. The Commune then voted to form a government directed by councillors elected by universal suffrage for short terms, who would be recallable at any time by the voters of their district. These councillors and all other government officials were to be paid salaries no higher than those paid to ordinary working men. On the urging of supporters of the International, the Commune decreed that means of production be democratically controlled and supervised by workers themselves. But the short-lived communal government was not able to do much. The people were preoccupied with organising neighbourhood militias, electing officers and preparing the defences of their surrounded, isolated city. In a little over two months, the reorganised French armies – with the assistance of the Prussians – forcibly took the city from its inhabitants. Thousands of working people were killed after the last communards had laid down their arms; thousands more were transported abroad to French penal colonies.

Karl Marx, writing from London, responded to those who claimed that the Commune had 'intended to abolish property, the basis of all civilization!' by saying,

> Yes, gentlemen, the Commune intended to abolish that class property which makes the labour of the many the wealth of the few. It aimed at the expropriation of the expropriators. It wanted to make individual property a truth by transforming the means of production, land and capital, now chiefly the means of enslaving and exploiting labour, into mere instruments of free and associated labour. [61]

Despite the swift defeat of the Commune, wealthowners had been shaken. Changes had to be made to weaken working-class opposition to capitalism. Trade union activity aimed at increasing wages or improving working conditions – which did not otherwise challenge capitalist control of the means of livelihood – was made legal. In Britain workers had won the right to form unions in 1824. Severe prohibitions on the right to strike were removed in 1875. In France, workers had won the right to strike in 1864. They were granted the right to organise unions in 1884. [62]

The most immediate response came from learned opinion. The labour theory of value was declared obsolete. Less than a year after the Commune, Leon Walras presented his work on marginalist economics to an audience in Paris. Using the symbols and language of calculus, Walras claimed to have found the source of price in the marginal utility of commodities to purchasers. Price, he said, was a function of marginal shifts in demand relative to supply: the more people demand a commodity in relation to its supply, the higher its price will be; the lower this marginal utility, the lower the price of the commodity. Marginal utility – demand for incremental purchases of a commodity – he said, could be measured using differential equations.

A similar theory had been put forward in England – a few months earlier – by William Stanley Jevons in his *The Theory of Political Economy*. In Austria, Karl Menger published a marginalist theory of value in non-mathematical language at about the same time. Soon afterwards, John B. Clark independently formulated marginalist theory in the US. Alfred Marshall also claimed to have done the same in those years. [63]

The time for marginalism, or differential economics, had obviously come. This can be partly explained by the hope that economics would benefit from the use of differential equations, just as physics, chemistry and engineering had. However, prior to the Paris Commune few believed that economics could legitimately aspire to the precision of the physical sciences. When Jevons published his paper a 'Notice of a General Mathematical Theory of Political Economy' in 1862 it had been 'received without a word of interest or belief'. [64] What had changed to make mathematical precision more plausible in the 1870s? Unlike engineers or chemists, economists could not point to practical applications for differential equations. Marginalism appealed to capitalists and conservative academics because it abandoned the labour theory of value. Basing prices on marginal utility was not likely to give comfort to the radical labour movement. Besides, the theory's arcane formulations, the symbols and notations of differential calculus, were Greek to most working-class readers.

Marginalists adopted the symbols of the most advanced mathematics. They illustrated their assertions with elegant curves and intersecting graphs, but their economic assumptions were even less realistic than Adam Smith's. In their models of 'pure competition', *homo economicus* is the central character. *Homo economicus* exchanges goods in competitive markets and moves freely from one line of work to another in response to marginal changes in prices and profits. He fully understands incremental changes in the marketplace and responds to movements in price and supply like a sensuous calculating machine, differentiating and integrating variables to maximise the utility he will receive from his expenditures.

How relevant is this hypothetical android to the real world? If everyone has access to means of livelihood and is free to move in pursuit of the most remunerative work, how can lack of skills and chronic unemployment be explained? If consumers fully understand market conditions, how could merchants buy cheap in one market and sell dear in another? It is argued that simplified models allow the theorist to isolate forces and to develop more logical or more scientific explanations of processes. Granting this, what was discovered from the marginalist model?

In their search for mathematical precision marginalists started with the assumption that prices are a function of marginal utility. How is marginal utility, a subjective determination, to be measured? It is measured by the prices people are willing to pay. So what have we learned? Prices are determined by marginal utility; marginal utility is measured by prices. Prices, then, are nothing more nor less than prices. Marginalists, having begun their search in the field of subjectivity, proceeded to walk in circles.

Adam Smith had pointed out a century earlier that price has little to do with the utility of a good to a consumer. Water and air have great utility but little or no exchange value. Pearls and rubies have little use value but great exchange value. Utility or use to a consumer cannot determine exchange value because it is the interests of sellers – not buyers – that determine the price of commodities. From a seller's viewpoint, the marginal utility of a commodity is beside the point. It can even be said that the less use the seller has for a good, the more he or she will see it as an exchange value. Despite being of little utility for sellers, commodities will not usually be given away. If sellers are independent producers, free to move from one line of work to another, they will attempt to exchange the products of their labour for a price that gives them the means to purchase goods that take at least as long to produce. If they cannot, they will turn their attention to producing goods that take less time and can be sold for higher prices. If sellers are capitalist producers, they will sell goods for their costs of production plus the average rate of profit or more. If they cannot, they will produce something else or go out of business.

Marginalists claimed to have found an explanation of prices in exchange, but they did not entirely ignore production. Here they pushed labour time, wage levels and profit rates into the background and emphasised 'opportunity costs'. Opportunity costs, they said, measure the revenue possible from the most favourable exchange. If one seller can get greater revenue applying his capital to the production of some other commodity, or if another seller gets a higher price for a similar commodity, the seller has a claim to the increased revenue as an opportunity cost.

Wealthowners warmly embraced the idea of opportunity costs. It remains a fixture of competitive market theory even though opportunity costs would not arise in the competitive conditions presupposed by the theory. If markets were characterised by

numerous small enterprises, none of which had the power to
influence supply or price and if producers were free to move from
less profitable to more profitable activities, prices would be
pushed toward points at which producers with average costs got
average profits. Nobody could claim opportunity costs.

Marginalists also put forward a theory of wages. Their basic
premise was that 'the marginal disutility of labour must in
equilibrium equal the marginal utility of wage income'.[65] This is
supposed to mean that a worker will agree to work an additional hour if the negative value of the loss of an hour's leisure
is less than the positive value of the additional wages. While a
comforting idea, this again ignores reality. Few workers have
the option routinely to bargain over wage rates or to choose
the hours they will work. Wages are either set unilaterally by
employers or are arrived at by collective bargaining. In the
absence of labour laws and trade unions, employers determine
how many hours will be worked. Even if the reality of capitalist
master–servant relations are ignored, it would still be impossible
precisely to compare or contrast the disutility of additional
labour with the utility of additional income.

Nonetheless, the smoke and mirrors of differential and integral
equations succeeded in creating an illusion that economic theory
was now grounded in mathematical precision. The abandonment
of the logical foundation for belief in the beneficial effects of
market forces was successfully obscured. Without the labour
theory of value, there was no longer the possibility that an
objective foundation could be established for the claim that competition leads to the exchange of equivalents. The emerging
profession of economics still claimed that market forces led to
general wellbeing, but this was now driven more by public relations than logic. Marginalists were content with the observation
that in free exchanges both buyers and sellers got what they
wanted. The concepts of marginal utility and opportunity cost had
transformed the market into an arena in which some manipulated
wants to make gains at the expense of others. In this, marginalism could not be faulted. That is capitalist reality.

Support for marginalism depended on the success of the
system it was commissioned to defend. From the 1870s on,
imperialist expansion allowed the capitalist powers of Europe
and North America to exploit resources from all continents.
Technological advances reduced the labour time required in
production, while a broadening franchise encouraged social
reform. A strengthened trade unionism made it possible for
workers in more prosperous nations to increase their real
income as capital increased its profits. Marginalists basked in
the reflected glory. Their dogmas went virtually unchallenged

until the deep depression of the 1930s made it obvious that market forces could not be relied upon to revive prosperity.

The Keynesian Revision

The revision of marginalist theory is identified with John Maynard Keynes. Keynes, who worked in the India Office before World War I, had observed that saving by buying and hoarding gold could lead to a decline in the money available for investment. In the 1920s, he suggested that other savings could be idle. He added that savings invested outside of the country had a negative impact on domestic economic activity. Little attention was paid to his challenge of the proposition that savings necessarily equalled investments – which was accepted by all classical and marginalist economists – until the economic collapse of the 1930s.

As the Depression deepened, Keynes became more critical of traditional free market assumptions. In *The General Theory of Employment, Interest and Money*, published in 1935, Keynes rejected the 'loanable funds' theory of investment.[66] The present rate of investment, Keynes said, does not depend on the rate of savings or on the 'loanable funds' available to investors; it depends on changes in aggregate demand. When aggregate demand is growing, businesses anticipate growth in their future profits and will be motivated to invest to expand capacity even if the rate of savings is declining. When aggregate demand is shrinking, businesses have little expectation of increased future profits and will not invest to expand capacity no matter how high the savings rate is.

Keynes went on to reject the notion that increased savings are required to push economies out of recession. When businesses are not investing, savings will remain idle, dampening economic activity just as if they had been hoarded. Even when savings are invested, the result is not necessarily a revival of economic growth. So long as businesses believe that aggregate demand is stagnant or declining, firms will not invest in additional capacity. They may invest in labour-saving machinery, but such investments, by increasing unemployment, further dampen demand.

Keynes concluded that it was wrongheaded to seek a revival of economic growth through policies designed to stimulate private investment. The reverse is required: to create a climate in which businesses will invest in increased capacity, governments must intervene to increase employment and aggregate demand. Keynes argued that government efforts to increase employment should be financed largely by government borrowing. Since business is not going to expand capacity during times of stagnating markets, the argument that government borrowing reduces the money available for private investment has little merit. If governments act to keep interest rates low, the cost of government borrowing can be kept down and businesses will have cheap credit.

Keynes also advocated tax increases: a more steeply graduated income tax, higher business taxes and higher tariffs on imported goods. He dismissed the argument that higher taxes necessarily harm the economy. He did agree that increased consumption taxes could reduce aggregate demand. This is especially the case when consumption taxes are raised to reduce the deficit. Such tax increases, advocated by proponents of fiscal responsibility, have the effect of transferring income from consumers to the creditors of government. However, if higher taxes come from income that would otherwise be saved and are used to increase pensions, unemployment benefits or other government transfer payments, or to increase spending on public works, consumer demand will rise and private investment will be stimulated.

Keynes also advocated government intervention to protect domestic industry. To objections that tariffs and other protectionist measures disrupt markets and increase costs, Keynes said that the Depression made the argument for protectionism compelling. Protectionism increases employment by making marginal domestic businesses profitable. If tariffs on imports are accompanied by restrictions on the movement of capital abroad, more funds, at lower interest rates, will be available to the government and to domestic companies. Keynes admitted that such policies may not be justifiable in the long run, but quipped, 'in the long run we are all dead'.[67]

John Maynard Keynes was not an enemy of capitalism. His father and mother had been born to prosperous business families. His father was a professor of moral philosophy and the financial administrator of Cambridge University. His mother was one of the first women to attend that university and in the 1930s became the first woman mayor of Cambridge. The young John Maynard, after graduating from Eton, studied mathematics at Cambridge and then transferred to economics where he found a patron in Alfred Marshall, the most acclaimed economist of the time. While still a student, Keynes explained his interest in economics by saying, 'I want to manage a railway or organise a Trust or at least swindle the investing public. It is so easy and fascinating to master the principles of these things.'[68]

Keynes joined the civil service, where he worked in the India Office, studying the colony's means-of-payment problems. His early interest in international monetary issues led to a lifetime of successful currency speculation. During World War I, Keynes joined the Treasury and became that department's main negotiator at the Versailles peace talks. His fame as a prescient economic analyst began with his resignation in protest against the massive reparation payments the Allies imposed on Germany. In *The Economic Consequences of the Peace*, Keynes argued that reparations were folly: Germany could make these payments only if it were allowed to maintain huge surpluses of exports over imports – surpluses which would be at the expense of the industries of France and England.[69] He predicted that reparations would provoke another world war.

In 1921, John Maynard Keynes was appointed chairman of the National Mutual Life Assurance Society, one of the oldest investment houses in London. Three years later, he became – like his father before him – bursar of King's College, Cambridge, responsible for the college's investment portfolio. His acumen as an investor resulted in substantial increases in the stipends received by College fellows. For Cambridge, Keynes followed a cautious investment strategy. Investing for himself, he won, lost and regained fortunes. By 1930, he was a wealthy, prominent and busy member of the British ruling class. Governments routinely sought his advice. When he argued a few years later that government action was needed to pull the country out of the Depression, few people would dismiss him as a Bolshevik dupe.

Keynes was appointed to the House of Lords during World War II. His proposals for war financing inspired government policy in Britain, Canada and the US. As Britain's chief negotiator at Bretton Woods, Keynes was the architect of post-war monetary policy. His interventionist policies allowed governments to smooth the transition from warfare to consumer goods production. The unemployment and social dislocation that followed World War I was largely avoided. During the 30 years after the war, in which governments followed Keynesian policies, capitalism experienced its longest period of sustained growth.

However, the seeds of rejection were germinating within the economics profession. In *The General Theory* Keynes had done little more than superimpose his observations on the traditional model of the individual in the market. He noted the tendency of the system to operate at less than full employment. He made no attempt to develop the logic of unequal property relations, of restricted access to resources or of oligopolistic control of markets. Although he had rejected the most untenable dogmas of *laissez faire* theory, he otherwise remained committed to the nineteenth-century free market view. After Keynes, students of economics still began with a theory of competitive individualism. They were taught to view capitalist control of markets as 'imperfect competition', as merely a deviation from 'perfect competition'.

Wealthowners had never been comfortable with government intervention that did not directly further their own interests. When they decided they had had enough of Keynesianism, many economists joined them in their retreat to nineteenth-century *laissez faire* positions. By the 1970s, the neoconservative reaction had gained enough influence in academic and business circles to restore the dogmas of the individual in the market to the dominant place they held before the 1930s Depression.

2   Corporate Oligopoly

The Decline of Individual Economic Activity

The free market theory revived by neoconservatives is based on the assumption that competitive individualism is the predominant form of economic activity. In fact, independent producers are a small minority. Nearly all industries, including communications, energy, finance, forestry, manufacturing, mining and transportation are dominated by a few large corporations.

Even agriculture, the traditional stronghold of independent producers, has come under the control of agribusiness. Although independent farmers still produce most food crops, 60 per cent of the food dollar goes to corporations that direct the flow of goods from farmers to consumers. Corporations like Cargill, International Multifoods and General Foods control 80 per cent of the market for primary products. The superabundance of brand names on supermarket shelves creates an illusion of choice and competition, but most packaged goods are actually produced by a handful of companies. Nestlé and Unilever produce and sell packed goods worldwide. Beatrice, Consolidated, Kraft and Heinz dominate the US market. [1] George Weston, Labatt and McCains are dominant players in the Canadian domestic market.

Retail trade, once a preserve of small shopkeepers, is now big business. Food distribution has long been dominated by chains like Safeway and Loblaws. In the last generation mom-and-pop convenience stores have been replaced by chains like Mac's and 7-Eleven. The same is true of drug stores. The local druggist is more likely to be a salaried employee of a chain than an independent pharmacist. In dry goods, independent shopkeepers have been pushed aside by department stores and chains like Canadian Tire. Independent retailers have not been helped by the spread of shopping malls. The dozen or more speciality shops in a mall make it appear that the independent shopkeeper is well represented, but most are either branches of large chains or franchises. In Canada, a mall may include up to ten shops owned by one company – Dylex. Few shoppers know of Dylex, which in the late 1980s had sales of C$2 billion a year. It operated under names like Tip Top, Harry Rosen, Big Steel, Fairweather, Susy Sheir/L.A. Express, Town and Country/Petites, Club Monaco, Alfred Sung, Bi-Way, Thrifty's and Drug World.

The hospitality industry is dominated by large corporations. International chains like McDonald's, Burger King and A & W along with national, regional and city-wide chains now dominate the restaurant industry. Hotel chains, associated with railways, airlines and international travel agencies, control the more expensive, better-advertised facilities.

Trucking is one industry in which the number of owner-operators has grown. But this is the result of deliberate corporate policy. Replacing hired truck drivers with owner-operators weakens unions, undermines wages and working conditions and allows companies to shift debt load to drivers. Increasing numbers of owner-operators, realising that a few large companies control transportation services, have joined together in unions to demand minimum mileage rates, maximum hours and safety regulations – just like other workers.

Independent practitioners continue to predominate in medicine, law and architecture – where competition is limited by onerous entrance requirements and strict regulations – but even here large, multi-city businesses are becoming common. In these, a few partner-owners employ dozens and sometimes hundreds of salaried professionals. In teaching, nursing, accounting and engineering, most people are salaried employees working for public institutions or for large corporations.

People who exchange their own products in competitive markets are not close to being a majority in any industrialised country. Most people work for wages or salaries. In the UK during the Thatcher years, the number of wage and salary workers did decline, but employers and the self-employed grew only fractionally from 7.4 per cent to 7.6 per cent of the economically active population. The UK was the exception. While the number of employers and self-employed in Canada and the US grew from 7 per cent of the economically active population in 1970 to 8 per cent in 1990, the number of wage and salary workers grew from 88 per cent to 90 per cent. In Japan the self-employed and employers fell from 19 per cent of the economically active population in 1970 to 14 per cent in 1990. During the same period the proportion of wage and salary workers rose from 64 per cent to 76 per cent. (Unpaid family workers declined from 17 per cent to 10 per cent.) [2]

The rise in self-employment since 1980 is not a sign of renewed economic independence. It is more a result of rising chronic unemployment and a preference by some employers for dependent contractors. People who cannot find full-time work try to hustle an income working out of their homes. Many barely supplement unemployment or social security benefits. Many more work long hours at sewing machines for less than the minimum wage. The more successful often work at their own computer terminals. They may consider themselves self-employed but they are likely to be dependent on one employer for most or all of their income. Dependent contractors are becoming common in construction. Here self-employed subcontractors do the same physical work as employees and are supervised by company foremen. The employers' aim is to get around union agreements and to evade payroll deductions for taxes, unemployment insurance and workers' compensation. In Canada, construction companies pay ostensibly self-employed contractors two thirds and sometimes as little as half of the prevailing union wage. [3]

Individual production is not compatible with capitalism. Capitalist industry cannot function without the combined activity of numerous people in numerous occupations. Before production can begin, facilities must be designed by engineers and built by construction workers. Investable funds must be accumulated and distributed by people working in the finance industry. Materials must be gathered, processed and refined by miners, loggers, farmers and smelter and mill workers. Materials are turned into manufactured goods by machine operators, assemblers, packagers, administrators, repair and maintenance workers. Goods are distributed to customers by workers in transportation, storage and sales. In theory, the individuals or groups in each of these steps could purchase goods from those in the preceding step and sell to those in the next step. But that is not how capitalism works. It is a system of wealth-owners' control over means of livelihood.

Domination by capitalists began with enclosures and took off with industrialisation. When capital mechanised industry, it socialised labour. Since then capital itself has been collectivised in giant national and transnational corporations. In capitalist law, corporations are deemed to be persons. They are actually hierarchic institutions, controlled by wealthowners, that command social labour. The more administrative control they have over materials, technologies and markets, the more profits corporations can make.

Adam Smith was aware of the capitalist drive for administrative control and condemned it. Alfred Dupont Chandler, while conceding that modern corporations have little in common with the theory of the individual in the market, was less critical. In *The Visible Hand: The Managerial Revolution in American Business*, he said, 'the assumption that the processes of production and distribution are managed, or at least should be managed, by small traditional enterprises regulated by the invisible hand of the market' has been outdated ever since the modern multi-unit business enterprise replaced market mechanisms with administrative coordination. [4]

Chandler, a professor at Harvard Business School, was no critic of capitalism. He edited the presidential papers of Dwight Eisenhower and extolled the virtues of big business in *Giant Enterprises and the Railroads* and in *Pierre S. du Pont and the Making of the Modern Corporation*. In *The Visible Hand*, he traced the rise of corporate power over the market to the late nineteenth century when the modern business

> enterprise came into being and continued to grow by setting up or purchasing business units that were theoretically able to operate as independent enterprises ... The internalization of many units permitted the flow of goods from one unit to another to be administratively coordinated. [5]

As giant corporations came to dominate business,

> the visible hand of management replaced the invisible hand of market mechanisms ... Whereas the activities of single-unit traditional enterprises were monitored and coordinated by market mechanisms, the producing and distributing units within a modern business enterprise are monitored and coordinated by middle managers. *Top managers*, in addition to evaluating and coordinating the work of middle managers, *took the place of the market in allocating resources for future production and distribution.* [6]

In the US the first giant multi-unit business enterprises were built by tycoons like du Pont, Rockefeller, Vanderbilt, Gould and Morgan. [7] The du Pont family built a chemical trust out of their Civil War explosives business and later assembled the companies that made up General Motors. John D. Rockefeller organised the Standard Oil trust that for decades monopolised the supply and transportation of petroleum products. In the 1880s, Standard Oil produced 85 per cent of US crude and refined petroleum; it had 20,000 oil wells, owned 5,000 tank cars and employed 100,000 people. [8] Vanderbilt and Gould acquired and merged railways, eliminated competitive bidding in freight rates and organised military-like managerial hierarchies to command these giant corporations. Their companies passed into the hands of J. P. Morgan, the most powerful banker of the era, whose railways at the turn of the century generated revenues equal to half of US government's receipts. [9] In *The House of Morgan*, Ron Chernow wrote that Morgan 'saw competition as a destructive, inefficient force and instinctively favoured large-scale combination as the cure'. [10] Morgan, he said, 'always favoured government planning over private competition, but private planning over either'. [11]

US patent law played a critical role in the consolidation of administrative control of markets. Patent-holders were not only rewarded with royalties, they were given an exclusive right to market the product or process for 17 years. Passed ostensibly to encourage individual inventors, these laws had the effect of legalising monopolies, particularly in the electrical and chemical industries. The use of patents to gain control of these industries is discussed in *America by Design*, by David Noble. [12]

General Electric, Westinghouse and Bell were pioneers in establishing technological monopolies. The founders of these companies – Thomas Edison, George Westinghouse and Alexander Graham Bell – not only patented significant inventions themselves, they bought additional patents from independent inventors or acquired these when competitors were taken over. [13] Edwin Prindle, an engineer and patent attorney who had represented all three companies in late nineteenth-century disputes, said, 'Patents are the best and most effective means of controlling competition. They occasionally give absolute command of the market, enabling their owners to name the price without regard to cost of production.' Prindle added that manufacturers should do what they can to get patent protection. 'If a patent can't be secured on a product, it should be secured on processes for making the product', and if this cannot be done, the product should 'be tied up in some way with a patent on some other product, process or machine'. [14]

The pioneers in technological monopolies quickly realised that they could not fully exploit their technical advantages so long as they were in competition with the others. By 1896, two of the three, Westinghouse and General Electric, had over 300 patent suits outstanding against each other. Concluding that overlapping patents were unprofitable, the two decided to pool their patents and divide the growing electrical business among themselves: 62.5 per cent was assigned to General Electric and 37.5 per cent to Westinghouse. In 1920, the Bell companies (AT&T and Western Electric) joined the cartel. All the patents held by the three companies were pooled and then reassigned, with each company getting exclusive control of all the patents in the section of the industry assigned it. General Electric and Westinghouse continued to share industrial equipment and consumer appliances; Bell was given control of telephones and telephone equipment.

World War I gave US chemical companies the opportunity to build technological monopolies. Before the war, US companies like Hooker and Dow had developed important electrochemical processes, but most of the patents in the expanding organochemi-

cal industry – then based on coal tar derivatives – were held by
German firms. Taking advantage of the exclusive possession provided by US law, German firms had methodically secured patents
on every chemical combination their scientists could devise. As a
result, no one else could make or market these substances in the
US. By 1912, 'ninety-eight per cent of applications for patents in
the chemical field had been assigned to German firms and were
never worked in the United States'.[15] This continued until 1917
when the US declared war on Germany. US patents held by
German firms were seized by the government and then sold to
US companies like Eastman Kodak, Union Carbide, Bausch and
Lomb and Bakelite. Du Pont benefited the most, acquiring 300
patents.

After the war, the US government imposed tariffs that effectively blocked attempts by German firms to re-establish their
dominance in the US market for organochemicals. By the middle
1920s, after nearly 500 mergers, three companies – Union
Carbide, Du Pont and Allied Chemical and Dye – dominated high
volume products. American Cynamid, Monsanto, Dow, Kodak
and Merck dominated smaller, more specialised fields.[16] Following the example of the electrical monopolies, each chemical company sought to patent all potentially profitable discoveries in the
part of the industry it dominated. Competitors and individual
inventors were given the choice of either selling their patent
rights to the dominant companies or being dragged through
expensive, drawn-out litigation.

Monopolies based on patent rights last only so long as the
patent is in force. To overcome the 17-year time limit, science-
based corporations institutionalised innovation. They set up
research and development departments and hired the best scientific minds money could buy to work on problems assigned by
top managers and patent attorneys. They also financed industrial
fellowships in universities. Scientists receiving these fellowships,
like those working in corporate research departments, were
obliged to sign over patent rights to the funding corporation.
Research and development departments and university fellows
were set to the task of redesigning products, processes and
equipment so that the corporations could register new patents
and thereby continuously maintain monopoly positions on the
most profitable technologies.

By 1925, Du Pont alone employed 1,200 scientists; the Bell
system, 3,600. By 1938, one third of all scientific researchers
were employed by 13 companies, half by 45 laboratories.[17]
David Noble commented, 'In the nineteenth century, scientific
ideas had given rise to industrial manufacture; now the industrial corporation undertook to manufacture scientific ideas.'[18]

In 1885, nearly 90 per cent of all patents were taken out by individuals. In 1950, three-quarters of all patents were issued to corporations. Corporations, by collectivising innovation, had made the individual inventor an anachronism.[19]

Transnational Corporations

During the 1970s, the US transnational corporations had revenue equal to 30 per cent of the planet's entire gross annual product.[20] In 1989 the revenues of the ten transnationals, with the highest sales (Mitsui, General Motors, C. Itoh, Sumitomo, Marubeni, Mitsubishi, Ford, Exxon, Shell and Nissno Iwai) totalled $1,000 billion – nearly twice as large as Canada's Gross National Product. The combined profits of the ten most profitable transnationals (IBM, Ford, Exxon, Shell, General Motors, General Electric, British Telecom, Dow, AT&T, Du Pont) at $40 billion equalled Iraq's entire Gross National Product in the year before the Gulf War.[21] In 1992 transnational corporations employed 73 million people, 10 per cent of global non-farm jobs and 20 per cent of jobs in more prosperous countries. The 100 largest transnationals controlled one quarter of all global output.

The power of these giant, privately-owned collectives is greater than the numbers imply. According to *World Investment Report 1994*, published by the United Nations, another 77 million people were indirectly employed by transnationals.[22] Proponents of competitive individualism say that most people work for small businesses. They do, but the presence of transnationals determines whether local, regional and national businesses prosper or fail. When a transnational opens a manufacturing plant or a materials processing operation in a region, numerous small businesses will spring to life supplying materials, manufactured components, transportation and business services for the transnational and consumer goods for its employees. When the transnational shuts down, small businesses lose their markets.

Control of global markets allows transnationals to pit governments against each other. By doing so they get the best credit terms and the lowest taxes, the most profitable materials supplies, the most favourable locations and the best transportation and communications facilities at the least cost to themselves. Transnationals benefit from the most advanced technologies – developed by men and women whose education was paid for by taxpayers in the most prosperous countries. They set up production facilities in poorer countries where skilled labour is cheapest. They focus their marketing efforts in countries where wages and prices are highest.

The power of transnationals over the market is most apparent in the petroleum industry. Seven transnationals (Exxon, Mobil, Texaco, Chevron, Amoco, Shell and British Petroleum) control oil wells throughout the world and own huge reserves of natural gas, coal and oil shale.[23] They are the major producers, the major distributors, the major refiners and the major retailers of petroleum products. Their combined sales in 1989 totalled $250 billion, their profits $11 billion. In the 1950s, they accounted for 60 per cent of the western world's oil production, for 90 per cent of production in Latin America and the Middle East and for three quarters of oil industry profits. Their dominant position has little to do with free, competitive markets. It began with concessions wrested from Cuba, Mexico, Indonesia, Venezuela and, later, from countries in the Middle East. They were nurtured with bribes, threats and direct military intervention by the governments of Britain, the Netherlands and the US. [24]

The 1991 Gulf War showed that threats to the security of petroleum supplies still provoke military intervention. But most of the time, petroleum transnationals prefer to manipulate markets peacefully. When demand for energy is thought to exceed supply, oil companies raise prices, claiming that this is the way the market rations a scarce resource. They lobby governments to provide tax concessions and outright grants to pay for new exploration and development, claiming this is the most efficient way to protect consumers from more severe future shortages. When times change and energy supplies exceed demand, oil companies lobby governments to fix minimum prices and to provide further tax concessions and grants – now ostensibly to ease the economic hardship in petroleum-producing regions. In either case, actual reserves and production levels are carefully guarded business secrets. The public has no way of knowing what is fact and what is not.

What is known is that control over the resource allows petroleum transnationals to profit from nearly any circumstance. When Iraq occupied Kuwait in August 1990, the price of a barrel of oil, which had been trading at $15, jumped to over $30. Oil companies claimed that shortages were forcing them to raise prices to consumers. As it turned out, oil production levels and stockpiles were so high that supertankers with nowhere to unload were being used as storage facilities. The supply glut caused the price of oil to fall to $20 a barrel. Despite the recession in 1991, oil companies were able to report record profits.

False claims of petroleum shortages are not new. In 1920, Standard Oil (now Exxon) initiated a propaganda war to force its way into UK-controlled Iraqi oil fields. Domestic petroleum production, the US public was told, would begin to fall off in three years. Standard Oil lobbyists solemnly declared that the country would shortly become dependent on the much more expensive fuel extracted from oil shale – unless supplies could be secured from abroad. To make the crisis more credible, the price was doubled to 35 cents a gallon. In some parts of the country gasoline was sold in one or two gallon allotments. Alarmed commentators spoke of making synthetic gasoline from wheat and others talked of going to war with Britain to get access to Iraqi oil. The British got the message and agreed to allow US oil companies into Iraq. Once US oil companies had secured a place in Iraq, the oil shortage miraculously disappeared. By the end of the decade, US domestic oil production had doubled.

In 1929, the Federal Oil Conservation Board recommended that domestic production be cut and imports increased, claiming that US oil reserves were being exhausted at an alarming rate. This campaign was vigorously endorsed (and perhaps initiated by) Andrew Mellon – President Hoover's Treasury Secretary. Mellon's family owned the controlling interest in Gulf Oil, one of the two main producers in the newly developed Venezuelan oil fields. If the government could be persuaded to ration domestic oil, the market for Venezuelan oil would expand. However, Mellon's scheme came to nought. Independent oil operators discovered Spindletop in 1930. East Texas wells were soon producing 10,000 barrels a day. The shortage became a glut and the price of crude fell from one dollar to ten cents a barrel.

In 1947, oil companies said prices had to be increased because supplies were running out. This time people were sceptical. A senate investigation committee found an unexplained quarter of a million barrels of crude in storage. By the mid-1950s massive new oil fields had been discovered in Texas and Oklahoma. The US was again pumping far more oil than could be sold. In 1959 domestic producers succeeded in getting a law passed to limit oil imports to a maximum of 12 per cent of domestic production. But because the law allowed imports only by companies that owned refineries, transnationals were given a new way to undercut smaller producers. Meanwhile, the big oil companies found new markets for Middle Eastern and Venezuelan crude in the expanding economies of western Europe and Japan. [25]

The oil giants were doing very well until the oil crisis of the 1970s – then their profits soared. In the early 1970s the public was traumatised by reports of the imminent exhaustion of petroleum supplies. In 1973, the Arab oil-producing states increased the price of crude from $3 to $11 a barrel. In

1979, the price was increased to $30. Oil companies claimed to be innocent victims of the Organisation of Petroleum Exporting Countries (OPEC). This was given credence in 1975 when the Saudi monarchy announced the nationalisation of oil lands owned by ARAMCO (a consortium of Chevron, Texaco, Exxon and Mobil, which controls Saudi Arabian oil fields). As it turned out the nationalisation was far from complete. The oil-consuming public was encouraged to believe that the Saudi royal family had a stranglehold on energy supplies, but the ARAMCO consortium continues to control exploration, production and distribution of Saudi crude.

If oil companies were subject to market forces, the steep rise in the cost of supplies should have squeezed their profits. What happened? In 1972, Exxon, the world's largest oil company, reported net income (profits after costs and taxes) of $1.5 billion. In 1973, after the price of crude had jumped from under $3 a barrel to $6 and then to $11, Exxon reported net income of $2.5 billion. In 1979, after the price had been pushed above $30, Exxon reported net income of $4.3 billion – nearly three times its profits before the original oil price increase. British Petroleum, one of biggest operators in the Middle East, weathered the storm even more successfully. 1972 had been a bad year for BP; its profits of $176 million were less than half of what they had been in 1971. In 1973, after the first jump in crude prices, BP's profits rose to $760 million. In 1979, after the second oil price shock, BP reported profits of $3.6 billion – a 20-fold increase over 1972.[26]

The reported profits of oil companies – from books that are used for tax purposes in their home countries – are only the tip of the iceberg. Operating around the globe, oil companies can move money from one place to another and from one account to another with no enforceable regulation from any government. They can and do increase charges to one affiliate and lower those to others to hide profits in one country and to take advantage of weaker regulations or more sympathetic tax laws in others.

Domestic Oligopoly

Oligopoly – control of an industry by a few companies – is not limited to transnational business. The US domestic economy has long been dominated by oligopolies. Table 2.1, based on data from the 1970s,[27] shows the extent of oligopolistic control of selected US industries.

Table 2.1
Number of Companies Accounting for 75 per cent or More
of the Business of Selected US Industries

Aluminium	3
Automobiles	3
Cereal foods	2
Cigarettes	4
Copper	4
Electric bulbs	3
Flat glass	4
Gypsum	3
Rubber tyres	3
Salt	2
Soap	3
Basic Steel	3
Synthetic fibres	4
Telephone equipment	1

Source: M. B. Clinard and P. C. Yeager, *Corporate Crime*, p. 33.

Competitive individualism has the status of a national ideology, but economic life in the US is actually administered by corporate oligopolies. In 1989, 200 corporations accounted for two thirds of all US industrial revenue. The 50 largest corporations got over half of all US industrial profits.[28] The chief executives of these corporations could easily and – as we shall see in Chapter 4 – often did fit into one room.

In Europe, oligopolistic control is more or less accepted. Government policies have favoured national companies large enough to compete in the world market. As the European Union has become more integrated, dominant companies in one country have merged with those in others. Giant corporations like Royal Dutch Shell, Philips, Unilever, Volkswagen, Electrolux, Nestlé and ICI dominate their industries. Governments actively promote the interests of these oligopolies and encourage others in aircraft production, railways and computers.

In Canada in 1991, ten non-financial corporations accounted for more than one fifth of Gross National Product. These were Bell Canada Enterprises, General Motors Canada, Ford Canada, Canadian Pacific, Imperial Oil, Alcan, Chrysler, George Weston, Noranda and the Thomson Corporation.[29]

Bell Canada Enterprises owned Bell Canada which had a monopoly of telephone transmission in Quebec and Ontario, as well as the controlling interest in telephone transmission in the

Maritime provinces. It owned a majority interest in Northern
Telecom, which had a near monopoly on the manufacturing of
telephone equipment in Canada. BCE also owned the controlling
interest in TransCanada PipeLines which, along with InterProvin-
cial PipeLines, monopolised the flow of petroleum products from
western Canada.

General Motors shared Canadian automobile production with
Ford and Chrysler. These three US-owned companies faced
growing competition from Japanese, European and Korean auto-
makers, but controlled two thirds of the Canadian automobile
market.

Canadian Pacific, along with the government-owned Canadian
National Railway, controlled cross-country rail traffic. In 1990,
CP's 1,500 tractors made it one of the two largest trucking
companies in Canada. Its fleet of deep sea ships was registered
abroad, so this company – so closely identified with Canada's
history – did not have to pay taxes here or meet Canadian safety
standards, working conditions or wage rates.

Imperial Oil, a subsidiary of US-owned Exxon, shared the bulk
of the Canadian petroleum business with Shell, Gulf and Petro-
Canada.

Alcan had a near-total monopoly of aluminium smelting in
Canada.

George Weston owned Loblaws, Super Valu and Real Canadian SuperStores, as well as the largest bakery chain in Canada.
Weston subsidiaries shared domination of the cross-Canada food
retailing business with the US-owned Safeway chain.

Noranda, the largest mining company in Canada, dominated
the non-ferrous metal business in Canada and in 1989 owned
the controlling interest in MacMillan Bloedel, Canada's largest
forest company.

The Thomson Corporation owned 40 daily newspapers across
Canada, including the *Globe & Mail*, as well as numerous week-
lies and biweeklies including the *Financial Times*. It also owned
more than 100 newspapers in the US and UK.

Five banks dominated Canadian banking. The Royal Bank,
Canadian Imperial Bank of Commerce, Bank of Montreal,
Toronto Dominion Bank and the Bank of Nova Scotia had
combined assets of over C$500 billion in 1991. Their profits
totalled more than C$3.5 billion. These banks' board of directors
meetings brought together top executives of Canadian and US-
owned national and regional corporations. During board meetings,
held several times each year, directors discussed and approved
policy decisions that affected every company in Canada that
relied on credit. During breaks in the meetings, these top corporate executives made friendships and connections. A few hundred

men and a handful of women developed common approaches to
consumers, workers and smaller businesses.

Oligopolies also dominate business within smaller regions.
While Jim Pattison Enterprises was not in the same league as
Alcan or Bell Telephone, in 1990 Pattison owned the largest car
dealership in British Columbia. Through Overwaitea and Save On
Foods, he owned the largest food retailers in the province. His
Neon Products and Seaboard Advertising had a near monopoly of
outdoor advertising displays. Mainland Magazines, Provincial
News and Mountain News, gave him a near monopoly of magazine distribution. Jim Pattison is a champion of the free market,
but his subsidiaries are not free to make the most profitable
exchanges in the marketplace. His car dealerships buy their signs
from his Neon Products. His food stores prominently display his
Gold Seal Salmon and Berryland canned goods. In 1990 all his
subsidiaries got their credit through Jim Pattison Enterprises –
and paid a surcharge of 1.5 per cent. [30]

Local markets are not immune to oligopolies. A small city will
usually have one, two or three machine shops, plumbing suppliers,
industrial laundries, bottling plants, feed distributors, travel
agents, stationers, music and record stores, wedding shops and
funeral parlours. These may be branches of large or small chains.
Whether they are or not, it will be in their interests to standard-
ise prices and services in the markets they share.

Oligopoly is typical wherever capitalist property relations
prevail. Despite the enthusiasm of free market theorists for competition, most entrepreneurs prefer to dominate markets. This can
be seen in the value that sellers and buyers of businesses place on
'good will'. What is good will if not favoured access to suppliers,
customers, technologies and skills? Good will has a monetary
value because it allows some businesses to overcome the competitive pressures that limit the profitability of the less favoured.

Oligopoly in Japan

In Japan, between one and three companies control 70 per cent of
the market in most industries. [31] Corporations are grouped into
economic organisations called *keiretsu*. The companies within each
group own each other's shares and supply each other with capital,
materials and equipment; their top executives meet regularly to
coordinate group activities. Six *keiretsu* – Mitsui, Mitsubishi,
Sanwa, Fuyo, Dai Ichi Kangyo and Sumitomo – dominate Japanese
business. Each includes scores of corporations in such diverse
industries as mining, smelting, steel, automobiles, machine tools,
computers and other consumer electronics, as well as some of the

world's largest financial and real estate companies. Each is tied to a
giant trading company, six of which handle over half of Japan's
non-oil imports. Well-known Japanese transnationals – oligopolies
in their own right – are merely parts of these empires: Toyota is
affiliated with Mitsui; Nissan with Fuyo; Nippon Electric (NEC)
with Sumitomo; Kirin with Mitsubishi; Hitachi with both Fuyo and
Sanwa.[32]

Government, through the ministries of Finance and International Trade and Industry, provides another level of administrative control. The Ministry of Finance uses selective tax and
interest rates to direct the flow of capital towards and away from
targeted industries.[33] The Ministry of International Trade and
Industry (MITI) has set import levels for materials and some
manufactured goods.[34] In the past, it has assessed business
conditions and made recommendations that selected industries be
emphasised and others phased out. Companies that followed its
advice were given grants and tax concessions.

In the 1960s, MITI initiated the shift from shipbuilding to
automobiles. In the next decade, it responded to rising oil prices
by directing business away from high energy use to the computer
industry. Six companies – Hitachi, Toshiba, Fujitsu, Nippon Electric, Mitsubishi and Oki – were picked to lead Japan's drive to
become a major computer producer. These six were given tax
incentives, preferential treatment in bank lending and were provided with a captive market through a government-backed computer leasing company, the Japan Electronic Computer Corporation,
which purchased their first computers. MITI also pressured steel,
machine tool and motor vehicle companies to buy Japanese computers. A few years later, MITI and the government-owned
telephone monopoly, Nippon Telegraph and Telephone, assembled
the consortium of computer companies that developed the semi-
conductor business. It took only a few years for these companies
to overtake the US industry.

It would, however, be wrong to conclude that Japan is a
centrally planned economy. As in other capitalist countries,
accumulation is private. The massive aggregates of capital that
dominate Japanese industry share a commitment to the national
economic interest but compete aggressively for market share.
Government is not monolithic either. The ministries of Finance,
International Trade and Industry, Post and Telecommunications
and Agriculture – each of which has a critical role in the
Japanese economy – often engage in unseemly bureaucratic turf
wars.

The influence of the Ministry of Post and Telecommunications comes from its control of the largest financial institution
in the world. The Japanese postal savings system holds more

personal savings than the total in all the savings accounts in Japanese commercial banks. It attracts savings by paying higher interest rates than those set by the Ministry of Finance for other financial institutions. Postal savings are then loaned to the Japanese government at less than the prevailing government bond rate, keeping government debt service charges low. The authority to license telecommunications companies has made the Ministry of Post and Telecommunications a rival of MITI in supervision of the electronics industry.[35]

The Ministry of Agriculture's influence is based on its close association with the National Federation of Agricultural Cooperatives (*Nokyo*), which inherited the structure of the Imperial Agricultural Association, set up in 1943 as a compulsory farmers' organisation. Most farmers remain members. *Nokyo* purchases crops, provides storage facilities and sells seeds, fertilisers, supplies and equipment. Payments for crops are credited to the accounts of farmers in the *Nokyo* bank. The bank supplies farmers with credit, organises the payment of their bills and transfers funds to the *Nokyo* mutual aid association – the largest insurance company in the world. *Nokyo*, while technically a farmers' cooperative, is thus really a government-supported conglomerate with a monopoly on all aspects of agriculture in Japan.[36]

Despite rivalries and competition, government and business work together. Top ministry officials meet regularly with officers of *Keidanren* (the Federation of Economic Organisations), the main big business lobby group; with *Nissho* (the Chambers of Commerce and Industry), for smaller businesses; and with *Sanken* (the Industrial Relations Study Council – which includes 20 senior representatives of *Keidanren* and *Nissho*). *Sanken* acts as the executive committee of the business elite, making the day-to-day decisions on issues. During the long years of uninterrupted Liberal Democratic Party rule, the ties between government and business were further strengthened by the career patterns of government officials. When top bureaucrats retired, they were hired as executives in politically sensitive industries like construction, road building and banking, or they were rewarded with safe LDP seats in parliament.[37]

The Liberal Democrats, a conservative and authoritarian party, ruled Japan from the 1950s to 1993. The LDP got its funds from big business and was run by top corporate executives and the former heads of government ministries. Government officials openly campaigned for the LDP. LDP governments concentrated on handing out the patronage on which their majorities depended but otherwise left the business of government to senior bureaucrats.[38]

Government and big business in Japan have had close rela-

tions throughout the modern era. When the Tokugawa Shogunate
was overthrown in the 1867 Meiji Restoration, the victorious
samurai leaders were determined to master western technology
and business organisation, but they had no interest in western
liberalism or in Adam Smith's already archaic model of the individual in the market. Having seized power in the name of the
emperor and in defence of traditional family and national values,
Japan's leaders praised obedience over freedom, mutual obligations over competition and loyalty over individualism.

They were encouraged in this by leading western thinkers,
including Herbert Spencer, a theoretician of rugged individualism. In response to a letter from Baron Kentaro in 1892,
Herbert Spencer expressed his dismay at a proposal to lift
restrictions on capital from abroad and on individual foreigners.
He wrote, 'I regret this as a fatal policy. If you wish to see
what is likely to happen, study the history of India.' [39] Kentaro
had sought his opinion because Spencer's Social Darwinist
theory of the survival of the fittest appealed to the aristocratic
extremists then in power in Japan. Spencer did not disappoint.
He advised that foreigners not be allowed to own land and that
they should also be prohibited from the coastal trade and the
distribution of imported goods within Japan. Although Spencer
was hostile to demands for public ownership in Britain, he
recommended that mining remain in the hands of Japan's military government.

Japan sent diplomats, students and scholars abroad to learn
from the West. They admired the quality of British goods and
the refinement of French culture. They noted that the US –
dominated by giant trusts – was becoming an economic super-
power. They were even more impressed with Germany's interventionist state and giant cartels. Japan's leaders concluded that
close cooperation between industry and government was the
quickest route to industrial strength. Industrialisation began
with the building of a scientifically educated bureaucracy in the
German manner. As the state apparatus was assembled, it
initiated investments in the steel industry, shipbuilding, muni-
tions, food processing and consumer goods. When businesses
became profitable these were turned over to private interests,
many ending in the hands of great merchant families who had
allied themselves with samurai leaders through marriages. [40]

By World War II, four family holding companies, called
zaibatsu – Mitsui, Mitsubishi, Sumitomo and Yasuda – dominated what was already the globe's fourth largest economy.
After the war, US occupation forces ordered the *zaibatsu* dismantled, but the results were not as expected. Workers' councils took charge of enterprises abandoned by *zaibatsu* repre-

sentatives. Then, when Mao Tse-tung's victory in China inspired rapid growth in support for the Communist Party among Japanese trade unionists, the occupation authorities decided that campaigns against war criminals had best be subordinated to the defence of capitalist property rights. A reconstituted police force, supported by criminal gangs – both including veterans of Japanese overseas campaigns – launched a wave of violence against the Communist Party and trade unions. The old ruling classes were pushed to form the unified governing party that would eventually become the LDP. The *zaibatsu* were allowed to reorganise as *keiretsu*. Professional managers were put in charge. Intercorporate ownership replaced family holding companies, but the system of interconnected trading, real estate, construction, financial and industrial enterprises remained intact. [41]

The *keiretsu* system has allowed Japanese companies to move resources from one industry to another without the bankruptcies and lay-offs that would result in Canada, Britain or the US. When changing market conditions dictate, major *keiretsu* shift capital and labour either away from or towards steel, aluminium, shipbuilding, automobiles, machine tools, computers, semi-conductors, musical instruments, or household appliances. The system of interlocking ownership between industrial corporations and financial institutions makes the managers of finance capital aware of industrial needs. It encourages cheaper credit. [42] During the late 1980s when US business was paying real interest rates of 4 or 5 per cent, Japanese business was getting credit for 2 per cent and less. The *keiretsu* system encourages enterprises to focus on long-term growth. Because shares are held by associated companies and 60 to 70 per cent of shares are rarely if ever traded, shareholder pressure for immediate returns is minimised. Although profit rates during the 1980s were less than half those of US companies, Japanese industry had a much higher rate of investment. By the end of the decade 15 to 20 per cent of Japan's GNP was being invested in machinery and equipment, compared with 6 to 7 per cent in the US and Canada. [43]

This higher rate of investment increased the efficiency of Japanese industry. By 1990 an automobile was assembled in 17 hours of labour in Japan; it took 26 hours in the US and 35 hours in Europe. [44] Not only did Japanese businesses devote more time to research, they were able to purchase and develop research done by others. Japanese companies became world leaders in developing and marketing new computerised consumer products such as laser printers, lap-top computers, refrigerators, cameras, vacuum cleaners, automatic rice cookers and bread makers. In the semi-conductor business, where US companies in the 1980s were spending 18 per cent of their revenue on new plant and equipment, Japanese companies were spending nearly 40 per cent. They were producing semi-conductors with the world's most advanced automated machinery in ultra-clean, dust-free production facilities where they were able to reduce defects to 20 to 30 per cent of output compared to 40 to 50 per cent in the US. [45]

Oligopolies and Market Theory

When means of livelihood are controlled by capitalists neither the assumptions nor the conclusions of free market theory hold. The right of wealthowners to deny access to materials, technologies, markets and credits means that people do not have the economic mobility assumed by the theory. Relations of domination and subordination take the place of the exchange of equivalents in the market. Because supply and price are administered in the interests of wealthowners, the search for the laws of self-regulating markets is futile. What is needed is not a physics of competitive exchange, but a sociology of capitalist power. Such a sociology will content itself with describing capitalist property relations and assessing their social consequences.

The unequal property relations of capitalism are designed to favour wealthowners. Great disparities in income are built into the system. A few get incredible material rewards which have little relation to needs or to any direct contribution to the wellbeing of others. They are scorers in a game in which losers must far outnumber winners. Losers include the unemployed who are denied the means of participating in consumer society. Losers include wage- and salary-workers who must submit to master–servant relations and spend most of their waking hours at exhausting and monotonous jobs. Losers include the self-employed who work longer hours for less pay. Those who lose the most are people in poor countries. Unemployed, naked, homeless, starving, penniless people have no demand. Demand in a capitalist market means having the money to buy commodities.

When people are denied access to means of livelihood, the invisible hand of market forces does not intervene on their behalf. Equilibrium between supply and demand has no necessary connection with human need. For example, assume a country of one million people in which 900,000 are without means of livelihood. One million bushels of wheat are produced. The entire crop is sold to 100,000 people at $10 a bushel. Supply and demand are in equilibrium, yet 900,000 people will face starvation.

Capitalist property relations mean that markets are dominated by oligopolies. Paul Samuelson, an influential US economist in the 1950s and 1960s, wrote that markets are dominated by oligopolies when 'anyone who buys or sells a good in large enough quantities [is] able to affect the price of that good'. He added,

> to some degree that means almost every businessman, except possibly the millions of farmers who individually produce a negligible fraction of the total crop. All economic life is a blend of competitive and monopoly elements. Imperfect, or monopolistic, competition is the prevailing mode. [46]

Oligopolistic power over markets is based on horizontal and vertical controls.

Horizontal controls allow oligopolies to control necessary steps in an economic process from material supplies to processing, manufacturing, transportation and distribution. Oligopolies establish horizontal control over materials by controlling more of the highest quality and most accessible supplies than they intend to market immediately. When competitors are left with lower quality or more expensive supplies, oligopolies can regulate supply so that output multiplied by price results in maximum income. Horizontal control over processing or manufacturing is based on exclusive possession of technologies, patents and franchises as well as on excess productive capacity. When control of a market is secure, oligopolies will usually delay innovation to maximise profits from existing plant and equipment. When control is challenged, oligopolies will speed the introduction of more advanced technologies, forcing competitors to make do with less marketable products and less cost-effective production processes. Excess capacity will make it possible for oligopolies to increase production and drop prices if necessary to drive unwanted competitors out of the business.

Vertical controls substitute administrative command for exchange between steps of economic processes. The largest oligopolies procure materials from their own subsidiaries, process and manufacture these in their own refineries, mills and factories, transport their own goods and then market these through their own distribution and sales networks. When vertical control is complete every step of the economic process is administratively regulated.

Oligopolies need not control all aspects of the economic process. Dominance can be maintained while control shifts from one step in the economic process to others. Standard Oil began by monopolising transportation of petroleum by rail. It later relied on its marketing networks, its refining capacity and its control of the crude oil supply. The big three US automobile companies relied initially on the most advanced production technologies. Their strength is now based on extensive dealership networks and customer loyalty. Like other mature oligopolies, they rely on the weight of capital itself: on expenditures for research and development, on access to the cheapest credit, on the extent and location of facilities, on exclusive agreements with suppliers and distributors and on the size of their advertising expenditures.

The few firms that share oligopolistic control of an industry need not actually conspire to control a market. They will usually sell similar goods produced with similar technologies at similar prices. When one firm raises prices, the others, facing similar conditions and invoking the concept of opportunity cost, will follow suit. In the meantime they will make a show of competing. Aggressive advertising is the preferred form of oligopolistic competition. In the US in 1990, $130 billion – a sum greater than the GNP of most countries – was spent on television and magazine advertising, on eye-catching displays and on celebrity endorsements.[47] Advertising creates an illusion of competition, but is designed to build the consumer loyalty that keeps smaller firms, which cannot afford expensive advertising campaigns, on the fringes of the market. Unlike competitive producers, whose prices are set by market forces, oligopolies can pass advertising and other cost increases to consumers.

For a competitive firm with no control over prices, rising costs mean lower profits. For oligopolies, rising costs often mean rising profits. This is certainly the case whenever prices rise by the same percentage as a cost. For example, if wages rise by 5 per cent and total wages account for 20 per cent of revenue, total costs would have increased by only 1 per cent. If oligopolies are able to increase prices by 5 per cent, they will get a windfall profit of 4 per cent. They also have the power to maintain and raise prices as costs fall. In free market theory, the higher profits resulting from labour-saving technologies are supposed to attract additional producers, causing supply to rise and prices to fall. When oligopolies dominate markets, horizontal and vertical controls block the entry of competitors, allowing dominant firms to maintain prices. Indeed, through most of the twentieth century increasing labour productivity has been accompanied by rising prices.

Chronic inflation is usually blamed on rising wages, expanding money supply and government deficits. The fundamental cause is oligopoly. Inflation benefits oligopolies in many ways.

Inflation allows oligopolies to cite the principle of opportunity cost: 'other companies are increasing prices, so we are as well'. Inflation allows oligopolies to increase the book value of their investments to justify higher profits. Inflation, by making past and present investment more expensive, acts as a barrier to future competitors.

It should not be concluded that oligopolies can set prices as high as they like. If prices are set too high, dominant firms from other industries would be tempted to move in and gain a share of the exceptional returns. Small producers – using more expensive materials or out-dated technologies – would be able to increase their share of the market and make the competitive rate of profit or better. The ability of oligopolies to set prices is narrowed further during times of economic decline. When the solidarity of dominant firms is shaken by slumping sales, attempts to increase prices can lead to a loss of market share. Cost-cutting becomes the favoured means to maximise profits. Control over crucial aspects of markets is maintained and extended through mergers and acquisitions.

When oligopolies dominate industries, market forces do not bring profit rates to an average. The more competitive the market, the closer profit rates will be to the average return on capital. The more complete and secure control of a market is, the higher oligopolistic profits will be. The spread between competitive and oligopolistic rates is obscured by the capital market. As shares are bought and sold in stock exchanges, higher profits are transformed into higher share prices. If, for example, the actual investment in an oligopoly is $500 million and its annual profit is $100 million, the real return on investment is 20 per cent. But if the average competitive return on shares is 10 per cent, the shares of the oligopoly will sell for $1 billion. Investors who buy the shares at the market rate will get the average competitive return. Only the original investors will get the higher oligopolistic rewards, either as a 20 per cent return on their original investment or as a capital gain of 100 per cent.

When a few companies regulate resource utilisation, control the development of technologies and have privileged access to credits and markets, it cannot reasonably be held that the free play of supply and demand pushes economies to equilibrium at full employment. With administered markets and exclusive, private possession of means of livelihood, no steady state can be sustained. Smaller firms are driven to grow so that they too can get oligopolistic returns. Dominant firms are driven to grow so that they can retain and expand their market share. Instead of equilibrium, periods of frantic growth are followed by periods of spiralling decline.

Growth has its benefits. The capitalist drive to accumulate
private wealth has generated an ever expanding volume and variety of goods with less and less labour. Capitalist growth has
electrified daily life, bringing labour-saving appliances, entertainment and education into homes. It can claim credit for a transportation revolution that enables common people to travel distan-
ces that only the most adventurous would have attempted 100
years ago. It has led to the development of means to eliminate
hunger, cold and pestilence. But capitalist growth has not come
without costs. To maximise short-term profits, corporations dump
the unwanted by-products of industry into the atmosphere, soil
and waterways. They deplete non-renewable resources at an ever
escalating rate. Capitalist growth, by the logic of exclusive possession, leads to worsening polarisation between rich and poor. In
the systemic drive to cut costs and maximise profits, oligopolistic
capitalism causes hardship and hunger. When oligopolies gain
control of resources, people are driven from land that has sustained them. Entire continents have been turned into low wage
areas. Even in the most prosperous countries, people are denied
access to means of livelihood. Chronic unemployment of 5 to 10
per cent is common during good times in western Europe and
North America.

In competitive markets, systemic unemployment is supposed
to be impossible. If everyone had unfettered access to means of
livelihood, people who lost their jobs due to increased productivity in some industries would find jobs in others. As new jobs
were created, the total supply of goods would increase, prices
would fall and real wages would rise. A new equilibrium would
be reached at full employment.

Why is this picture so out of focus?

Unemployment is systemic because social means of livelihood
are controlled by wealthowning minorities and because the products of social labour are privately appropriated. For the majority
who rely on income from labour, the system is an oligarchy: a
wealthowning minority sets the conditions of employment and has
the power to deny work except on their terms. For wealthowning
minorities, the system remains private and competitive. Each
capitalist collective is responsible for maximising its own profits.
None is concerned with the impact of cost-cutting measures on
total labour income or on the markets for goods. So long as
growth in output is matched by growth in aggregate demand – as
it was from the end of World War II to the 1970s – the
contradiction between social production and private appropriation
is obscured. However, when the drive to maximise private profit
provokes a shift in total income from labour to capital, chronic
unemployment becomes intractable.

When capital expands faster than labour income, productive capacity expands faster than the markets for most goods. When markets are stagnating or declining enterprises become even more determined to cut costs. Businesses 'downsize' and 'outsource'. They cut employment, speed the introduction of labour-saving technologies, contract out work to lower-cost producers and relocate factories in lower-wage areas. Employment, real wages and consumer demand fall further. The profits of particular firms may rise, but the aggregate income on which profits can be realised falls.

The contradiction between the way particular firms maximise profits and the way the system as a whole realises profits is aggravated by the tendency of claims on capital to rise faster than the capacity of enterprises to generate surplus. When capital's share of total income rises, increased income in the hands of investors will spark speculative growth in share prices and property values. As share prices grow, enterprises will have to generate more revenues for dividends. Meanwhile, the availability of liquid capital will have made borrowing easier. Equity issues and credits will be directed towards mergers and acquisitions and to investments in labour-saving technologies. Claims on capital by shareholders, bondholders and creditors will rise even though markets for consumer goods are not growing. As claims on capital exceed the capacity of enterprises to generate surplus, bankruptcies and plant closures will further reduce labour income and consumer goods markets.

Growth in these circumstances can be revived only by intervention from outside the capitalist marketplace. For wealthowners, the stimulation of choice is militarism. Military spending generates lucrative opportunities for profit-making for enterprises producing capital goods and consumer goods. If militarism leads to success in war, wealthowners on the winning side can benefit from the destruction of means of production on the losing side. Unlike other forms of government spending, military spending is not based on and does not encourage demands for income redistribution. Militarism reinforces the relations of command and obedience upon which minority control of economic life depends. The authoritarianism it encourages can be turned against anti-capitalist movements.

A Note on Oligopoly in the British Columbia Forest Industry

In British Columbia oligopolistic control of timber supplies allows a few companies to overexploit the resource and underemploy labour. A system of Tree Farm Licences gives less than a dozen integrated timber companies exclusive cutting rights to three-quarters of British Columbia's timber supply. Control of the resource keeps the price of logs artificially low. A history of militant trade unionism keeps labour expensive. To keep labour costs to a minimum, investments have been concentrated in mechanised logging and in automated mills producing pulp, paper and minimally processed dimension lumber. Companies export high-volume, low-cost products to the US, Europe and Japan.

Clear-cutting – the mechanised cutting of all trees in an area – is one consequence of oligopolistic domination of the industry. The larger the cut block, the lower the costs of moving machinery and equipment from site to site. Because all trees are cut down, logging crews do not have to take the time to determine how to safely fall selected trees or to decide what stands, soils, slopes or streams should be preserved. 'High-grading' and the diversion of saw logs to pulp mills are other consequences. In the 1980s, during a time of 'sympathetic administration' by the provincial government, high-grading – removing only the best logs and leaving the rest to burn or rot – was common, as was the pulping of larger logs that could have been cut into higher value wood products. These destructive practices were prohibited by the regulations governing Tree Farm Licences, but timber oligopolies convinced the government to look the other way. According to the Truck Loggers Association (independent logging contractors) British Columbia lost up to 100,000 jobs and tax revenue in excess of $1 billion annually.[48]

In the early 1990s a less sympathetic government was elected. High-grading was made impractical by dwindling timber supplies. The pulping of large logs was made uneconomic by a combination of slumping pulp prices and rising prices for scarce mature, old-growth timber. Instead, the most valuable timber was exported either as raw logs or as barely processed, squared cants. Clear-cutting of large blocks of 250 hectares and more continued. In 1993, timber companies removed 79 million cubic metres of wood. According to the British Columbia government forest service (itself strongly influenced by industry pressure), 65 million cubic metres was the maximum sustainable cut. Environmentalists and more critical foresters estimate that present cutting rates will eliminate large stands of accessible old-growth rain forest in British Columbia soon after the first decade of the next century. Industry representatives claim old growth will last 50 years. In either case, present cutting rates are far beyond sustainable levels.

Defenders of existing oligopolies like to point out that the forest industry is the most important employer in British

Columbia.[49] It is, but it is the forest resource that is responsible for the employment opportunities. The dominant companies have actually done what they can to cut jobs. Their control of the resource has blocked the development of a secondary manufacturing industry. In 1993 wood manufacturing actually employed a smaller portion of the British Columbia workforce than it had in 1981. Employment has also fallen in logging and processing. Between 1979 and 1989, labour-saving technologies resulted in a net loss of 10,000 jobs even though the annual timber cut continued to rise.[50] In 1984, 1,000 cubic metres of wood created 1.04 jobs in British Columbia, 2.2 in the rest of Canada and 3.55 in the US. By 1987 each 1,000 cubic metres cut in British Columbia generated only 0.95 jobs.

The public that owns the forests need not choose between preservation and jobs as is claimed by the supporters of the timber oligopolies. The choice is either high short-term profits or sustained forestry. Selection logging would maximise long-term employment in forestry.[51] Selection logging can include the removal of some mature timber, the thinning of stands to encourage more rapid growth of the healthiest trees and clear-cuts of up to a few hectares. Mature rain forests add wood fibre at a rate of 2 to 3 per cent a year. If enough mature trees are left standing to die and fall to nourish new growth an equivalent of all the wood fibre in the mature forest could be removed during the course of 50 to 100 years and the forest would contain as much fibre as it did to begin with. Not only would the forest ecosystem be self-sustaining, the more valuable tightly-grained heartwood from mature trees could be harvested forever.

When the same forest is clear-cut and replanted, a second-growth forest may be ready to cut in 60 to 80 years if the untested hypotheses of the industry's silviculture experts are correct. However, the artificially planted second growth will not have the genetic diversity that protects old growth from the ravages of disease. Countless plants and animals with unknown roles in forest ecosystems will have been destroyed. Nutrients generated naturally in a mature forest will not be available. The spongy organic debris that holds water and is slowly transformed into soil will have dried up and been blown away after being exposed to the direct rays of the sun in the clear-cut. The soil that had accumulated in the mature forest will no longer be protected by multi-layered canopies. Rapid snow melt will have washed it away. If, despite all this, the plantation thrives, it will contain less wood fibre than the mature forest. Trees will be smaller and not suitable for higher value wood products. The cost of planting trees and of applying fertilisers and pesticides to the weak and vulnerable plantation when carried for a period of 60 to 80 years will have all but cancelled the revenues the plantation generates.

Selection logging designed to allow forests to sustain and regenerate themselves would unquestionably increase the labour required to remove a given volume of wood. Why is that to be avoided? Higher logging costs mean more jobs for loggers. Rising log prices would make it less likely that trees would be transformed into pulp or into low-priced dimension lumber. Higher value products like clear beams, windows and doors, panelling, cabinets, furniture, musical instruments and boats would more likely be produced. More skilled jobs would be created.

The benefits of selection logging and value-added manufacturing may seem obvious to people concerned with the health of ecosystems and with maximum long-term employment opportunities. These are not so obvious to executives of timber oligopolies who are paid to concern themselves with the return on capital right now. From their perspective, the greater the immediate profit, the greater the value of the forest as capital. If they get a 20 per cent return for 15 years from clear-cutting, timber companies can recover their investment, keep their shareholders happy and accumulate sufficient funds to invest in some suitably profitable venture somewhere else when this resource has been exhausted.

For the oligopolistic strategy to be rational, reality must be turned upside down. Short-term profits must be considered more important than present-day employment and long-term economic health. Old-growth timber must be treated as though it was cheap and abundant. It is actually scarce and valuable. The price of wood – unlike that of most other raw materials – has gone up relative to the price of manufactured goods for most of this century. It will continue to rise as the globe's forests shrink.

Supporters of capitalism cite what they call the tragedy of the commons to explain the wanton plundering of forests, fish and waterways, but common property is not the problem. When property was held in common by tribes, clans and villages, people took no more than their share and respected the rights of others. They cared for common property and when necessary acted together to protect it against those who would damage it. Under capitalism, there is no common property. (Public property is a form of private property, property owned by a government as a corporate person.) Capitalism recognises only private property and free-for-all property. Nobody is responsible for free-for-all property until somebody claims it as his own. He

then has a right to do as he pleases with it, a right that is
uniquely capitalist. Unlike common or personal property, capitalist property is not valued for itself or for its utility. It is
valued for the revenue it produces for its owner. If the capitalist owner can maximise his revenue by liquidating it, he has the
right to do that.

3 Corporate Hierarchy

Hierarchies of Wealth

Aristotle defined oligarchies as systems in which 'men of property have the government in their hands'.[1] In his time – more than 2,000 years ago – oligarchies ruled because they controlled land, merchant capital and armed men. Today, oligarchs rule because ownership of capital gives them control over means of livelihood and command of social labour.

According to the *Globe and Mail*, half the value of all the companies on the 1984 Toronto Stock Exchange's 300 composite index was controlled by nine families: Thomson, Bronfman (CEMP), Desmarais, Bronfman (Edper), Reichman, Weston, Black, Southern and Seaman.[2]

Ken Thomson controlled assets of C$12 billion. He was probably the richest man in Canada. His 400 publications – including 40 daily newspapers in Canada and 100 in the US – made him the leading newspaper publisher in the world. He was also the biggest retailer in Canada, owning the Hudson Bay Co., Zellers, Fields and Simpsons, a total of more than 800 stores. He was a substantial shareholder in 47 of the largest shopping malls in Canada, owned a number of hotels, 17 office towers and a score of industrial buildings. In the early 1980s, his investment in North Sea oil provided Ken Thomson with an income of C$3.3 million a day, which alone would have made him one of the richest men in the world. He inherited the core of his interests from his father, Lord Thomson of Fleet, a businessman originally from Sudbury, Ontario.

The brothers Charles and Edgar Bronfman controlled CEMP investments, Seagram Distillers and real estate giant Cadillac Fairview. Their Canadian companies had assets of C$5 billion. They also held a 23 per cent share in the US chemical giant, E. I. du Pont de Nemours – slightly more than the 22 per cent held by the du Pont family itself. Their father, Sam Bronfman, amassed a fortune from alcohol and real estate.

Edward and Peter Bronfman are the sons of Sam's brother and business partner. In the early 1960s, Sam Bronfman decided to pass ownership of Seagram distillers to his own children. He bought out his brother's sons with $15 million. From that modest beginning, Edward and Peter began buying shares in Canadian companies. In 1978 they won control of holding company

Brascan which had liquid securities of $400 million. They used these to construct a pyramid of holding companies headed by Edper Investments, Brascan and Hees International. Their financial managers then perfected the practice of paying for takeovers with what would later be called 'junk bonds'. High-yield preferred shares in companies already in the Edper stable were exchanged for the common shares of companies being acquired. By 1984 Edward and Peter Bronfman controlled 100 companies with assets of close to C$100 billion, employing more than 100,000 people. These included Noranda, the largest mining company, and MacMillan Bloedel, the largest forest company in Canada, as well as Chateau-Gai Wines, Catelli Spaghetti, Habitant Soups, Five Roses and Ogilvie flour, the Toronto Blue Jays and John Labatt breweries. John Labatt controlled 40 per cent of Canada's beer market and owned both Dominion and Silverwood dairies, making it the country's largest dairy. Their financial and real estate interests included Royal Trustco, London Life, Royal LePage and Bramalea Ltd. The equity in Edward and Peter Bronfman's investment arm, Hees International, equalled the combined equity of all other investment firms on Toronto's Bay Street.

Albert, Paul and Ralph Reichman owned Gulf Canada, Hiram Walker Resources and Abitibi-Price but were primarily real estate developers. In the 1980s they had large minority holdings in real estate giants Trizec and Cadillac Fairview. Their own Olympia & York generated C$1 million a day from more than 100 skyscrapers and shopping centres. Outside Canada, they owned 10 per cent of the office space in Manhattan, including the World Trade Center. They were starting the construction of Canary Wharf, the largest real estate development in London's history.

Paul Desmarais controlled industrial and financial companies with assets of close to C$50 billion. Through Power Corporation he held the controlling interest in Montreal Trustco, Credit Foncier, Investors Group and Great West Life Assurance, as well as La Presse, Canada's largest circulation, French-language newspaper. He also held the single largest block of shares in Canadian Pacific.

Galen Weston, who divided his time between Canada and the UK, ran his family's North American business. His father, Garfield Weston, a Canadian who moved to the UK, amassed the family wealth. In the 1980s their holdings in Canada included Weston Bakeries, Loblaws, Super Valu, Real Canadian Superstores, National Tea, Holt Renfrew, Kelly Douglas, Atlantic Wholesalers, British Columbia Packers and E. B. Eddy Forest Products. Their brand names included Wheat Thins, Ryvita crackers, McCormick cookies, Neilson's chocolates,

Clover Leaf salmon, Twinings Tea and White Swan paper products. Total sales of their Canadian companies were more than C$8 billion. Their Associated Foods in Britain had sales of C$5 billion.

Conrad Black in the 1980s owned Dominion Stores, Norcen and Hollinger. Born to a family with substantial holdings in E. P. Taylor's Argus empire, he was just beginning to build his newspaper empire.

The Southerns and Seamans, both from Calgary, completed the *Globe and Mail* list of the nine wealthiest families in Canada in 1984. The Southerns owned ATCO, the world's largest builder of mobile housing units. They and the Seamans made millions during the 1970s oil boom.

A list of the top corporate oligarchs in Canada at the time would not be complete without the inclusion of the Irvings from New Brunswick, the Eatons of Toronto and the Richardsons of Winnipeg. The *Globe and Mail* did not include these families because their holdings were held privately in companies whose shares were not publicly traded on Toronto's stock exchange.

The family of K. C. Irving dominated economic life in New Brunswick, owning 400 companies with assets of C$10 billion and employing 25,000 people. In the 1980s the family's holdings included Canada's largest oil refinery, 3,000 service stations, pulp and paper mills, sawmills, food processing companies, a fleet of ships, trucks, construction companies, more than a million acres of land and every TV station and daily newspaper in New Brunswick.

The Eaton family owned the 300-store T. Eaton Co., the largest privately-held department store chain in North America. The Eatons had substantial holdings in downtown shopping malls across the country, shared control of the Eaton-Bay Trust Company and owned the controlling interest in Baton Broadcasting. Baton owned Toronto television station CFTO and Glen Warren Productions, which gave it the largest ownership stake in CTV, Canada's major private television network.

The Richardson family began as grain merchants in Winnipeg in the last century. In the 1980s they owned Richardson Greenshields – Canada's largest commodity broker and second-largest stock broker. Their Pioneer Grain with its 520 grain elevators, three terminal elevators and fleet of ships was the largest privately-owned grain merchandising company in Canada.

Hal Jackman should perhaps also be included. A prominent Toronto Tory, Jackman owned the majority of shares in National Victoria and Grey Trustco, Empire Life and Dominion of Canada General Insurance. He also owned Algoma Central Railway.

When these four are included, 13 families dominated Canadian corporate business. In *Controlling Interest*, Diane Francis listed 32 families who together controlled businesses with a revenue of C$123 billion in 1985 – 50 per cent more than the federal government's revenue in the same year. [3]

Is Canadian corporate business dominated by 9, 13, 32 or perhaps 200 families? The number is not critical. The point is that domestic corporate business was and is run by and in the interests of a very small number of very wealthy families.

As time goes by, relative position shifts: some families fall, others rise to the top. The Reichmans' Olympia & York empire has collapsed. Slumping commercial real estate prices, unwise investments in companies controlled by Robert Campeau and the debt burden and low occupancy in Canary Wharf pushed the company into bankruptcy. Edgar and Peter Bronfman's empire began unravelling in 1993, a victim of the slump in commercial real estate and declining returns on industrial investments in Canada. Conrad Black, in contrast, is moving up. Paul Desmarais, after selling his shares in CPR has not yet made a major move. No matter who is rising or falling, super-wealthy families are still ultimately in control. Their ownership of corporate assets gives them the right to set the priorities of economic activity and to use surpluses produced by social labour as they see fit.

A few dozen families could not control economic life without structures of social control. These structures are based on hierarchies of wealth and command. Below the few super-wealthy families are a second tier of corporate oligarchs including the chief executives of major corporations and lesser but still wealthy shareholders. Taxation figures give a rough estimate of the numbers in these top two tiers. In 1980, 7,742 Canadians reported income of C$200,000 or higher. The 7,563 who paid income taxes averaged close to C$300,000 from dividends and capital gains and C$150,000 in salaries. A mere 0.08 per cent of taxpayers – less than one of every 1,000 Canadians – they got 22 per cent of all capital gains, 20 per cent of all foreign investment income and 12 per cent of all dividend income. [4]

Below the second tier of top corporate oligarchs are a third tier: the owners of smaller but still substantial amounts of corporate assets; chief executives of smaller companies; middle level executives of larger companies; top civil servants; and prosperous independent business people and professionals like doctors and lawyers who have accumulated significant investments. Although top government officials are usually not paid as much as top corporate executives, their incomes do allow them to build investment portfolios. Their ties with private business are strengthened by movement back and forth between the upper rungs of government service and corporate management. The people in this third tier would have been included in the 250,000 Canadians – 2 per cent of taxpayers – who reported income of C$50,000 or higher in 1980.

Below them are the bottom rungs of management – the non-commissioned officers of corporate oligarchy – perhaps a million people in 1980. These are the people who actually direct the working lives of the majority. The system of hierarchic control would not function without them, but in income and lifestyle they have more in common with the wage- and salary-earning majority. They too labour in the interests of others. The bottom rung of the oligarchic pyramid could also be said to include all owners of corporate assets. In 1980, slightly more than a million people, 7 per cent of taxpayers, reported taxable dividends. However, many of these were working people who dabbled in stocks but who earned their income almost entirely from wages and salaries. Many others were pensioners whose income from investments was modest.

In the United States in 1983, 420,000 families each owned assets of more than $2.5 million. Just 0.5 per cent of the US population, they owned 35 per cent of US wealth – up from 25 per cent two decades earlier. This group would include the wealthiest shareholders and the top corporate executives. Another 420,000 families each owned assets of $1.4 million to $2.5 million. This group would include middle level wealthowners, higher ranking executives of large firms, chief executives of smaller firms and prosperous professionals and small business people. An additional 7.5 million families each had assets of $206,000 to $1.4 million. This group would include most of the people in the bottom rungs of the corporate oligarchy. These income groups combined accounted for 10 per cent of the US population. The remaining 90 per cent owned only 28 per cent of the country's wealth, an average of $40,000, accounted for largely by the value of their homes.[5]

Despite the myth of equality and upward mobility in the US, most of the wealthiest people, as recorded by *Forbes*, were the heirs to fortunes that had been in their families for generations. In 1990, the du Ponts, whose wealth comes from chemicals and General Motors, had assets of $10 billion. The Rockefellers, whose wealth comes from the old Standard Oil trust and from banking, had assets of $8 billion. The Cargill/MacMillans, with wealth from grain merchandising and agribusiness, had assets of $7 billion. The Mellons, inheriting fortunes from steel, machinery, Gulf Oil and the Aluminum Company of America, had assets of $4.4 billion. The Hearsts, whose wealth is from newspaper publishing, had assets of $4.3 billion. The size of these family fortunes is exceptional; the fact their wealth was inherited is not. Among the very wealthy, three out of four can trace their family wealth back 100 years. In the 1980s three quarters of corporation directors who had personal assets of $10 million or more were themselves the sons or daughters of rich parents.[6]

The Management of Labour

The men in command of US corporations like to think of themselves as rugged individuals. They are actually bureaucrats in command of large hierarchical institutions. The executives of major transnational corporations direct the labour of as many people and control as much revenue as most governments. In the 1970s, 'General Motors employed more persons than the states of California, New York, Pennsylvania and Michigan combined'. Exxon, the largest US transnational, employed three times as many people abroad as were employed in the US foreign service.[7]

In his *Concept of the Corporation* – a study of General Motors, written in the 1940s – Peter Drucker said,

> Like the army or like any other social institution, the things that really count are not the individual members but the relations of command and responsibility among them ... An institution must have an esprit de corps which induces its members to put the welfare of the institution above their own and to model themselves upon an institutional idea of conduct.[8]

Drucker, an enthusiastic supporter of capitalism, brushed away the claim that corporate organisation brings managers with exceptional individual ability to the top. He said,

> No institution can possibly survive if it needs geniuses or supermen to manage it. It must be organized in such a way as to be able to get along under a leadership composed of average human beings ... No institution has solved the problem of leadership, no matter how good its formal constitution, unless it gives the leader a sense of duty, of the importance of his trust and a sense of mutual loyalty between him and his associates; for these enable the average human being – and occasionally somebody well below average – to function effectively in a position of trust and leadership.[9]

Drucker, an influential teacher of the generation of managers now in command of corporations, added,

There is a remarkably close parallel between General Motors'
scheme of organisation and those of the two institutions most
renowned for administrative efficiency: that of the Catholic
Church and that of the modern army as first developed by the
Prussian General Staff between 1800 and 1870 and later
adopted everywhere.[10]

A similar point was made by Alfred Chandler in *The Visible Hand*.[11]
The industrial corporations of the late nineteenth century, he said,
adopted the organisational structure of the United States Armory at
Springfield, Massachusetts. Chief executive officers played the role
of generals; below them, senior managers commanded corporate
divisions; junior managers commanded departments. Foremen and
supervisors were the non-commissioned officers. Just as the actions
of soldiers in far-flung battlefields are directed by military hierarchies, the activities of workers in numerous factories and shops
are directed by corporate hierarchies.

Top-down hierarchies were a consequence of the collectivis-
ation of capital. In the days of the owner-entrepreneur, employers
usually had face-to-face contact with employees and direct knowledge of the work done. With the consolidation of multi-unit
business enterprises, owners were no longer in daily contact with
their employees and rarely possessed the technical knowledge to
direct labour intelligently. Authority had to be delegated to managers who understood the work. The early approach was to
promote skilled workers into supervisory positions and then into
management. This was soon deemed unsatisfactory. The class
arrogance of wealthowners in the late nineteenth century made
them doubt the managerial ability of former workers. Growing
class polarisation made them doubt their loyalty.

The engineering profession provided the solution. In the
early years of the nineteenth century there were fewer than 100
engineers in all the United States. Most of them trained in
military colleges and worked as independent consultants. As the
factory system spread, industrialists encouraged the establishment of professional engineering schools to train managers who
understood mechanical processes and who would be committed
to the interests of capital. In 1880, 85 colleges were granting
engineering degrees. By World War I, 4,000 engineers were
graduating each year in the US, most to become salaried
managers in corporate enterprises.[12] Their task was to apply
their technical understanding so as to arrange work processes in
ways that would maximise profits for shareholders. The elite
private universities they attended had taught them to 'always be
subservient to those who represent the money invested in the
enterprise'.[13]

In the 1890s, an engineer, Frederick Taylor, formulated a system he called 'scientific management'.[14] Born into a prosperous Philadelphia family, he worked as a factory manager while still a youth. He had already advocated a system of 'differential piece rates', which, he claimed, could increase output and reduce costs to employers. He would later design a prototype of a modern assembly line. His innovations were driven by a belief that workers were not sufficiently disciplined. In his time – before assembly-line production had become common – employers decided what would be produced, but the tempo and order of the work was typically directed by the most experienced craftsmen.

The goal of scientific management was to put an end to workers' control of work. Taylor urged managers to assume 'the burden of gathering together all the traditional knowledge which in the past has been possessed by the workmen and then of classifying, tabulating and reducing this knowledge to rules, laws and formulae'. After this was done, he claimed that mechanical and human processes could be reorganised so that optimum standards were established to maximise profits. The management of capital would be made as precise as other sciences.

Taylor knew that his system would require more highly specialised managers. He insisted that employers would nonetheless save money because the elimination of the need for thinking on the job would allow workers to give undivided attention to repeating the tasks assigned by others. He justified the required hardening of relations of command and subordination by claiming, 'one type of man is needed to plan ahead and an entirely different type to execute the work'. He added, 'Even if the workman was well suited to the development and use of scientific data, it would be physically impossible for him to work at his machine and at a desk at the same time.'[15]

The men in command of the rapidly growing multi-unit enterprises liked what they heard of Taylorism. However, it was quickly determined that his approach to labour relations was too heavy-handed. Taylor was an engineer confident of his method and convinced of the accuracy of his calculations. He saw no need for subtlety or guile and never got beyond the carrot of differential pay and the stick of fines, suspension and dismissal. When he was given opportunities to apply his system, unionised workers went on strike and unorganised workers refused to follow orders and engaged in acts of petty sabotage.

New schools of management, established in the early years of the new century, tackled the problem of applying the principles of scientific management.[16] Future managers studied industrial psychology and learned to foster a paternalism intended to encourage workers to identify with the companies that employed them. Cafeterias, safety programmes, athletic and cultural events as well as injury compensation, pension and unemployment insurance plans were proposed to win the cooperation and allegiance of workers.

However, the goal was still to remove all brain work from the shop floor. Workers were to be transformed into compliant and alert levers, conveyors or grippers who could be made to work at tempos set by machinery. Workers were no longer participants; they became objects of production. Robbed of control of their own living-time, commanded by others, driven to the limits of physical endurance by time-and-motion experts, workers found little self-esteem or social identity in work. Pay was the only consolation. Life was reduced to consumption.

To this day, the flow and the pace of work in scientifically managed enterprises is predetermined by engineers and time-study experts. Each worker is assigned a few repetitive tasks. The aim is to utilise every minute at work in the interests of the employer. Bells or buzzers signal the start and end of the work day and the duration of coffee and lunch breaks. Workers often need permission to relieve themselves. In short, scientifically managed workplaces are forced-labour camps. Robert E. Wood, the chief executive officer of Sears, spoke plainly when he said, 'We stress the advantages of the free enterprise system, we complain about the totalitarian state, but ... we have created more or less of a totalitarian system in industry, particularly in large industry.' [17]

Workplace totalitarianism is masked by the legal fiction that the employer–employee relation is based on private, mutually agreed contracts between equal individuals. However, the employer's right to property is not matched by a worker's right to employment. The rights of property are recognised in residual rights of management. Workers, in contrast, leave their rights at the door when they enter the workplace. In the US, the law allows employers to 'dismiss their employees at will ... for good cause, for no cause or even for cause morally wrong, without being thereby guilty of legal wrong'. [18] Because of the fiction that the workplace is private, capitalist law does not even protect workers from discipline or job loss for complaining about unfair treatment – unless the matter in dispute is covered by union agreement or anti-discrimination legislation.

The anti-worker animus inherent in capitalist property rights and in scientific management has been given a new twist. Unable to find enough people content to be treated like machines, management set out to eliminate people entirely from the production process. As people are replaced by automated machines, people without capital are denied even the right to consume.

Automated machinery not only cuts labour costs, it further

reduces management dependence on skilled workers. Numerical control – a method of programming machine tools that breaks jobs down into elements which can be transformed into mathematical equations – continues Frederick Taylor's project. It has succeeded in taking mental preparation of work from machinists and made it the exclusive prerogative of engineers and mathematicians. So far, the quality of work done with numerical control has not lived up to expectations. The elimination of skilled operators also eliminated the human response to unforeseen circumstances. Moreover, the cost benefits have been less than expected. Computer-directed machinery requires substantially larger initial capital outlays. The savings in direct labour time are offset by higher costs for planning, scheduling and supervision. [19]

Computerised machinery has eliminated many jobs in continuous process operations – in oil refineries, pulp mills and chemical plants – and many others in telecommunications, mail sorting, billing and inventory control – wherever a sequence of routine operations is repeated many times. Robots, however, have not been as universally applicable as their early proponents claimed. Although more and more robots are being used in manufacturing operations where highly precise, unchanging motions are required, pre-programmed automatic machines cannot respond to unanticipated changes. For most manufacturing operations, robots are more expensive than human beings and less reliable. Despite management complaints about labour turnover and absenteeism, complex state-of-the-art machines are subject to breakdown and require costly maintenance.

Computerisation has succeeded in tightening management control over the workplace. Managers with access to master terminals can now know precisely what workers are doing at each terminal. This is particularly oppressive for workers at retail check-outs, switchboards and word processing and data entry stations. For these workers, mostly women, computerisation has meant permanent surveillance. Under constant pressure to keep pace with pre-assigned levels of key strokes or entries regardless of the particular problems, workers are denied even the semblance of personal control over their work or bodily movements. An epidemic of repetitive strain and stress-related occupational illnesses indicates that the information revolution has taken workplace tyranny to new levels of refinement.

The Japanese Work Group

In Japan, the image of the rugged individual is not superimposed over the institutional reality of business. Managers are expected to put the interests of their company first, to do what their superiors expect and to work well with subordinates. Problem-solving is treated as a group activity. The manager's job is to motivate and mobilise the team under him. When a consensus is reached, the group's decision is passed on by the manager to his superiors for decision or action. Although authority does reside at the top of hierarchies, the collegial system allows Japanese corporations to benefit from the energy and expertise of lower-level managers in ways that are not possible where the boss is determined to make decisions himself.

The work-team is the basic unit of production. Tasks are assigned to the team, not to individuals. Because the team makes routine production decisions and is responsible for both the tempo and quality of work, it is sometimes held up as an alternative to traditional scientific management. It is actually another version. The team takes on some of the tasks of lower management, but the effect is to put more pressure on workers. Because the team as a whole is responsible for the work, each worker must be able to do all the jobs assigned. Team members who complete their tasks are expected to move immediately to assist other team members, so what remained of free time is lost. Competition among work-teams and peer pressure within groups are aggressively encouraged by management. 'Foremen in a typical plant in the 1980s were expected to explain the slogan: "Use every minute, use every effort!" ' [20] at the daily morning assembly. The result, at its most extreme, is *karoshi* – death by overwork.

Self-management within the strictly predetermined tasks of a work-team is only one aspect of the Japanese system of scientific management. Like Taylorism the system is designed to maximise management control over workplaces. It not only harnesses collegiality to this end, it relies on institutionalised divisions within the workforce, on bonuses tied to enterprise profits, on company unionism and on strict control and surveillance of all employees.

In large Japanese companies the workforce includes regular workers as well as temporary, part-time and contract employees. Most skilled workers plus lower level management are included in the regular workforce. Their pay is determined largely by years of company service. The salary differentials between regular workers and managers is narrow, usually less than two to one for people with the same seniority. Bonuses for regular workers, based on company profitability, can amount to anywhere from a quarter to several times basic pay. Regular workers are consequently inclined to identify with management and to see their interests as tied to the growth and profitability of the company. However, regular workers in large companies account for only a third of the workforce. They are paid two or three (or more) times as much as temporary, part-time and contract workers, who often do exactly the same work.

The institutionalised division of the workforce effectively discriminates against women. Because regular employees are nearly always hired directly out of school, women who quit their jobs after marriage or childbirth rarely get back into this relatively privileged strata. Those who resign their regular workforce positions do not always leave voluntarily. In many companies – despite laws prohibiting the practice – women are subject to compulsory retirement at marriage, when pregnant, or at age 35 – whichever comes first. Those who then re-enter the workforce will be eligible only for 'temporary' work. As temporary workers, they may work alongside regular workers for years, doing the same work at lower pay with no benefits. No matter how many years they work, they will be subject to lay-off or dismissal at the company's discretion. It is no surprise that women in Japan are considered to be more militant trade unionists and have provided the bulk of support for left-wing political parties.

For regular workers, the carrot of better treatment is accompanied by the stick of management control. In return for lifetime employment, Japanese employers insist on regulating the private lives of their employees. They often expect to be told where employees go for lunch, how they spend their evenings and where they go on vacations. At work, the use of video cameras and other electronic eavesdropping equipment is common. Honda is notorious for these practices. The Honda headquarters, opened in Tokyo in 1985, 'is equipped with systems that tell the employer when a worker arrives, how much he pays for lunch and what he is doing and where he is at any particular time.' [21]

In some companies, surveillance is deliberately intimidating. Toyota hired ex-members of the military as foremen and team chiefs. They were given the authority to read, at their discretion, the diaries that new recruits were compelled to keep. [22] Employees at Matsushita Electric – which produces Panasonic, Quasar and Technics – were compelled to sing a company song, 'Grow industry, grow, grow, grow' before and after each shift. To relieve employee stress, the owner, Konosuke Matsushita, installed a 'self-control' room supplied with staves that employees could use to beat a stuffed dummy of himself. [23]

Not all aggression in Japanese industry is cathartic. In 1969, women assembly-line workers in Sony's Shibaura plant were physically assaulted by security guards and thrown out of the plant for complaining about working conditions. In 1982, several workers at Nissan who complained about working conditions were severely beaten by company and union officials. [24]

Japanese trade unions are not much of a counterweight to management. Most unions are company-based, with membership open only to regular employees. They rarely take aggressive stands against management. When they do, top management encourages loyal employees to set up alternate unions. This is not difficult. Many regular employees identify with management. University graduates hired as management trainees begin as production workers and remain in the regular workforce after being promoted. They are supported by other regular employees when they run for union office.

The workers most in need of union representation, non-regular workers who account for 40 per cent of the workforce in large enterprises, are not eligible for membership of enterprise unions. They are paid less for doing the same work. They do not get the bonuses or the seniority-based pay rises paid to regular employees. They do not get employer-paid medical benefits. They have no access to company housing or health and recreational facilities. When business slows, they are subject to lay-off with little notice.

Much is heard of the Japanese system of lifetime employment. Only regular employees, and in practice only those in large companies, can expect to benefit from this commitment. Even for regular employees, it is not what it appears to be. For all but top corporation officers, lifetime employment ends at the compulsory retirement age of 55. Pension benefits do not begin until the age of 60. Retirees do get a lump-sum payment of up to four years' basic salary – not including bonuses. Often a retiree will use this lump sum to purchase the company house he has lived in for years. If he does not, he will have to find alternate accommodation. In all likelihood the retiree, faced with no income until age 60, will ask to be re-hired as a non-regular employee, doing the same work as before, at a lower wage.

Theories of a Managerial Revolution and of Contending Elites

Is the control of labour simply a management function or is it designed to serve the interests of wealthowners? Theorists of a managerial revolution claim that wealthowners have lost economic power.

The theory of a managerial revolution was advanced in the 1930s and 1940s by A. A. Berle and G. C. Means, James Burnham and John Kenneth Galbraith.[25] They pointed to the growth of multi-unit corporate enterprise and asserted that it was no longer practical for individual owners to direct business. The wide dispersal of shareholdings, they claimed, meant that ownership no longer included control. Corporate business, they said, was now controlled by a managerial elite. This managerial revolution, they prophesied, would result in a more humane capitalism. In their view the recurring booms and busts of entrepreneurial capitalism, provoked by the old preoccupation with short-term profit maximisation, would be replaced by social engineering. Out of professional self-interest, the highly educated managerial elite would pursue policies of long-term growth and institutional stability.

Advocates of a managerial revolution were right to point out that many large corporations have no identifiable majority owners. But does this mean that wealthowners have lost control of companies? After several generations, a dominant family's holdings may be dispersed among numerous people. Names will have changed through marriage. Nonetheless, founders' shares may still be voted as a block by trust companies or law firms. When shareholdings are widely held, a holding of 20 per cent or even 5 per cent can give effective control. True, this often allows top management to organise the votes needed to dominate shareholders' meetings, but there is little in recent business practice to suggest that managers put institutional interests or managerial concerns ahead of profits.

Top executives have frequently used their control of shareholders' meetings to pursue their own interests. They have initiated mergers, acquisitions and leveraged buy-outs and gained generous fees, bonuses and stock-options by doing so. When these burden companies with debt service charges that exceed revenue, the losses are passed to shareholders, workers and the managers who did not directly benefit from the deals. The same happens when any other controlling shareholders pursue immediate gains at the expense of the longer-term viability of the enterprise. Executives who arrange to be paid seven-figure salaries, supplemented by larger bonuses and stock options, leave less income available for ordinary shareholders. Does this put top management on a collision course with other wealthowners? Not necessarily. It can reaffirm the right of those who control great wealth to enrich themselves at the expense of those who have less.

Despite the claims of the theory, managers are rarely in a position to pursue managerial group interests. They work in top-down hierarchies in which chief executive officers answer to owners of capital. Everyone else does what he or she is told. Where corporations are controlled by a dominant shareholder or group of shareholders, the chief executive is directly responsible to them through the board of directors. Where the controlling shareholders' vote is in the hands of top officers, management must still answer to outside shareholders, to creditors and to wealthowners generally. Whoever has the controlling interest, management is driven to maximise short-term profits just as it was in the 1890s and 1920s. If corporate managers really acted as theoreticians of a managerial revolution, they would have blocked the lay-offs and plant shut-downs of the 1980s and 1990s to protect their own managerial empires. Their failure to do so shows they do not see themselves as a distinct class. They acted like other wealthowners.

For chief executives, the commitment to wealthowners begins long before they reach the top. Executives are not picked off the street. They are usually the sons, and occasionally the daughters, of wealthowners. They attended exclusive private schools where they met and befriended the sons and daughters of other wealthowners. They went on to prestigious universities where they met people who helped them in their careers. When they entered the business world, their family wealth, education and personal connections eased their climb to the top. [26]

Managers who come from less privileged families will probably have graduated from business schools that preach the priority of wealthowners' interests. The few who came from the ranks will have learned during their climb that success in the business world is measured by the ability to advance the interests of major shareholders. If they did not begin with substantial shareholdings, they are likely to have accumulated handsome investment port-folios during their climb. As they moved up the corporate ladder their stock options and other opportunities for profitable invest-ment will have grown along with their salaries. By the time they reach the top, most of their income will come from shareholdings in their companies. They will have little reason to see their interests as distinct from those of other wealthowners.

The belief that a new managerial capitalism would better serve the interests of the people was reinforced by the theory of contending elites. This was put forward in the 1940s by the sociologist Talcott Parson and the economist Joseph Schumpeter and later elaborated by Parson. The theory holds that pluralist democracies are characterised by contention among elites for position, privilege and group interest. [27] According to the theory, no single elite dominates pluralist society on its own. Elites from business, regions, government, trade unions, the military, the media and cultural, religious, health care and educational institu-tions contend for influence. Power depends on, and is moderated by, alliances and compromises between the elites. The result is the greatest good for the greatest number. Advocates of this theory claimed they had formulated a value-free, descriptive, scientifically objective theory of how pluralist democracies actually worked.

As an explanation of democracy, the theory had a curious origin. It can be traced back to the writings of Vilfredo Pareto and Robert Michels. Pareto, an Italian engineer turned sociology professor who wrote at the turn of the century, was passionately contemptuous of democracy. He argued that populations are naturally divided into an upper stratum or elite that has the capacity to govern and a more populous lower stratum fit only to be led. He could not help noting from his study of history that minority rule was typically founded on property ownership or military power and that the possession of great wealth automatically placed individuals in the elite even if they did not otherwise possess any apparent leadership qualities. Yet he claimed that leadership was otherwise a function of innate personal qualities. Elites, he said, are set apart by their intelligence, their ability to govern and especially by their virility – willingness to use violence in pursuit of power. He then went on to distinguish between elites that govern and those that do not. He concluded that declining virility among governing elites is the major cause of the social upheavals which bring new elites to power. The masses, he said, participate in these changes only as pawns. [28]

Pareto's claim to have demonstrated scientifically that democracy was unnatural attracted the interest of better educated supporters of political privilege. Electoral democracy is now more or less universally accepted as the most legitimate form of government. Yet it is easy to forget that until the twentieth century the educated classes nearly unanimously accepted Aristotle's claim that democracy – which he called government by the poor – meant little more than mob rule. Nonetheless, by the end of the nineteenth century most working men in western Europe had won the right to vote. The movement for votes for women was close to victory. Meanwhile, the reaction against democracy was becoming more aggressive. During the early part of this century, people who believed that political rights should be the privilege of minorities found 'scientific' comfort in Pareto's theory of natural elites. In English-speaking countries, Pareto appealed to the advocates of social engineering. The most enthusiastic social engineers looked for work in large corporations, especially in the colonies. The more radical proposed to replace the anarchy of the market with planning by scientific experts, but they had little in common with rising socialist movements. Advocates of social engineering shared the capitalist view that the majority should be commanded by minorities. In Italy, Mussolini liked Pareto's theory so much that he made him an official philosopher of fascism.

Robert Michels was the other major inspiration for the theory of contending elites. In *Political Parties*, a study of the German Social Democratic Party written just prior to World War I, Michels formulated what he called the iron law of oligarchy.[29] Unlike Aristotle who identified oligarchy, rule by the few, with rule by the rich, Michels saw the distinction between a powerful few and the powerless many as an unavoidable result of social organisation. He argued that because large numbers of people are incapable of making decisions without delegating authority, all large organisations, including trade unions and socialist parties, are led by oligarchies. Unlike Pareto, who began by identifying with elites, Michels at first claimed sympathy for democracy. But, by insisting that democracy can only mean that all members participate equally in making decisions, he made democracy impractical in all but the smallest social groups. In the end, he too became a supporter of Mussolini.

The defeat of fascist powers in World War II and the subsequent Cold War against Communism made opposition to democracy unacceptable, even among conservative wealthowners. Minority control of economic and political life persisted, but the theory of contending elites allowed minority control to be incorporated into what was called democracy. According to the theory, business was not run by capitalists but by a managerial elite. This was no cause for concern because all large organisations are inevitably run by elites. Elites are actually democratic. Leadership qualities are more or less equally spread among elites. Membership of elites is a result of individual abilities. Minorities may rule, but pluralist, electoral democracy provides elites with a framework in which to contend in a fair and even-handed manner without violence or bloodshed.

The theory of contending elites became the official ideology of Keynesian welfare capitalism. However, it was not the objective, value-free description of social relations claimed by its proponents. This is most obvious in the way the theory obscures the power of capital. Perhaps the formulators can be excused. They were writing in the years following World War II. Ruling classes had publicly espoused the cause of democracy. Keynesian government intervention was encouraging steady growth in living standards and greater access to higher education. Steeply graduated income taxes were redistributing income and growing trade union membership made it appear that workers' organisations could counterweight the power of capital.

The theory of contending elites seemed reasonable until the neoconservative reaction swept the capitalist world in the 1980s. Wealthowners reasserted their right – indeed their duty – to pursue their interests regardless of the impact on workers, the poor, communities and the environment. The neoconservative governments they put in power deregulated business, lowered corporate taxes, slashed high income tax rates, cut social spending and increased the taxes paid by most wage and salary earners. The assault battered other elites. The military establishment in the US became stronger, but other scientific, educational, cultural and public elites dependent on government funds were weakened. Trade unionism, according to pluralist theory, has a special role in balancing the economic power of the managerial elite. Trade unionism could not maintain itself in the face of the anti-labour onslaught. Unions that had represented 35 per cent of US workers in the 1940s were reduced to 22 per cent by 1980 and to only 16 per cent in 1990.

The neoconservative reaction made it clear that elites do not contend as equals. Those elites favoured by wealthowners prosper; those that are not, do not.

The Managerial Elite in Japan

In post-war Japan, business, government and politics have been run by closely knit, university-educated managerial elites. Nearly half the presidents of the 1,500 largest firms are graduates of the old Imperial universities, Hitotsubashi, Kyoto and Tokyo. [30] Graduates of Tokyo University alone account for over half of all executives in 43 of the top 50 enterprises in Japan. They hold nearly 90 per cent of the top positions in the Ministry of Finance, 75 per cent in the Foreign Ministry, 75 per cent in the National Land Agency and 70 per cent in the Ministry of Transportation. Graduates of the most prestigious universities prefer to be hired by government ministries because this places them at the centre of political and economic life. Here they will get the most benefit from *jinmyaku*, webs of personal connections that include mutual obligations to class mates and earlier graduates of their school. Patrons will speed their rise up the hierarchy. Those who reach the top of government departments will be offered secure parliamentary seats and lucrative positions in private business. [31]

This government-business elite does appear to be a meritocracy. Membership requires graduation from an Imperial university, admissions to which are based on merit, or more precisely on scores obtained in entrance examinations. The more prestigious the university, the more difficult the entrance requirements. Nonetheless, those born with wealth have a far better chance of being accepted. They will have attended exclusive private kindergartens and similarly exclusive elementary, middle and high schools. All of which will have focused on teaching the pupil to do well on entrance exams. Furthermore, at each level it is understood that the greater the financial contribution made to the school by parents, the more likely the student will successfully move to the next level.

For the children of the less wealthy, admission to a top university requires a childhood of 'examination hell'. Pre-school children will be provided with tutors to prepare them for the entrance examinations for exclusive kindergartens. If successful, they will spend their time in kindergarten memorising correct answers for the entrance examinations for exclusive elementary schools. In elementary school, they will memorise answers to examinations for top middle schools; and in middle school they will prepare for examinations for the best high schools. Once in high school, they will be urged to spend all their waking hours preparing for university entrance examinations. In addition to attending school six days a week, the student will be enrolled in a private cram school in the evenings, on Sundays and during summer vacation. After graduating from high school, young adults will sometimes write the examinations for their favoured universities three or four years in a row until their marks are high enough. To get to this point, poorer parents must have motivated their child to excel in school, paid for a string of tutors and provided a suitable space and environment for long periods of solitary study. Now they will have to pay the tuition fees charged by the best private cram schools while they support the high school graduate for several more years. [32]

Those who succeed in getting to university can relax: students who attend classes rarely fail. The years at university are a breathing space between examination hell and the demands of the business world. Students are expected to have a good time and to make the friendships and connections that will aid them in their careers. Friendships and carefully cultivated mutual obligations will be as important as their university degrees. Those fortunate enough to have gained entrance into the old Imperial universities, if themselves not the offspring of the *zaikai* – the top oligarchs in industry, finance and trade – or of big landowners, will seek out opportunities to get to know such people.

The combination of the early focus on memorisation and hierarchical grading and then the emphasis in university on the building of personal connections prepares the graduate for life in the Japanese business world. Rote learning may not encourage pupils to be creative, but it does prepare them to give the answers their superiors are looking for. Hierarchic grading – by making pupils constantly aware of who is above and below them – conditions them for work in stratified institutions.

Personal networking at university will have prepared future managers to rely on mutual obligations with people above and below them.

The collegial system of management is aided by cultural monolithism. Japan does not claim to be a pluralist society. Orthodox opinion considers dissent contrary to the national spirit. Aside from complaints about endemic corruption, the only opposition voices regularly heard are those of rightists, who are extremists in their defence of existing power relations. Much of the official trade union movement acts in the interests of employers. During the 1970s and 1980s, the teachers' union did criticise Japanese social relations, but it was a lonely voice. [33] Means of communication are almost entirely in the hands of one company, *Dentsu*, which controls advertising for newspapers and television. *Dentsu*, the country's leading public relations firm, represents major conglomerates and national business coalitions. It ran election campaigns for the Liberal Democratic Party when it was in power, was the main polling organisation in the country and was the government's primary source of information on the attitudes and opinions of the people. [34]

Does the theory of contending elites apply to Japan? Rivalries between competing *keiretsu*, government departments and graduates of different universities are aggressive and sometimes destructive. But, as they vie with each other for position and privilege, members of the Japanese governing classes share a common interest in the accumulation of wealth for the system and for themselves. The system of closely held interlocking ownership shields managers from pressures to meet the short-term demands of shareholders. Ambitious managers look instead for opportunities to identify themselves with policies that lead to long-term growth in revenue or in market share for their companies.

Success in Japan is usually measured in institutional terms, but incredible private fortunes have also been made. Japan had more billionaires than any country except the US. Industrial growth has produced wealthy and powerful industrialists like Konosuke Matsushita of Matsushita Electric, Kanichiro Ishabashi of Bridgestone Tires, Soichiro Honda of Honda Motors, Eiji Toyoda of Toyota and Akio Morita of Sony. It has also produced non-industrial fortunes. Yoshiaki Tsutsumi was the world's richest landlord in 1990. He owned railways, hotels, golf courses and ski resorts. Taikichiro Mori was the world's richest economist, owning Tokyo office buildings. The billionaires are just the tip of the iceberg. Below them are thousands of others who possess lesser but still great fortunes. As in other countries, money in Japan talks and buys the hands and brains of others. [35]

The power of wealth can also be seen in recurring financial scandals. Corruption is common in all capitalist countries, but in Japan it was the glue that bound the Liberal Democratic Party to private business and government ministries. The LDP was plagued with bribery scandals from the time it was put together by big business in 1955 until it lost power in 1993. The most powerful faction leader in the LDP during the 1970s and 1980s, Kakuei Tanaka, controlled the party's most extensive patronage network. Tanaka entered politics as a successful building contractor. He used his connections in business to get contributions for the LDP and rewarded his contributors with generous government contracts. He built a following within the ministries he headed by finding attractive positions in private industry for officials loyal to him. Meanwhile, he used inside information on government plans to make a personal fortune buying and selling real estate. Letting others in on these opportunities allowed him to strengthen his patronage machine within the LDP. Even after being found guilty of accepting bribes from US aircraft maker Lockheed and spending a few days in jail, Tanaka continued to dominate the LDP. He was instrumental in choosing the next three prime ministers. A fourth, Noboru Takeshita – who resigned as prime minister in the late 1980s after the Recruit kick-back scandal – had inherited Tanaka's machine and remained one of the two most influential politicians in the LDP until its defeat in 1993.[36]

The Social Consequences of Private Power

Frederich Hayek, the most erudite of neonconservative ideologues, argued against government planning by writing, 'though the pursuit of the selfish aims of the individual will usually lead him to serve the general interest, the collective action of organised groups is almost invariably contrary to the general interest'.[37] Claiming to oppose all collective action on philosophical principle, he contrasted what he called the 'spontaneous order' with a 'made order'. He defined the spontaneous order as the result of the unplanned activities of individuals pursuing their own self-interest. A made order, he said, is the result of deliberate, collective decisions, of a kind that inevitably disrupt the spontaneous order in unpredictable ways.[38]

The argument has some merit. Individuals acting alone influence the lives of few others. However, government action is not the only organised human activity. Hayek is wilfully wrong when he assumes that capitalist societies consist of governments on one side and private persons on the other. His position requires acceptance of the legal fiction that corporations are individual

persons. In fact corporations are capitalist collectives that organise human activity. Transnational corporations are among the
largest human collectives ever assembled. Their social impact is
made no less disruptive by private ownership. If anything, it is
made more irresponsible.

The social impact of ostensibly private corporate decisions is
most obvious when significant harm is done to others. The
polluting of Love Canal, the incinerating of people in Ford Pintos
and the gas poisoning of thousands in Bhopal, India, are well
publicised examples of unconscionable damage done to others in
the pursuit of what corporate oligarchs insist are their own
private interests. [39]

During the 1930s and 1940s, as theories of a new socially
conscious management were becoming popular, Hooker Chemical
was dumping 20,000 tons of wastes from the manufacturing of
pesticides, plastics and caustic soda into a large ditch called Love
Canal in Niagara Falls, New York. The ditch was then covered
with earth and donated as a gift by the company to the Niagara
Falls School Board – which then legally assumed all responsibility
and liability for the site.

A residential neighbourhood grew next to the hidden dump.
Unaware of the danger, the community planned to build a school
on the land. Before this could be done, residents close to the area
began suffering from a multitude of unexplained maladies: respir-
atory problems, nervous disorders and rectal bleeding. By the
mid-1970s the incidence of cancer among women was above the
national average. Pets kept in backyards close to the canal were
losing their fur and dying of internal tumours while still young.
The area was afflicted with an unusually high proportion of
miscarriages and births of deformed or retarded children. Traffic
signs near the canal warned motorists to watch for deaf children.
The State of New York responded to the public outcry by buying
several hundred uninhabitable homes. No criminal charges were
brought against Hooker officials either for dumping the toxic
chemicals or for foisting the problem onto unsuspecting taxpayers.

The Ford Pinto shows how corporate cost–benefit analysis can
overlook serious harm done to others. This car's fuel tank could
burst into flames when hit from the rear. Ford engineers calcu-
lated that the problem could be corrected at an additional cost of
$11 a car, but top executives rejected the engineering proposal
after receiving a cost–benefit analysis that concluded it would be
cheaper to pay out $200,000 for each of the 180 anticipated
deaths a year. Between 1971 and 1976 Ford continued to build
cars that burst into flames after rear-end collisions at virtually any
speed. Changes were not made until Ford's Canadian subsidiary

discovered that the problem could be solved by placing a $1
plastic baffle between the fuel tank and the differential housing.
Despite their indifference to human life, no Ford executive was
prosecuted for murder or for criminal negligence.[40]

The Union Carbide disaster in Bhopal, India in 1984 showed
that the power of corporations is even more devastating in poor
countries. An explosion and subsequent poison gas leak killed
more than 2,500 people and blinded and injured thousands more.
A *New York Times* investigation concluded that the disaster was a
direct result of cost-cutting measures by Union Carbide: training
of personnel had been curtailed; plant staff had been halved on
each shift, making it physically impossible to run the plant safely;
instead of repairing a system that cooled chemicals, it was shut
down. Of the plant's three main safety systems, one had been out
of operation for weeks; another had been inoperative for days.
Monitoring instruments were unreliable: alarms went off an average of 20 times a week; supervisors on duty consequently ignored
warnings of the coming disaster.[41]

Partisans of corporate power claim that such events are
exceptions and that most corporations act in a responsible and
lawful manner. Evidence however suggests that the private
power of the corporate oligarchy encourages a wilful ignoring of
the law. Criminologists Marshall Clinard and Peter Yeager
reported that 60 per cent of the largest corporations were
charged with some form of illegal behaviour and that nearly half
of the largest manufacturing corporations were charged with
multiple violations. Their study, *Corporate Crime*, was made
during 1975–6 and partly funded by the Law Enforcement
Assistance Administration of the US Department of Justice.
Corporate Crime, concluded that

> violations were far more likely to be committed by large
> corporations ... large corporations [accounted] for almost
> three-fourths of all violations, nearly twice their expected per-
> centage. Large corporations, moreover, accounted for 72.1 per
> cent of the serious and 62.8 per cent of the moderately
> serious violations.[42]

Clinard and Yeager argued that

> size, delegation and specialisation combine to produce an
> organisational climate that allows the abdication of a degree of
> personal responsibility for almost every type of decision ... At
> all levels of the corporation there may be an institutionalisa-
> tion of irresponsibility that permits the corporation to function
> as if encumbered by blinders and may allow individuals in the

corporation to remain largely unaccountable, often legally as well as morally ... Executives at the highest level can absolve themselves of responsibility by the rationalisation that illegal means of attaining their broadly stated goals have been devised without their knowledge ... To the extent that middle and lower level managers feel that illegal behavior is a necessary part of their job, indeed perhaps that they are coerced into it, the sense of moral responsibility may be blunted at this level also. [43]

Clinard and Yeager reported that consumer products sold on the US market during the early 1970s caused 20 million injuries a year. They add that 1 million to 5 million of these could have been avoided with stiffer product standard regulations. [44]

Workers are the most frequent victims of corporate irresponsibility. The employer-sponsored US National Safety Council reported that more than 14,000 people were killed at work each year during the early 1970s – twice as many Americans as were killed in Vietnam. The Council estimated that another 100,000 deaths a year could be attributed to occupational diseases, including up to 40 per cent of all cancer deaths. Injuries were more frequent. The 1972 *President's Report on Occupational Safety and Health* reported that 'at least 390,000 new cases of disabling occupational diseases develop each year'. The US Department of Labor estimated that another 5.6 million workers were injured on the job annually.[45]

The publication of this information provoked a corporate backlash. After the Reagan victory in 1980, funds for regulatory agencies were cut and regulations were watered down. The Reagan government, committed to the primacy of shareholders' interests, insisted that business functioned best when it regulated itself.

Self-regulation led in part to the grounding of the *Exxon Valdez* in Alaska's Prince William Sound. Exxon, in its quest to maximise profits, shipped the maximum volume of oil at the lowest possible cost. Despite petroleum industry studies that showed groundings were much less likely to cause major oil spills if vessels had double hulls, Exxon shipped Alaskan oil in cheaper single-hulled supertankers and reduced crew sizes to the bare minimum. When the single-hull, 200,000 ton *Exxon Valdez* ran aground in 1989, only one officer – a third mate not certified to navigate a tanker through the sound – was on watch. Exxon had received a Coast Guard waiver exempting it from the regulation requiring certification for all officers. Meanwhile, government cutbacks (encouraged by giant corporations like Exxon) meant that only one person was on duty in the

Coast Guard station. Its radar was not able to cover all of Prince William Sound.

The largely cosmetic clean-up job cost Exxon $2 billion, but the corporation remained profitable. The cost to the fishing and tourist industry is estimated to be in excess of $1 billion. The cost to the ecology of the area is beyond calculation.[46]

Corporate Militarism

Warfare is the most destructive collective human activity. Should warfare be blamed on governments or on capitalist profiteering? In earlier times, trading corporations in Portugal, Spain, Holland, Britain, France, Denmark, Italy, Germany and Japan all relied on armed force to assert their control of markets. By the end of the nineteenth century, European companies controlled the trade of most of Asia and Africa. US public opinion condemned European imperialism, but as the nineteenth century ended, US corporate interests were looking abroad for control of resources and markets.

In 1900 US armed forces occupied Puerto Rico, Cuba and the Philippines and took part in crushing the Boxer Rebellion in China. In 1903 US troops intervened to carve Panama out of Colombia and the Panama Canal Zone out of Panama. In 1904 US troops intervened in the Dominican Republic, returning in 1911 and 1914. US troops fought in Cuba in 1906 and 1909, returning in 1912 and remaining until 1917. US troops intervened in Honduras in 1909 and 1911. They intervened in Nicaragua in 1910, 1912 and 1913. These invasions had little to do with the interests of the US public. The aim was to secure rights to land and resources for US companies and to collect debts owed to private US bondholders.[47]

In 1914 US troops temporarily seized Veracruz in Mexico. In 1916 troops crossed the border from Texas in pursuit of Pancho Villa. Faced with a loss of its Mexican supply of sisal fibre, the US sought an alternative source. US troops invaded Haiti in 1914 and remained until 1934. US forces intervened in the Dominican Republic in 1916 and remained until 1924. They invaded Nicaragua in 1922, remaining until 1924, and again in 1926, remaining until 1933.

After World War II, direct military control of other nations fell into disrepute. During the war, the Allies had claimed to be fighting Nazi subjugation of other nations. After the war, the USSR was denounced for dominating the countries of Eastern Europe. The old imperial powers – Holland, France, the UK and Portugal – did fight to hang on to their empires, but national liberation movements were stronger and more determined than ever. Meanwhile, the US insistence that its indebted allies give it equal access to colonial markets made the rewards of direct rule not worth the cost. Former colonies won their independence one after the other.

The US itself continued to use military force when capitalist property relations or corporate domination of markets were challenged. Between 1946 and 1954, US troops fought peasant insurgents known as 'Huks' in the Philippines. From 1950 to 1953, US troops fought in Korea under cover of the UN banner to hold back the Communist north. In 1958 US troops intervened in Lebanon to prevent the fall of a friendly government. In 1965 21,000 US marines invaded the Dominican Republic to overthrow Juan Bosch, the elected president who had annoyed US business interests. Between 1964 and 1973, US troops fought in Vietnam. At the peak of this invasion, more than 500,000 US soldiers fought to stop the unification of Vietnam. Millions of civilians died as more bombs were dropped on that poor country than were dropped in all of World War II.

US marines landed again in Lebanon in 1982, claiming to be a peace-keeping force, but the Muslim majority soon concluded that the US was siding with Christian war lords. In 1983 US armed forces invaded the tiny island of Grenada and installed a government that agreed to give it control of the island's main air base. US forces invaded Panama in 1989 and arrested its president on charges of drug running. Thousands of civilians were killed. Panama has not yet recovered from the invasion and the preceding embargo. Promised economic assistance failed to materialise. The drug trade has not abated. The aim of the invasion seems to have been to reassert US control of the Panama Canal.

The US government also engaged in covert efforts to protect and promote its business interests abroad. In 1953, the CIA organised a coup in Iran that overthrew elected Prime Minister Mossadegh after he had indicated his intention to nationalise the oil fields. Democracy was replaced with the authoritarian rule of the Shah. In 1954 armed forces financed and advised by the US overthrew the government of Guatemala which had embarked on a programme of land reform. A US-organised invasion force landed in Cuba in 1961 but was routed at the Bay of Pigs. In 1964 a US-backed military coup in Brazil ousted democratically elected and reform-minded President Goulart. In 1973 democratically elected President Allende of Chile was murdered in a military coup led by officers receiving aid and advice from US government and business interests. Allende was a moderate socialist who favoured land reforms, higher minimum wages and protection for domestic Chilean industries.

During the 1980s the US funded a not-so-covert war against the Sandinista government of Nicaragua. The Sandinistas – named after Commander Sandino who had fought US invaders in the 1930s – had come to power in 1979 after a successful guerrilla war against the brutal and nepotistic dictator Anastasia Somoza whose family had been installed in power by US marines. The Sandinista coalition of socialists, patriots and Catholics expropriated the property of the ex-dictator and his cronies, redistributed land to peasants and organised agricultural cooperatives. The Reagan Administration and private US business interests responded by financing, training, arming and billeting thousands of anti-Sandinista *contras* just outside Nicaragua's borders. From these havens, protected by US air power, *contras* surreptitiously crossed the border, burned crops, bombed buildings and shot peasants. US forces took a more direct role in mining Nicaraguan harbours, killing merchant seafarers, fishermen and other civilians. The interminable military pressure worsened conditions for the people and forced the Sandinistas to concentrate on the survival of the regime. In a free election, called by them, the Sandinistas got more than 40 per cent of the vote, but lost the presidency. In a first for a Central American government that had come to power by force of arms, the Sandinistas showed their respect for democracy by accepting the election results and agreeing to act as a parliamentary opposition.

During the same time, El Salvador, Nicaragua's neighbour, was wracked by a prolonged struggle for political and land reform. Here the US financed, advised, trained, armed and occasionally provided logistical support for a government representing one of the most brutal landowning oligarchies in Central America. Top political and military leaders were closely associated with death squads that methodically murdered priests, nuns, an archbishop and tens of thousands of workers, students, teachers and peasants. Representatives of two of the death squads explained their philosophy with demented frankness, saying,

This country's society is divided into three classes: a superior creative class composed essentially of specialists and large landholders; a smaller class that tries to imitate this superior class; and an inferior rustic class that is made up essentially of workers, poor peasants, students and small businessmen. Another group exists that we hold in low regard and consider very small – the dangerous intellectual class that tries to contaminate the above-mentioned classes. The superior capitalist class in our country is naturally the strongest and its destiny, without question, is to govern and regulate the inferior classes. And what is more, it has a duty to exploit, dispose of, conquer and even exterminate elements of these inferior classes when the benefits of capitalism require such. [48]

Officially, US leaders insist they intervene in other countries only to rid them of terrible dictators or to protect US citizens from drugs and unspeakable crimes. They claim that countries that have lost wars to the US have prospered as a result, citing the economic success of Japan and Germany. But these are exceptions. After World War II, the US encouraged their development to undermine support for Communism. Others have not been so fortunate.

The countries of Central America and the Caribbean, the most frequent theatres of US military action, are among the poorest in the world. Domination by US military and business interests has strengthened the *latifundia* system in which vast tracts of land owned by wealthy local landowners and foreign corporations supply the world market with cheap crops. To keep the price of exports low, *latifundia* owners pay wages so low they provide only the barest subsistence. Land on which food could be grown by peasants is deliberately left idle, so that rural people have no alternative but to work for any wages offered. [49]

Property relations in these countries are like those that provoked the eighteenth- and nineteenth-century potato famines in Ireland. Nearly all land was owned by Anglo-Irish landlords. The Irish, driven off their ancestral lands, had little choice but to hire themselves out as seasonal labourers at less than living wages. The crops they planted, weeded and harvested were consumed in England. They were allowed only the tiniest plots to grow potatoes for themselves. When potato blight swept Ireland, more than 1 million died in famines; another million fled to the US, Canada, Australia and England. Eventually Irish people responded by rising in armed struggle for national liberation. [50]

People who are denied sustenance from their own lands do not forever suffer in peace. US governments and business leaders blame Russians or Cubans for armed uprisings in Central America. But people who grow food for others while their children die of malnutrition and despair do not need to be told by foreigners that their conditions are intolerable. Insurgents have fought for independence and social reform from the beginning of US intervention – before either the Cuban or Russian revolutions. Insurgency, motivated by the demand for land reform, continues to the present day in virtually every country of Central America. (The Philippines – which has a similar history of US military intervention and a similar system of land ownership – has a similar history of insurgency.)

Militarism and Oil

The Middle East has been another focus of corporate militarism.
The people of this region have the misfortune of living in the
homeland of three major religions and on the planet's largest
known reserves of petroleum.

For 300 years until the nineteenth century, the countries of
the Middle East were united in the Ottoman Empire. When
Napoleon conquered Egypt at the end of the eighteenth century,
the empire's prosperity was legendary, but its power was already
in decline. In the nineteenth century Britain took control of
Egypt as well as strategic enclaves on the Persian Gulf, including
Kuwait and Bahrain. Russia annexed lands in the north Caucasus,
west of the Black Sea and north of the Danube.

In World War I, the Ottoman Empire sided with the losers,
Germany and Austria, against their enemies, Britain and Russia.
After the war, the victorious allies dismantled the Ottoman
Empire. Greece and other Balkan nations became independent.
Turkey was reduced to its present boundaries. The national interests of Arabs and Kurds were disregarded. Arabs had been promised independence by the British and French in return for military
support against the Ottomans, but the discovery of oil made Arab
control of the eastern Mediterranean inconvenient.[51]

Large oil-bearing formations had been discovered in Persia
(Iran) by a French geologist in 1901. Similar formations were
observed in Iraq a few years later. Although the deposits had not
yet been developed, the men who made the treaties ending the
war understood that oil would be essential for industrial growth
and military power. Rather than granting Arabs independence, the
British and French decided to take control of these lands.
Borders were decided arbitrarily and had little to do with linguis-
tic or economic realities. Iraq, Palestine and Trans-Jordan became
British Protectorates. Syria and Lebanon were ceded to France.
Most of Arabia was allowed formal independence (oil had not yet
been discovered there) and the Saudi family was proclaimed
protector of Islam's holy places.

A French geologist is credited with discovering oil in the
region, but the British got the most productive oil fields. This
was partly corrected by a series of treaties involving first
France and Britain and later the US. Britain got half the Iraq
Petroleum Company, France a quarter and a consortium of US
oil companies the other quarter. Five per cent of the shares of
each partner went to C. S. Gulbenkian, an Armenian businessman, who had originally promoted the company. Neither the
government of Iraq nor domestic business interests were given

any ownership of the oil fields. Kurdish interests were not even considered.

The Kurds – descendants of the ancient Medes who speak a Persian language, closely related to the dominant languages in Iran and Afghanistan, but not to Arabic or Turkish – had been promised autonomy. However, their leaders' support for Turkey during the war and immediately after gave the victorious allies the pretext needed to disregard the national interests of a people living over some of the world's richest oil deposits. The British claimed the Kurdish area of Mosul, which includes present-day oil-rich Kirkuk, and attached it to Iraq. The French annexed three Kurdish administrative areas to Syria. The Kurds – now divided among Turkey, Iraq, Iran, Syria and the Soviet Union – were left with no country to call their own. Ataturk's republican government rewarded Kurds for their loyalty to Turkey by declaring them to be 'Mountain Turks' and making it a crime to speak Kurdish. Uprisings resulted in the death of tens of thousands and the flight of hundreds of thousands of Kurds from Turkey to Iraq. In Iraq, indigenous Kurds rose in rebellion against the British. The British responded by sending the Royal Air Force to bomb their towns and cities.

The treaties carving up the area did give the government of Iraq the right to collect oil royalties, but these did not cover the interest payments on what Britain insisted was Iraq's share of the old Ottoman debt. To extract more revenues, taxes were levied on the impoverished people. When disaffected people, especially the Shia in the south and the Kurds in the north, refused to pay, their villages were bombed by the RAF. The bombings began in 1920 when Winston Churchill was Secretary for War. He recommended 'the construction of special aeroplanes for this purpose'. To the commanders of the air force, he said,

> You will naturally make the tools you require for the job and exactly those tools *ad hoc*. The question of chemical bombs which are not destructive of human life but which inflict various degrees of minor annoyance should also be the subject of careful considerations.[52]

A. T. Harris, a young squadron leader – who would command the World War II bombing of German cities – got first-hand experience bombing civilian targets in Mesopotamia in the early 1920s. He distinguished himself by altering aircraft to make bombing more accurate.[53]

The bombing attacks did more than annoy civilians. According to Peter Sluglett, 'The casualties may appear unimpressive by today's standards, but over a two week period 144 people were killed, an unspecified number wounded.'[54] By 1923, the bombing of civilians had become a public scandal. George Lansbury, the socialist publisher of the *Daily Herald*, denounced 'this Hunnish and barbarous method of warfare against unarmed people'.[55] The Beaverbrook and Harmsworth newspapers demanded that Britain get out of Mesopotamia. Even the crusty imperialist, Lord Curzon, former Viceroy of India, objected to the bombing of civilians for non-payment of taxes. Nonetheless, the RAF would continue such raids until Iraq was granted formal independence.

Iraq was declared independent in 1932, but the Royal Air Force stayed to defend a king installed by the British until a republic was proclaimed after an uprising in 1958. Syria got its independence from France after World War II. Lebanon, administered by France until 1946, has since been split by civil war between supporters and opponents of a French-imposed constitution that gave political control to the Christian minority.

During the oil crises in the 1970s much was made of the wealth of Arab sheikhs, but the Arab world is far from wealthy. Some mini-states have substantial oil wealth, as do some larger states. Most Arabs, however, live in countries that do not have access to the funds required for rapid industrial development. The few fabulously wealthy families in the region have comfortably adjusted to class realities within boundaries imposed by European powers. They prefer to invest their surplus funds in Britain, the US and Europe where political systems are more stable.

Israel's existence is in part explained by the determination of transnational corporate interests to weaken the Arab world. The modern state of Israel traces its origins to the Balfour Declaration of 1917. When preparing to dismember the Ottoman Empire, Lord Balfour, the British Foreign Secretary, publicly promised British Zionists a homeland in Palestine. Because Britain at the time was also promising Arabs self-determination, the declaration had a rider that the rights of the existing non-Jewish inhabitants of Palestine would be protected.[56]

Prior to the late nineteenth century, few Jews actively claimed Palestine as a homeland. The successes of European colonialism and a racist backlash in Europe against citizenship rights for Jews led to the rise of the Zionist movement. Zionists held that Jews would not be accepted as full members of the European community of nations until they controlled their own state. They considered African and South American locations and eventually decided that the Jewish state must be in Palestine. Jews at the time were a small minority in Palestine, as they had been for 2,000 years. For most of that time they lived in peace with their Muslim and Christian neighbours, who, like them, considered the land sacred to their religion.

Zionism remained a minority movement among Jews until World War II. In 1939, Jews were one third of the population of Palestine and owned 10 per cent of the land. After the Nazis began their campaign to exterminate Jews, hundreds of thousands fled Europe. Most wanted to settle in North America, but the US and Canada refused to accept more than a token number of Jewish refugees. In desperation, European Jews flooded Palestine. The British were uneasy: they had agreed to the Balfour Declaration, but Palestinians violently objected to Britain giving their lands to refugees from Europe.

In 1947, the United Nations General Assembly voted to partition Palestine into an Arab and a Jewish state. In 1948, the British withdrew from Palestine and Israel declared itself an independent state. In a series of wars, Israel – armed and financed by the US – seized lands the UN had assigned to Palestinians and other lands from Jordan, Syria and Egypt. The Jewish seizure of Arab lands is justified on religious grounds by some Jews and some Christians. It is condemned on religious grounds by virtually all Muslims. After the religious arguments are cancelled against each other, Israel appears as a twentieth-century variant of nineteenth-century colonialism: a predominantly European people has taken the land of a non-European people.

Corporate capitalism has had more practical reasons to support Israel. Support for a Jewish homeland was consistent with the strategy of keeping the Arab world weak and divided so that petroleum transnationals could control Middle Eastern oil. During the Cold War, the Israeli military provided the US with a reliable and effective force that could contain Arab regimes hostile to US interests without putting US troops in a situation where they had directly to confront allies of the USSR.

The precise level of US aid to Israel is kept secret, but it is known that during the early 1980s, US military aid amounted to the equivalent of $10,000 per Israeli soldier per year. Israel was the largest recipient of US foreign aid, getting 40 per cent of the total during the 1980s. R. T. Naylor estimated that 'by 1985 every Israeli had received in real terms twenty times the amount given by the US to the average European under the Marshall plan'. US aid accounted for 20 per cent of Israel's annual Gross National Product, nearly $1,000 each year for each man, woman and child in the country – a level of aid that alone explains most of the economic success of Israel compared to its Arab neighbours.[57]

During the Gulf War, Israel was made to stand on the

sidelines. Perhaps the collapse of the Soviet Union has reduced the importance of the Israeli military to transnational capital. However, the war showed that basic policy had not changed. The fury of the bombardment of Iraq was designed entirely to protect western oil interests. Human rights and justice were beside the point. The US and its allies allowed Saddam to remain in power. After driving his forces from Kuwaiti oil fields, they did little to stop him from driving Kurds from their ancient homelands and nothing to stop his regime from organising a brutal, environmentally destructive campaign to exterminate the Shiite marsh Arabs who had heeded George Bush's call to rebel against Baghdad.

Militarism at Home

Although governments direct the military, and the people pay, wealthowners reap the benefits. Militarism transforms tax dollars into profits for military contractors and creates an authoritarian political climate that justifies oligarchic rule. In 1960 Republican President Eisenhower, himself a retired general, more or less admitted this when he warned that 'a military industrial' complex had become a major threat to US democracy. By the time Ronald Reagan left office, the staggering military budget left no doubt that the military-industrial complex was in effective control of the US government.

Military contracting is a cost-plus business. Because cost is often less a consideration than precise specifications and delivery time, profits are typically higher than in production for civilian markets. Out of the tens of billions of tax dollars annually handed to military contractors, a few tens of millions are routinely recycled to swing politicians into line. Companies like General Dynamics, Grumman, Lockheed, Rockwell International, McDonnell Douglas, Northrop and United Technologies, each of which have received military contracts worth billions a year, have been major contributors to political campaigns. Some of the money they spend on lobbying goes to promote particular weapons systems or specific locations for defence industries. Some goes directly into the campaign coffers of politicians. There is nothing illegal about this; such donations if properly reported are tax deductible.[58]

Weapons manufacturers are not alone in their dependence on militarism. Contracts from the US military provide assured revenues for US aircraft, computer, metal, chemical and specialist plastics manufacturers. Numerous other industries, including those producing medical equipment, fuel, clothing, housing and recreational weapons, profit from the provision of goods and services to the military and for its civilian support personnel.

Nonetheless, military spending distorts capital markets. As investments flow to the higher profits in military production, enterprises not so favoured are weakened. Money spent on the military increases government debt while adding little to social infrastructure and less to a country's capacity to satisfy non-military consumer demand. On the rare occasions that military research has had civilian applications, the direct funding by government of civilian research would most likely have been less expensive. Much of the relative economic decline of US civilian industry in the 1980s compared to Japan and Germany can be explained by military spending and the preoccupation with military research.

In the short run military spending does add to civilian employment. In the long run it is the most ruinous form of government economic intervention. Adam Smith had no doubt about that. Writing of the impact of the wars that followed the Restoration of 1660, Smith said,

> Had not those wars given this particular direction to so large a capital, the greater part of it would naturally have been employed in maintaining productive hands ... More houses would have been built ... more manufactures would have been established and those which had been established before would have been more extended; and to what height the real wealth and revenue of the country might, by this time, have been raised, it is not perhaps very easy even to imagine.[59]

Similar comments can be made at present. In 1983, Amir Jamal, a Tanzanian governor of the International Monetary Fund, said that

> a two per cent reduction in defence expenditure by the industrialised countries could meet the minimum unsatisfied needs of poor developing countries. Ninety-eight tanks instead of a hundred, ninety-eight bombs instead of a hundred, ninety-eight missiles instead of a hundred. Is this such a huge sacrifice?[60]

The US public has been conditioned to back the military, but militarism also damages civil society in the US. It is no coincidence that the expansion of the military budget under Reagan and Bush was accompanied by a decline in the quality of life for a majority of Americans. Money spent on the military is money diverted from education, job training, services in inner cities or for a national health care system. More than that, militarism undermines concern for the wellbeing of others; it glorifies winners and stigmatises losers. Because militarism makes might right, it leads to contempt for the rule of law.

Was it surprising that Richard Nixon approved the Watergate break-in, when CIA operatives under his direction had routinely engaged in much more serious violations of the law in other countries? Reagan's willingness to ignore the Congressional ban on arms shipments to the *contras* and to Iran was entirely consistent with his government's refusal to heed the World Court's condemnation of the mining of Nicaraguan harbours.

US wealthowners – who are accustomed to using economic power and military force to enrich themselves at the expense of poor, mostly non-white people abroad – are not likely to have much sympathy for poor, mostly non-white people at home. The worsening racial polarisation in the US, the flight of jobs and income from African-American and Latino communities and the decay of social services in inner cities are predictable consequences of the militaristic world view: our guys win, you lose.

Internal violence is another predictable consequence of militarism. A country that sees violence as the solution to problems abroad encourages its citizens to use violence to solve their problems at home. Militarism has an especially corrosive effect on non-white communities where most economic opportunities have been lost to capital flight abroad and to lower-priced immigrant labour at home. African Americans and Mexican Americans have lived in the United States for generations. Their expectations and aspirations are entirely American. No more willing than white Americans to accept the wages paid in Mexico or Bangladesh or to refugees and illegals in the sweatshops of Los Angeles, they see no future in industry. For many young men in these communities, the military offers the only acceptable legitimate career. Those who join are taught that violence is not only acceptable but honourable. They learn that armed force is used to impose the will of the US government and business on defenceless, poor people. When their country tells them that is the road to glory is it surprising that some turn to private violence or the drug trade at home as no-less acceptable lifestyles?

4 The Political Power of the Oligarchy

Wealthowners and Politicians

In more prosperous countries, wealthowners remained in the background during the decades of sustained growth that followed World War II. During those Keynesian times politicians and public servants set the political agenda. With the neoconservative reaction, wealthowners once again took centre stage. They were cheered on by politicians singing the praises of the individual in the market. Politicians have always been eager to do the bidding of wealthowners. Although capitalists, as Adam Smith said, are a tiny minority 'whose interest is never exactly the same with that of the public', candidates for public office need money to get elected, and capitalists do have money. [1]

Ronald Reagan, a politically ambitious and modestly successful actor, understood that money was the key to success. [2] He ingratiated himself to conservative wealthowners during the 1940s by volunteering to be a stool pigeon for the FBI. As an executive member of the actors' union, he learned the private political opinions of his co-workers and then fingered some as liberals and leftists. He was rewarded for this back-stabbing by being made host of General Electric's Television Theatre. Reagan made the most of this opportunity. He travelled the country making speeches urging voters to support the stockpiling of nuclear weapons – weapons that the government would buy from General Electric. Business groups paid him $20,000 an appearance. His enthusiasm for big business was further rewarded when Twentieth Century Fox paid him $2 million for a parcel of land, three times its assessed market value and 30 times what Reagan had paid for it. The future president could now afford to devote all his attention to politics.

Given the choice, corporate oligarchs usually prefer to see their own people – like George Bush – in public office. Bush was born into a wealthy family, attended a prestigious prep school, graduated from an Ivy League college and went on to make his own fortune in the oil industry. He rose to the top ranks of the Republican Party, was made boss of the Central Intelligence Agency, became vice president and then was elected president. Nobody ever doubted his commitment to wealth.

In Canada, Brian Mulroney successfully challenged Joe Clark for the leadership of the Conservatives when he was not even a Member of Parliament. But he was president of the Iron Ore Company (a subsidiary of US-owned Hanna Mining Company), a director of the Canadian Imperial Bank of Commerce and a director of Standard Broadcasting. In the 1984 election, Mulroney's party collected C$21 million from supporters, more than twice the contributions collected by either the Liberals or New Democrats. Half of the Conservatives' donations came from corporations. Most of the remainder came from corporate executives and shareholders. Mulroney did not fail to repay his supporters: he lowered taxes paid by the rich and raised those paid by the working majority; he kept interest rates high so that creditors could maximise returns from their wealth; he signed a trade agreement with the US that favoured transnational capital at the expense of domestic industry.[3]

The power wealthowners have over politics is secured by control over the media. In the US, three giant corporations (NBC, CBS and ABC) dominate network radio and television broadcasting. A handful of similarly large corporations dominate the movie industry. Where local newspapers, radio and TV stations are not part of conglomerates, they are owned by wealthy families. In 1990, the fortunes of three of the six richest Americans came from ownership of means of communication: John Werner Kluge's money was in Metromedia (radio and TV stations); the Cox fortune was in 18 daily newspapers, 7 major TV stations, 13 radio stations and a cable TV network; Newhouse money was in 29 daily newspapers, 17 magazines (including *The New Yorker* and *Vogue*), Random House publishers and a cable TV network.[4]

In English-speaking Canada, two corporations, Thomson and Southam, dominate the daily press. The Thomson chain owns the Toronto *Globe and Mail*, the Winnipeg *Free Press* and 40 other dailies. Southam owns fewer papers, but its 15 are usually in larger centres. These include the Montreal *Gazette*, Ottawa *Citizen*, Hamilton *Spectator*, Calgary *Herald*, Edmonton *Journal* and both the Vancouver *Sun* and *The Province*. Radio stations, when not part of networks like Standard Broadcasting or Selkirk, are usually owned by prominent local wealthowners.[5]

Corporate capital is increasing its hold on television broadcasting. Cutbacks by the Conservative government weakened the CBC and strengthened the two privately-owned networks. CTV is controlled by the Eaton and Bassett families of Toronto and the Griffiths family of Vancouver. Global is owned by Izzy Asper of Winnipeg. In cable television, Rogers is methodically building a private monopoly. The CBC is itself subject to heavy corporate pressure, from advertisers and from pro-corporate political appointees on its board.

Regardless of the integrity of individual journalists, the policy and tone of the media is set by corporate owners and advertisers. Free speech for the media means little more than the freedom to say or write what brings the largest audience. The point is to sell a product (advertising). Information and entertainment are presented in ways designed to please advertisers and to portray capitalism in the most favourable possible light. The corporate media, despite its monopoly on social communication, does not even pretend to give differing opinions a fair airing.

The oligarchy's control over social communication does not end with the media. Schools and other educational institutions are also used for public relations by corporate oligarchs. In the US, the Joint Council on Economic Education, ostensibly a charitable organisation, funds economic education for teachers and provides books, pamphlets and movies as teaching aids. In 1974, 20,000 US teachers participated in its workshops. These are not limited to teaching the skills required in business. The aim is to make teachers present corporations in an uncritical light to their students.

> Although it has not been able to bring about active acceptance of all power elite policies and perspectives, on economics or most other domestic issues, it has been able to ensure that opposing opinions have remained isolated, suspect and only partially developed.[6]

Funding for this propaganda arm of big business comes from the American Bankers Association, AT&T, the Sears Roebuck Foundation and the Ford Foundation.

Scholarly discourse is also heavily influenced by wealthowners. Most scholars prefer to live in comfort while doing their work, so private family foundations have a critical role in determining research priorities. In 1974, 26 US foundations each dispersed funds from endowments of more than $100 million. The Rockefeller, Carnegie, Ford and Russell Sage foundations had been around for decades. More recent, stridently pro-capitalist foundations like the Pew Memorial Trust, Lilly Endowment and Smith Richardson foundations played an important part in preparing the neoconservative climate in the academic world, in politics and in the media.[7]

Chambers of Commerce, Manufacturers Associations and trade associations help corporate oligarchs mould public opinion. Such organisations lobby for corporate interests in local communities. They play an important role in passing the prevailing views of wealthowners to the middle and lower rungs of management. In this they are aided by a variety of business-oriented fraternal organisations like the Shriners, Kiwanis and Rotary clubs and by aggressively pro-capitalist religious groups like those led by Jerry Falwell and Pat Robertson.

In pursuing their collective interests, wealthowners claim they are simply exercising their rights: their right to run their TV stations, movie studios and newspapers as they see fit; their right to have their point of view heard; and their right freely to associate in pursuit of their uncommon interests. But corporate oligarchs are not just another interest group. When they decide to act in concert, they have means to impose their interests on everyone else.

Through the Trilateral Commission, wealthowners were able to set the global political agenda for the next generation. The Trilateral Commission, formed in the 1970s, brought together top business and government leaders from western Europe, Japan and North America. Organised by Prince Bernhard of the Netherlands and David Rockefeller, chairman of the Chase Manhattan Bank, the Commission became the forum in which transnational corporate oligarchs got together to set the priorities for the neoconservative reaction.[8]

Opposition by corporate oligarchs to the egalitarianism of welfare capitalism was expressed in a book-length report, published for the Commission in 1975. The problem with the world, it said, was 'an excess of democracy'. 'People no longer felt the same compulsion to obey those whom they had previously considered superior to themselves in age, rank, status, expertise, character, or talent.' Just as troubling, 'previously passive or unorganised groups in the population, blacks, Indians, Chicanos, white ethnic groups, students and women ... embarked on concerted efforts to establish their claims to opportunities, rewards, and privileges, which they had not considered themselves entitled to before'. Such developments, the report claimed, undermined the system,

> The effective operation of a democratic political system usually requires some measure of apathy and non-involvement on the part of some individuals and groups ... In itself, this marginality on the part of some groups is inherently undemocratic, but it is also one of the factors which has enabled democracy to function effectively.[9]

The report in effect said that democracy works best when the interests of most people are not being served. The director of the

US National Association of Manufacturers was presumably making the same point when he said a few years earlier, 'Legislators have tended to be more receptive to the public interest than they have been to business.' [10] This fault in the system could be corrected, according to the Trilateral Commission, if the US returned to the good old days when 'Truman had been able to govern the country with the cooperation of a relatively small number of Wall Street lawyers and bankers.' [11]

The Trilateral Commission was only briefly in the spotlight. Prince Bernhard became more discreet after being named in a Lockheed bribery scandal. David Rockefeller's reputation was tarnished by the decline in the prestige of US banking. Nonetheless, the Trilateral Commission had done its job. In all major capitalist countries, corporate oligarchs united in the conviction that the demands of other interest groups had become excessive. Inspired by the Trilateral Commission, they set out to make governments more responsive to the demands of the most demanding of all interest groups – wealthowners. They launched campaigns against trade unions, social services, graduated income taxes, regulations, minimum wages and government-directed full employment strategies. They looked forward to the time when lower wages would leave more for the rich and high unemployment would put ordinary people in their place.

(Do not get the wrong impression. This was not a conspiracy. It was merely the deliberate application by wealthowners of economic and political power in their own interests. Only enemies of the established order engage in conspiracies.)

In the United States, the neoconservative reaction was led by the Business Roundtable, an organisation of chief executive officers of large corporations. [12] The Business Roundtable was formed in 1973 as a merger of the Construction Users' Anti-Inflation Roundtable and the Fair Law Study Committee. Both these groups shared a common hostility to unions and to the National Labour Relations Board which they claimed favoured unions. The merged Business Roundtable had 192 members, including the chief executive officers of General Motors, Exxon, Ford, Mobil, Texaco, Standard Oil of California, IBM, General Electric and Gulf Oil – nine of the top ten corporations in the US (only Chrysler was absent). It included chief executive officers of 17 of the top 20 and 39 of the top 50 corporations. Companies represented on the Business Roundtable controlled $1.3 trillion in assets in 1978 – half the US Gross National Product.

The Business Roundtable was and is discreet. It relies less on press conferences and public speeches than on lobbying. It sends chief executive officers of the world's largest companies to meet with congressmen, senators, cabinet members and the president.

Although not as publicly strident as the National Association of Manufacturers or the US Chamber of Commerce, the Business Roundtable has pushed for the same narrow, self-serving, oligarchic interests. It has opposed anti-trust legislation, environmental regulations and the Occupational Safety and Health Administration. It has supported tax cuts for the rich and has consistently called for cuts in government services. In short, the Business Roundtable was the source of the right-wing policies of the Reagan and Bush Administrations.

In Canada, the campaign to impose the corporate oligarchy's agenda on government was led by the Business Council on National Issues and the Fraser Institute. The BCNI – modelled on the Business Roundtable – includes the chief executives of 150 corporations, many of them US subsidiaries. In the early 1980s, the companies represented in the BCNI employed 1.5 million people and had annual revenues of $275 billion – half of Canada's GNP. [13]

The adoption of the BCNI agenda by the Mulroney government is documented by Linda McQuaig in *The Quick and the Dead*. The Mulroney government adopted BCNI opposition to the National Energy Program, to controls on foreign investment, to subsidised passenger rail service, to regional development programmes and to foreign aid spending. In 1986 the BCNI, urged the government to cut tax rates on corporations and on higher incomes and to make up the lost revenue by including services in the federal sales tax. Mulroney responded by pushing the Goods and Services Tax through Parliament.

The corporate lobby also inspired Mulroney's Free Trade Agreement with the US. The BCNI had initially favoured a sector by sector trade agreement, but after meeting with US Trade Representative William Brock it changed direction. Brock insisted that the US would agree only to a comprehensive trade agreement that removed restrictions on US ownership of Canadian companies and gave the US freer access to Canadian raw materials. Fearing charges of a sell-out to US interests, the BCNI agreed to make it appear that the initiative for such an agreement had come from Canadian business. Mulroney played along by publicly taking the initiative to urge the US to begin talks on a trade agreement. In the end the agreement was what US big business had wanted.

While the BCNI, and the Business Roundtable in the US, quietly lobbied politicians, the Fraser Institute focused on winning public support for the corporate agenda. The Fraser Institute claims to represent the interests of the individual in the free market but it is funded by large corporations like MacMillan Bloedel, Noranda, BC Telephone, Canadian Pacific, the Canadian

Imperial Bank of Commerce, the Royal Bank, Imperial Oil, IBM and General Motors of Canada. It has received contributions from Southam, the owner of Vancouver's two daily newspapers, and from BCTV, the owner of two of the four major TV channels in British Columbia.

The Fraser Institute was launched by officers of the Council of Forest Industries and the BC Employers Council after Dave Barrett's New Democratic government legislated a tonnage tax on minerals and removed some legal sanctions against unions. Big business – accustomed to extracting resources with virtually no return to the public and expecting to be able to use the courts against workers whenever it suited their purposes – decided the NDP had to go. The Fraser Institute was assigned the task of mobilising small business and the lower ranks of corporate management against the NDP, against unions, against human rights, against taxes on business and against virtually all regulations designed to protect the public from unrestrained profiteering.

The primary goal of the Fraser Institute is to convince people that all other rights must be subordinated to the right to enjoy wealth. Walter Block, a leading Fraser Institute ideologue, has argued that the right to enjoy property implies the right to discriminate. Block said no property owner should be compelled to sell a house, rent an apartment or offer a job to anyone whose looks, sex, creed, colour or lifestyle is distasteful to him. Block does not have Bernard Mandeville's sense of humour, but he shares his contempt for the disadvantaged and for common decency. In one of his books, Block said,

> Consider the sexual harassment which continually occurs between a secretary and a boss ... while objectionable to many women, [it] is not a coercive action. It is rather part of a package deal in which the secretary agrees to *all* aspects of the job when she agrees to accept the job, and especially when she agrees to *keep* the job. The office is, after all, private property. The secretary does not have to remain if the 'coercion' is objectionable.[14]

The Neoconservative Reaction

Keynesian policies were abandoned in the 1970s. Prior to that, in the decades following World War II, governments found that steadily improving social benefits could be paid for out of rising employment, rising real wages and rising government revenue. Nonetheless, corporate oligarchs succeeded in convincing politicians that full employment policies were causing inflation and placing an unfair burden of taxation on business.

The Labour government in Britain, the Democrats in the US and the Liberals in Canada moved to the right to accommodate wealthowners' demands. They cut corporate taxes, lowered marginal tax rates on high personal incomes and took steps to reduce growth in government transfer payments to the poor. They agreed that employment is best left to the market and to business. Corporate oligarchs were not satisfied. They turned to more aggressive neoconservative politicians who held that the old Keynesian parties remained committed to government intervention and were too weak to say no to 'special interest groups', like trade unions, teachers, health care workers, women and minorities. Pluralist parties were abandoned. Wealthowners gave their support to parties determined to govern in the interests of only one interest group – wealthowners.

To justify government for the rich, neoconservatives revived discredited nineteenth-century *laissez faire* dogmas, claiming these were fresh, new thoughts on a new reality. To make a case that lower taxes on business and the rich would benefit economies, they deliberately confused profits and wealthowners' income with savings and productive investment. Adam Smith could perhaps be forgiven for having said 'Parsimony and not industry is the immediate cause of the increase of capital.'[15] When petty capital was more common, small masters did have to choose between consuming the revenue from their labour or adding it to their capital stock. However, once enterprises began to employ large numbers, the claim that investment had anything to do with savings or with parsimonious living was worse than dubious. In the mid-nineteenth century, John Stuart Mill, the great free market theorist, had already more or less recognised this. He did continue to equate savings with investments, but added, 'it continually happens that the person who has capital is not the very person who has saved it, but some one who, being stronger, or belonging to a more powerful community, has possessed himself of it'. Enforced privations, he said, 'though essentially the same with saving, are not generally called by that name, because not voluntary'.[16]

In the present day, equating wealthowners' income – dividends, interest and executive salaries – with 'savings' or 'investments' stretches the meaning of words beyond recognition. How can top corporate oligarchs be considered paragons of parsimonious living when they typically spend more on themselves than is available to dozens of ordinary working families? Would it not be more reasonable to view wealthowners' income as funds removed from social production to private conspicuous consumption?

The claim that wealthowners' income is a legitimate reward for the 'risk' taken in investment is equally egregious. Risk is a consequence of virtually all human action: when we get up and exert ourselves, we risk pulling muscles or getting a heart attack; when we cross the street, we risk being hit by a car. Corporate oligarchs rarely risk life or limb in the course of their duties. When they make mistakes in judgement or when unforeseen developments cause their businesses to fail, corporate oligarchs will in most cases still live more comfortably than most working people. More serious consequences will be suffered by working people who lose their jobs.

Risk is only one of the dubious neoconservative concepts. George Gilder's defence of hypocrisy suggests that neoconservatives should not be read literally. According to Ronald Reagan's favourite economic writer,

> hypocrisy – the insincere profession of unfulfilled ideals – is the means by which the influence of ideals is extended beyond the small circle of true believers ... Hypocrisy might also be described as manners or exalted as civilization ... Hypocrisy can make us better than we are. [17]

However, it can be accepted that Gilder sincerely believed there was little point in being rich unless the poor were suffering. The same can be said for Friedrich Hayek and Milton Friedman. These two Nobel Prize winners can take credit for reviving the nineteenth-century free market dogmas that justified the neoconservative assault on the poor by the rich.

Friedrich Hayek, an Austrian who had written scholarly works on economics, theoretical psychology, philosophy, political science and law, moved to Britain in the 1930s and later taught at the University of Chicago. He was best known for *The Road to Serfdom*, originally published in Britain in 1944.[18] A condensed version of this pamphlet, published by *Reader's Digest* during the early years of the Cold War, inspired conservative US business people to speak out against the popular Keynesian policies of the time.

In *The Road to Serfdom* Hayek argued that totalitarianism is the inevitable result of government economic planning. Dismissing the Keynesian argument that growth in aggregate demand requires government planning for full employment, he said that no planner or group of planners can understand the needs and circumstances of all the myriad individuals in a nation. The state, he said,

> should confine itself to establishing rules applying to general types of situations and should allow the individuals freedom in

everything which depends on the circumstances of time and
place, because only the individuals concerned in each instance
can fully know these circumstances and adapt their actions to
them. [19]

In *Law, Legislation and Liberty*, published in three volumes from
1973 to 1979, Hayek repeated his earlier arguments but he now
made it clear that his sympathies were with wealthowners.[20]
Governments, he said, should limit themselves to protecting 'the
stability of possession' and 'the inviolability of property'.[21] To
make it impractical for them to do much else, he proposed that
governments be required to have two chambers: one with the
right to pass laws but with no administrative power; the other
with administrative power but no right to pass laws. This inspired
the campaign by the Alberta Conservative Party and the Reform
Party for a 'triple E' Senate. If they had succeeded, an annoying
and useless – but fairly harmless – patronage pasture would have
been transformed into an 'elected, equal and effective Senate'.
Two houses of parliament would have been locked in more or less
permanent dispute, effectively blocking any government initiatives
not overwhelmingly endorsed by the rich and powerful.

Hayek, like other neoconservatives, claimed the authority of
Adam Smith in his opposition to government. To do so, he had
to overlook a profound change in the nature of government. In
Smith's day government was openly and unashamedly an instru-
ment of wealthowners. Less than 10 per cent of British men –
and no women at all – had the right to vote. When Smith
opposed government interference in the economy, he was
opposing the imposition of wealthowners' interests on everybody
else. Today, when neoconservatives oppose state interference,
their aim is the opposite: to stop the representatives of the
people from interfering with the interests of wealthowners.

Hayek, who claimed to favour the individual over the collective on principle, did not hesitate to defend the collective rights
of wealthowners. He defended corporate control over means of
livelihood and even defended monopolistic super-profits.[22] His
solicitous concern for the corporate or collective interests of
capitalists was in sharp contrast to his hostility to the collective
interests of working people. Trade unions drove him to distrac-
tion. Perhaps aware that his denial of the collectivist character
of corporate activity made his argument shaky, Hayek complained that 'it is inexcusable to pretend' that corporations have
as much power to influence governments as trade unions.[23] To
show how frightening the power of unions was, Hayek went all
the way back to the turn of the century. He claimed that 1906
labour legislation in Britain, that limited the right of employers

to sue unions for losses during strikes, 'is the chief cause of the progressive decline of the British economy'.[24] Does the unwillingness of present-day British wealthowners to dirty their hands with industrial activities or to live in manufacturing centres away from London have nothing to do with this? Did the loss of empire, the decline of sterling as the world's reserve currency, the debt burden of two major wars and the competition from the technologically more advanced industries in Germany, the US and Japan have less impact?

Hayek had come a long way. In *The Road to Serfdom*, he called himself a liberal, not a conservative, because 'a conservative movement, by its very nature, is bound to be a defender of established privilege and to lean on the power of government for the protection of privilege'.[25] A generation later, the government of Margaret Thatcher – inspired by Hayek – did exactly that. Although he still claimed to espouse the liberal principles of Adam Smith, David Ricardo and John Stuart Mill, Hayek's defence of wealthowners had more in common with positions taken by John Locke, Bernard Mandeville and the mercantilists. Like them, Hayek believed in the utility of poverty (for others) and rejected aspirations for equality. He had nothing but contempt for politicians who strive 'to remove all sources of discontent'.[26] His major criticism of Keynesian governments was that they tried to redistribute income from the rich to the poor.

Milton Friedman, who also taught economics at the University of Chicago, had doggedly preached the old market dogmas during the days of Keynesian hegemony. His determination to remain in the nineteenth century was rewarded in 1977 with a Nobel Prize in economics. Friedman took advantage of this acclaim by writing the best-seller *Free to Choose*. Here he said shopping is more satisfying than voting. After you vote in an election, he said, 'you end up with something different from what you thought you voted for'. But, 'when you vote daily in the supermarket, you get precisely what you voted for and so does everyone else'.[27]

Was Friedman complaining about the dishonesty of politicians? Not at all. In *Tyranny of the Status Quo*, published in 1983, Friedman congratulated British Columbia Premier Bill Bennett for misleading the people. Immediately after winning a provincial election in which he had campaigned to make no changes, Bennett privatised highway maintenance, eliminated social programmes and cut government employment by 25 per cent. Friedman said he admired this duplicity because 'had Premier Bennett spelled out his intentions to cut personnel and funds before the election, he would have aroused immediate and vocal opposition.'[28] Brian Mulroney would also have pleased Friedman. When running for prime minister in 1984 he said he would never sign a free trade agreement with the US. Once elected he began negotiations for just such a treaty.

During these neoconservative times, election results have been disappointing. Do people always get what they want when they shop? Shoddy and dangerous merchandise is not uncommon. Even when products are exactly as advertised, shoppers do not always want everything they get. Do consumers who buy bleached newsprint and toilet paper really want tons of dioxins, furans and other organochlorides in rivers, lakes and coastal waters? Do consumers who purchase automobiles really want traffic jams, air pollution and the greenhouse effect?[29]

Friedman was unconcerned. For him, shopping was the source of individualism, the meaning of life. In Friedman's world view, the penniless, the downtrodden, the victims of injustice count for little. Only those with money to spend are real citizens. The problems that vexed him are those that sap the vitality of shoppers: inflation, taxes and government debt. Inflation dilutes purchasing power. Taxes shift dollars from shoppers to governments. Government debt aggravates inflation and leads to higher taxes. The culprits, according to Friedman, are social programmes. When governments bow to demands from unions for increased employment and from the poor for increased social spending, the results are inflation, taxes and debt. When unions push wages above market rates, income is taken from others and less is available for investment.

In his quest to prove the perfidy of unions, this Nobel Prize-winning scholar chose two typical unions. The first was the Airline Pilots Association. The 'airline pilots in the United States', Friedman said, 'received an annual salary, for a three-day week, that averaged $50,000 a year in 1976'. This, he claimed, came less from their skill and responsibility 'than from the protected position they have achieved through a union'.[30] His second typical union was the American Medical Association. 'Physicians', Friedman said, 'are among the most highly paid workers in the United States. That status is not exceptional for persons who have benefited from labour unions.'[31]

Friedman had not always believed that collective bargaining gave typical union members the income of medical doctors. In an earlier book he had said, 'Many unions are utterly ineffective. Even the strong and powerful unions have only a limited effect on the wage structure.' The price of labour, Friedman said, is not set by unions. Like that of any other commodity, the price of labour is determined by conditions of supply and demand.[32]

Why then was Friedman so hostile to unions? Because

> higher wages for one group of workers must come primarily
> from other workers ... Unions or their equivalent, such as the
> American Medical Association [have been able] to raise their
> wages 10 to 15 per cent above what they otherwise would
> have been, at the cost of reducing the wages earned by the
> other 85 or 90 per cent by some 4 per cent below what they
> otherwise would have been. [33]

How do the relatively high incomes of doctors or pilots come at
the expense of lower-paid workers? Most poorly paid workers are
employed in enterprises in the personal service industry, in fast-
food outlets and in retail shops. The higher pay of doctors and
pilots is not a cost to the employers in these industries. When
people working in other industries are paid more, enterprises
providing consumer goods and services benefit from the increase
in potential revenue.

Why indeed was Friedman criticising the relatively high pay
of pilots and doctors? He did not condemn the rapid increase
in corporate executive compensation during the 1970s and
1980s. He was an enthusiastic advocate of higher returns for
wealthowners. If the income of some high paid occupations
actually did come at the expense of lower-paid workers, Friedman would have applauded. He consistently claimed that ordinary US workers are paid too much. In the 1950s, he was
already complaining that industrial wages in the US were too
high. In the 1970s he actively campaigned against minimum
wage laws.

Minimum wages, Friedman said, by raising wages above
market levels, force employers to cut back on hiring to remain
competitive. Do they? Since minimum wage laws apply to all
employers, how can some get a competitive advantage over
others? Logic aside, why did north eastern US states, where
minimum wages were higher, have lower unemployment rates in
the 1960s and 1970s than south eastern states, where minimum
wages were lower and unions weaker? Why was the drop in
relative minimum wages during the Reagan and Bush years
accompanied by rising chronic unemployment? The answer is
not complicated. Wages are costs for some businesses. They are
potential revenues for others. When workers are paid more, the
market for goods and services increases and employment generally rises.

Friedman was unwilling to see the obvious because he, like
other neoconservatives, began with the assumption of a fixed
wages fund. This wages fund is supposed to be equivalent to

savings. The idea of a fixed wages fund appeared in Adam
Smith and became popular in the nineteenth century as an
argument against the demands of the emerging trade union
movement. For the wages fund to be fixed at a predetermined
level it had also to be assumed that the distribution of income
between capital and labour was fixed and that labour, capital
and resources were fully employed. Only then would it be
logical to conclude that wage gains for some workers would
come at the expense of others or of the funds available for
investment. If wages rose at the expense of profits, or if profits
rose at the expense of wages, the wages fund could not be said
to be fixed. If additional labour, capital and resources could be
utilised both wages and the wages fund would increase.

The idea of a fixed wages fund was not seriously challenged
until statistics gathering became more refined in the late nineteenth century. As more thorough information was gathered,
statisticians found that total wages, profits and investment had
all risen over time. The proportion of total income going to
capital and to labour was not fixed. It varied over time and
place. As wage income grew, profits rose, fell and rose again.

Still, the theory of a fixed wages fund remained a handy
weapon in the arsenal of anti-trade union arguments until it was
thoroughly discredited during the 1930s Depression. It then
became obvious, to all but the most dogmatic, that the basic
assumption behind the theory – static equilibrium at full
employment – in no way described existing economies. Leading
economists like John Maynard Keynes concluded that capitalist
systems rarely, if ever, operate at full employment. Because
labour, capital and resources are underutilised, higher income
for some need not come at the expense of others. When such
increases are a result of increases in the production of goods
and services, more is made available to all.

Hayek and Friedman preferred to ignore most of the twentieth
century. They campaigned to revive the steady state, full employment assumptions of neoclassical economics. Nonetheless, they
accepted Joseph Schumpeter's concept of 'dynamic disequilibrium'. Schumpeter – a contemporary of Keynes – argued that
innovative entrepreneurs continuously disrupted equilibrium. By
devising new methods of production and discovering new products or new wants, innovators unleashed processes of 'creative
destruction' that made existing enterprises unprofitable and generated the dynamic disequilibrium and relentless change that char-
acterises capitalism.[34] Hayek and Friedman liked Schumpeter's
concept of the innovative entrepreneur. They seemed not to
notice that dynamic disequilibrium is incompatible with their
assumptions of static equilibrium and a fixed wages fund.

From the perspective of particular enterprises, the idea of a fixed wages fund seems to make sense – especially in times of economic decline. Higher wages can be covered by increased production and higher prices when markets are expanding, but when markets are stagnant or declining, enterprises may not be able to increase production or prices. Higher wages for some workers in the enterprise will then mean lower wages for others, lower total employment or lower profits. The thought of lower profits horrifies wealthowners. However, lower profits are not as calamitous as they would have people believe.

Through most of the 1970s and 1980s, Japan's major industries had lower profit rates than their US counterparts; they invested more and grew faster. Two hundred years ago, Adam Smith observed that 'The rate of profit does not, like rent and wages, rise with the prosperity and fall with the declension, of the society. On the contrary, it is naturally low in rich and high in poor countries and it is always highest in countries which are going fastest to ruin.' [35]

In the 1930s Keynes said,

> There are valuable human activities which require the motive of money-making ... But it is not necessary for the stimulation of these activities ... that the game should be played with such high stakes as at present. Much lower stakes will serve the purpose equally well, as soon as the players are accustomed to them. [36]

Corporate oligarchs are rarely willing to accept less. Their structural need to maximise profits was encouraged by dogmas of neoconservative theology of private greed. In the late 1970s inflation rates of 20 per cent and more convinced many people that neoconservatives had a point, that costs were indeed getting out of control. Criticisms of Keynesianism poured out of boardrooms into the political arena. Wealthowners succeeded in persuading governments – and many voters – that rising wages, expanding social services and high taxes were suffocating business and drastically cutting the savings and investments on which future economic growth depended.

What were the facts?

Table 4.1 shows that corporate profits in the US rose more than 50 per cent faster and interest income more than twice as fast as Gross National Product during the 1970s. Government spending did grow faster than GNP (largely because of the impact of higher interest rates on debt service charges), but wages lagged behind. Contrary to neoconservative myths, the rich were not being decimated by the welfare state. It was workers who were being squeezed by a shift in income to wealthowners.

Table 4.1 Growth in Income Categories in the US, 1970–80

	%
Gross National Product	169
Gross Wages and Salaries	149
Corporate Profits After Taxes	265
Net Interest Income	388
Federal Government Spending	202

Source: *Statistical Abstract of the US, 1990*, US Department of Commerce, Tables 497, 694 and 696.

Table 4.2 Growth in Income Categories in Canada, 1970–80

	%
Gross National Product	248
Total Wages and Salaries	250
Corporation Profits	401
Interest and Misc. Investment Income	631
Federal Government Expenditures	307

Source: *Canadian Economic Observer, Historical Survey 1990–91*, Statistics Canada, Ottawa, Tables 1.1, 1.10.

Thatcher and Reagan

In the United Kingdom in the 1970s, income growth followed a similar pattern. Company profits and government spending grew faster than GNP. Wages and salaries lagged behind.[37] Nonetheless, Margaret Thatcher came to power in 1979 claiming that the Labour government and greedy unions were destroying the spirit of free enterprise.

Her government was elected with only 43.9 per cent of the vote – the smallest vote for any majority party since 1922 – yet Thatcher set out to radically change Britain. Keynesian policies were officially abandoned. The government would no longer take responsibility for the maintenance of employment or of aggregate demand. Deregulation, privatisation and restraint became watchwords of the day. 'Deregulation' meant that profits would be put ahead of the interests of consumers, workers and communities. Wellbeing would be left to market forces. 'Privatisation' meant transferring publicly owned assets and services to privately owned corporations to be run in the interests of wealthowners. 'Restraint' meant the majority would no longer be mollycoddled.

It meant cutting government employment and limiting funding for education, housing, healthcare and the poor.

Taxes on higher income Britons were lowered and taxes on the working majority were raised. Thatcher's first Social Security Minister, Reg Prentice, explained, 'If you believe economic salvation can only be achieved by rewarding success and the national income is not increasing, then you have no alternative but to make the unsuccessful poorer.' [38] In this the Conservatives succeeded. Between 1979 and 1988 income for wage and salary workers lagged behind GNP; corporate profits, dividends and interest payments grew nearly twice as fast. The top 20 per cent of households, who had received 35 per cent of national income at the beginning of the Thatcher era, had increased their share to 40 per cent by 1992. The share of national income received by the poorest 20 per cent fell from 10 per cent to 5 per cent. [39]

Thatcher's ministers claimed to have been inspired by the writings of Adam Smith. They seemed not to notice that Smith had written,

> Our merchants and master manufacturers complain much of the bad effects of high wages in raising the price and thereby lessening the sale of their goods both at home and abroad. They say nothing concerning the bad effects of high profits. They are silent with regard to the pernicious effects of their own gains. They complain only of those of other people. [40]

Thatcher's policies were pernicious. Her Tories claimed that putting more money in the hands of the rich would increase savings and investment. What happened? When the Conservatives came to power in 1979, 12 per cent of personal disposable income was saved; by 1988 this had fallen to 3 per cent. [41] Two million manufacturing jobs were lost. Unemployment rose from 1.2 million to 3 million. [42] Growing numbers of people, unable to find work, were left homeless. Thatcher's policies did not even lower inflation. [43] Unions were weakened by anti-labour legislation, but domestic prices increased by 90 per cent between 1979 and 1988 – a rate exceeding that in most other industrialised countries. Thatcher had promised to restore Britain's economic glory. By 1989, the UK had fallen further behind Germany, the Scandinavian countries, Austria, France, Belgium and Holland in industrial output and in living standards; and was in danger of being overtaken by Italy. [44]

In the US, Ronald Reagan's election in 1980 announced the official adoption of neoconservative policies. The supply-side economists Reagan brought to the White House set out to reduce taxes and government spending on social services. They claimed that government spending caused inflation by increasing demand without increasing the supply of goods and services. Non-inflationary economic growth, they argued, required growth in 'the supply side'. This could best be accomplished by increasing the funds available for private investment. Cutting the taxes paid by businesses and the top income brackets, they claimed, would do that. However, Reagan had also promised to cut the deficit. No problem. The most acclaimed supply-sider of the time, Arthur Laffer, famous for the 'Laffer curve', claimed to have graphically shown that tax cuts for the rich would reduce the deficit because the resulting increase in investments and economic growth would mean more revenues for government. Ronald Reagan was impressed. He cut taxes paid by the wealthy and eagerly awaited the economic growth that would reduce deficits. [45]

Did anyone believe this happy fantasy? Perhaps not, but otherwise reputable economists outside of Reagan's circle of supply-side zealots claimed that future prosperity required increased income for wealthowners and lower incomes for everyone else. The business community was nearly unanimous in this view. The May 1982 issue of *World Financial Markets*, a newsletter published by Morgan Guaranty Trust, echoed Laffer's position, when it said, 'increased consumption taxes are preferable to tax increases that deter savings and investment'. The editors of this prestigious newsletter argued that the

> necessary condition for a return to non-inflationary growth is the curbing of excessive real wage growth. To restore adequate profit margins – to provide an incentive for investment and the resources to finance it ... real wage increases [must] be kept below productivity gains for several years.

Governments, the newsletter said, should 'set the tone for wage settlements by adopting a tough posture in public sector negotiations'.

Were Reagan's policies good for the economy? Middle income Americans were faced with substantial tax increases. Even the poorest families paid 2 per cent more of their income as taxes to the federal government at the end of Reagan's two terms than they had when he came to office. [46] The heavier tax load came at a time when the earning power of wage and salary workers was declining. Minimum wages were being reduced and repealed. Reagan's decertification of the Air Traffic Controllers signalled the government's determination to put employers' interests ahead of collective bargaining rights. Meanwhile, better-paid jobs were being lost to capital flight and the shift to service industries. The result was that the income of 80 per cent of US families declined.[47]

When measured in real purchasing power, the income of blue-collar workers in the US in 1988 was lower than it had been in the 1970s. As better-paid manufacturing jobs were transferred abroad, two incomes became necessary to maintain a 'typical' American life-style. Industrial workers who owned their own houses were fortunate. By 1990 one fifth of full-time workers in the US were living below the poverty level, many on the streets because they did not have the money for any accommodation.[48]

The rich, however, were doing much better. In *The Politics of Rich and Poor*, Kevin Phillips explained, 'In the wake of the 1978 capital gains reductions and the sweeping 1981 tax cuts, the effective overall, combined federal tax rate paid by the top 1 percent of Americans dropped from 30.9 per cent in 1977 to 23.1 per cent in 1984.'[49] Phillips, a former chief political analyst for the Republican Party, reported that the top 1 per cent increased their share of after-tax income from 7 per cent in 1977 to 11 per cent in 1990. Their share of wealth went from 15 per cent to 27 per cent – higher than at any time since the years just before the 1930s Depression.[50]

When running for office, Reagan had denounced the Carter administration for allowing the annual federal deficit to reach $80 billion. In eight years under Reagan, the annual federal deficit rose to more than $250 billion. This was a direct consequence of the massive growth in military spending. Reagan – a former lobbyist for the military-industrial complex – was committed to giving the military what it wanted. In the last year of the Carter administration, the Defence Department's budget was $134 billion. By 1988, it was nearly $300 billion. Corporate oligarchs who had loudly denounced the Democrats for running up outrageous deficits were silent. They did not complain because Star Wars, the black hole in Reagan's budget, did not transfer funds to the poor, it transferred the poor's tax dollars to high-tech military contractors.

Despite Reagan's claim that he stood for fiscal responsibility, accumulated federal debt rose from a third of GNP when he took office to a half by 1988. Annual interest paid by the federal government grew from $75 billion, 13 per cent of expenditures in 1980, to $214 billion, 20 per cent of expenditures, in 1988.[51] These rapidly rising debt service charges represented another kind of privatisation: the privatisation of tax revenues. In effect, money was collected from the majority of poorer taxpayers and handed to the rich. Over half of interest income went to the richest 10 per cent of the US

population. For the very rich, rising federal debt service payments were made even sweeter by cuts to the maximum
marginal tax rate on interest income from 70 per cent to 28
per cent.[52]

Did the transfer of income to the rich increase the rate of
savings as supply-siders claimed? Not in the least. In 1980, 7
per cent of personal disposable income in the US was saved; by
1988 this had fallen to 4 per cent.[53] It is not hard to
understand why. Ronald Reagan had ushered in a new age of
unrestrained conspicuous consumption. Greed and hedonism
took on a spiritual intensity. Meanwhile, the decline in real
wages and the increase in taxes for middle income earners cut
into the savings of the very people who are responsible for
most personal savings.

What was the effect on investment?

Table 4.3
Growth in Constant-Cost Net Stock of Fixed Non-Residential Private Business Stock of Reproducible Tangible Wealth

	%
1950–9	38
1960–9	46
1970–9	37
1980–9	26

Source: Survey of Current Business, October 1990, p. 32,
US Department of Commerce.

Table 4.3 shows that the total net value of investments grew at a
slower rate under Reagan than in any other recent decade. Why
did rising income for wealthowners not lead to a more rapid
growth in means of production?

Only people confused by neoconservative dogmas should be
perplexed. Income at the disposal of the rich has little to do
with productive investment. Most funds for means of production are generated within enterprises, from pre-tax corporate
revenue, from depreciation and depletion allowances and from
undistributed corporate profits. When wealthowners do invest
their own funds, their aim is usually to increase their personal
income. During the Reagan years, such investments were
directed toward mergers and acquisitions and leveraged buyouts.
Few new means of production were created. Huge amounts of
capital were plundered from existing enterprises. During the
second half of the 1980s US non-financial corporations paid

out $600 billion more to shareholders and bondholders than they took in from stock exchange transactions.[54]

Deregulation and Fraud

Reagan's campaign against government regulations was designed to favour business at the expense of consumers and the public. After deregulation in the telephone industry, competition for long distance customers caused rates to fall. Most of the benefit went to large businesses. To compensate for the loss of long distance revenue, telephone companies took advantage of their monopoly position in local markets to raise local rates. As a result most people paid higher monthly telephone charges. In air travel, deregulation meant businesses benefited from lower fares for high volume flights between large cities. Individuals travelling between smaller cities paid higher fares for less frequent flights. Competition increased for a time. When the dust settled from rate cutting, fewer airlines were left. Some went bankrupt, others were swallowed by more successful competitors. Airline workers had their wages cut and lost their jobs.

In the savings and loan (thrift) industry deregulation led to a remarkable transfer of income to a few wealthowners. Before deregulation, S&Ls – privately-owned local banks – were restricted by law to accepting deposits at regulated interest rates and providing low-interest mortgages for local real estate. Such activity was far too prosaic for the high-rollers surrounding Ronald Reagan. They decided to give more Americans opportunities to participate in the glamour, risks and rewards of the high stakes financial market. In 1980 S&Ls were deregulated. Ceilings on deposits interest were lifted. Deposit insurance in S&Ls was raised from $40,000 to $100,000. Limits on the proportion of commercial real estate mortgages were removed, as were limits on holdings of stocks and bonds.

As S&Ls were freed to compete for deposits in the money market and to invest these wherever they chose, a new breed of S&L owner began buying out the local business people who had operated formerly staid and conservative S&Ls. The new owners were looking for opportunities to get their hands on massive amounts of federally-insured deposits. They paid top dollar for S&Ls. What had been called thrifts fell into the hands of pathologically greedy men like Charles Keating and Don Dixon, con-men like Mario Renda and Franklin Winkler and organised crime figures like Morris Shenker and Michael Hellerman. They had discovered a win-win game: if loans went bad, nobody would lose – except US taxpayers.

The plundering of S&Ls is detailed in *Inside Job*, by Stephen Pizzo, Mary Fricker and Paul Muolo.[55] Deposit brokers played a central role. They moved federally-insured deposits from one financial institution to another. Shadier brokers passed blocks of deposits to thrifts on condition that these moneys would be loaned back to their associates. Some thrift owners and managers procured deposits from legitimate brokers and then loaned these to the principals of other thrifts who in turn did the same for them. To make it look like loans were backed with real collateral, looters flipped real estate back and forth, increasing its book value each time. In one case a property initially assessed at $2 million was flipped back and forth until it was appraised at $175 million.[56]

In accounting systems used by financial institutions, outstanding loans are assets. Consequently, the more dubious and fraudulent loans an S&L made, the faster it grew. S&Ls became the glamour stocks of the early 1980s. Some people did get rich. The more insured deposits they moved, the more loans they made, the bigger the kickbacks, fees and profits they made. Rolling in other people's money, S&L owners, deposit brokers and real estate speculators bought sumptuous mansions, luxury yachts and politicians from both parties. It was fun while it lasted, but loans eventually have to be paid. How would they be repaid? Loans spent on high living rarely generate revenue. The market value of the collateral was only a fraction of the money that had to be repaid. Borrowers weighed the options, defaulted and walked away. When they did, S&Ls were left with over-valued real estate and without the cash flow needed to pay interest on the deposits they themselves had borrowed to make the loans. By 1987 the deposit brokering pyramid had collapsed. When the dust settled, 1,700 S&Ls declared bankruptcy.[57]

Fraud was not responsible for all the bankruptcies. Some S&Ls failed because owners and managers, deciding not to look gift horses in the mouth, had taken all the certified deposits they were offered. They then accepted overvalued property as collateral for loans on the assumption that real estate prices would rise forever. However, in many cases speculative stupidity was a cover-up. By late 1990, the Justice Department was sifting through 21,000 criminal referrals arising from S&L failures.

In 1984 the Federal Home Loan Bank Board had warned of shady and fraudulent practices and had called for reregulation, but its advice was rejected and its investigations blocked by free market ideologues in the Reagan Administration. Donald Regan, White House Chief of Staff, was particularly aggressive in opposing investigations of S&Ls. Prior to working in the White House, Regan had been boss of Merrill Lynch – the largest deposit broker in the US, a company that made millions in fees and commissions peddling deposits to S&Ls. Aware of the climate in Washington, individual looters courted friends in high places. Colorado real estate speculators took advantage of their connections with Neil Bush (the then vice president's son) to cheat Silverado Savings & Loan out of $100 million. But they were small fry. The manipulators of Texas and Lousiana S&Ls – responsible for bankruptcies that cost US taxpayers billions – had made large contributions to the election campaign of House Finance Committee Chairman Jim Wright. Wright did what he could to block investigations into these S&Ls.

Charles Keating was even better connected. He built a spectacular S&L business in Arizona and California by borrowing certified deposits and then buying junk bonds from Michael Milken. Rolling in money, Keating built palatial estates for himself in Arizona and the Bahamas. In the five years in which he ran Lincoln Savings & Loan in California, 'he and his family personally collected $41.5 million in salary, benefits and perks'. [58] The White House was impressed. Ronald Reagan expressed his admiration for Keating and George Bush openly consulted him. California Governor Deukmejian and California Senator Cranston received large campaign contributions from Keating. Mother Theresa used his private jet while flying in the US. Alan Greenspan – later head of the US Federal Reserve Board – was employed by Keating as a consultant. But Keating benefited most from the friendship of Attorney General Edwin Meese. When federal investigators first began making a criminal case against Keating, Meese cut their budget and diverted funds from S&L investigations to the campaign against obscenity (a campaign that received generous contributions from Charles Keating). In the end, the bankruptcy of Keating's S&Ls cost US taxpayers $2.5 billion.

When the new Bush Administration acted in 1989, it reregulated thrifts and took over half the industry's assets. The largest bank nationalisation in US history left the government owning billions of dollars worth of overvalued real estate. In theory the properties forfeited should have been sold to reduce the taxpayers' bill, but the Bush Administration was caught in a dilemma: the properties were so numerous that putting them on the market could punch the bottom out of an already sinking real estate market. Some of the overvalued properties were toxic waste sites. Once the government seized these as collateral for loans, taxpayers became responsible for cleaning them up. The deposit insurance fund covered only a small fraction of the total losses. Congress voted to give taxpayers responsibility for the rest. The cost will be somewhere between $300 billion

and $500 billion – equivalent to at least a third and possibly
more than half the value of the entire accumulated federal debt
when Ronald Reagan became president in 1980. [59]

Brian Mulroney

When Brian Mulroney won the federal election in 1984, his first
priority was what he called tax reform. He cut corporate taxes,
increased the ceiling on minimum taxable gains and lowered the
marginal tax rates on the highest incomes. Meanwhile, middle-
and lower-income Canadians had to pay more taxes. Federal
revenue from income taxes, which had totalled C$30 billion when
Mulroney came to office, rose to C$60 billion in 1990. Revenue
from consumption taxes also doubled, from C$14 billion to C$28
billion. Federal revenue from income and consumption taxes combined, which had equalled 10 per cent of GDP in 1984, rose to
13 per cent by 1990. Federal taxes on businesses fell from 2.1
per cent to 1.8 per cent of GDP. [60]

Conservatives claimed that these changes were necessary
because high tax rates on upper-income Canadians and on business were stifling economic initiative. Were they? It is true that
throughout the 1970s, government receipts were a higher percentage of GDP in Canada than in the US and higher than the
average for Group of Seven countries (US, Japan, Germany,
France, UK, Italy, Canada). However, real GDP had grown faster
in Canada than in the US. Fixed capital formation, as a percentage of GDP, was higher in Canada than the Group of Seven
average and substantially higher than in the US. [61]

Despite the aggressiveness of neoconservative ideology, the
evidence does not indicate that high taxes retard investment or
growth. In the late 1940s and 1950s in Canada federal business
taxes, at 5 per cent of GDP, were more than double what they
were in the early 1980s. Steeply graduated income taxes could
take as much as three quarters of the highest incomes. Nonetheless, the country was going through a prolonged period of
economic growth. Investment had not been inhibited, but higher
taxes did annoy wealthowners. Before Mulroney came to power
the idea that those who benefit most from the system should
pay the most taxes had already been abandoned. In 1980, the
average income of the top 7,742 Canadian income earners –
when the full value of their capital gains is included – was
C$438,000; on this they paid an average of C$110,000 in
income taxes, or 25 per cent. [62]

Mulroney, like neoconservatives in the UK and US, claimed to
stand for sound economic policies. His aim was actually to make
the rich richer. In this he succeeded. In 1980, 40,000 taxpayers

reported incomes of C$100,000 or more. A mere 0.27 per cent of taxpayers, they got 3.5 per cent of all Canadian income.[63] In 1990, 57,000 taxpayers reported incomes of C$200,000 or more. Only 0.30 per cent of taxpayers, they got 5.2 per cent of all assessed income, 31 per cent of all dividend income, 27 per cent of all mortgage interest, 31 per cent of all foreign investment income and 41 per cent of all taxable capital gains.[64]

To make the rich richer, Mulroney had to take from everyone else. He justified increased consumption taxes and higher income taxes for the majority by pointing to the high cost of social programmes. The truth is that in every year since 1986 tax revenue exceeded total spending on social programmes and all other government functions. In 1990 the federal government would have had a surplus of C$13 billion if it had not paid C$41 billion in interest on the federal debt – a sum substantially greater than the C$27 billion the federal government paid in total transfer payments to provinces for medical care, education and regional development and nearly equal to the C$42 billion in federal payments to persons for pensions, family allowances and unemployment insurance.

Mulroney claimed that these heavy debt service charges were the result of overspending by past governments. When Mulroney came to office, the net federal debt was C$160 billion, equivalent to one third of Gross Domestic Product. Debt had grown rapidly in the later Trudeau years. Tax concessions to wealthy individuals and corporations beginning in 1974, when Jean Chretien was finance minister, resulted in a loss of revenue estimated at C$14 billion a year.[65] Meanwhile, high interest rates in the second half of the 1970s and early 1980s significantly increased the cost of servicing the annual deficits and explain most of the rest of the rising debt.

After five years of Mulroney, net federal debt had grown to C$320 billion. No effort was made to get at the sources of the problem. The Mulroney government deliberately kept short-term interest rates two to four percentage points higher than US rates, as much as 5 per cent higher than German and 6 per cent higher than Japanese rates.[66] Corporate oligarchs did not object. They agreed that interest rates had to be kept high to attract the foreign money needed to fund the public deficit. They were prepared to accept the obscenity of a rich country borrowing from abroad to pay current expenses, so long as they did not have to pay more to fund the public services Canadians overwhelmingly demanded. As the foreign debt grew, they continued to press the Mulroney government for more tax breaks for businesses and the wealthy. Despite their anti-deficit rhetoric, corporate oligarchs continued to favour Mulroney with campaign funds. He had organised a win-win game for them. Tax cuts had increased their incomes; high interest rates had increased the returns on capital. Meanwhile, they could smugly point to the growing debt burden as an argument against social spending.

John Crowe, governor of the Bank of Canada, claimed that high interest rates were necessary to fight inflation. However, high interest rates are themselves a cause of inflation. High rates on Government of Canada bonds pushed up rates on provincial, municipal and corporate bonds. Because most businesses operate on borrowed money, higher interest rates work their way through the pricing system just like any other cost increase. For Crowe this was beside the point. Like other neoconservatives, he derived his policies from a free market model in which resources are fully employed and credit comes entirely from within the system. If such a closed system is assumed, it can then be deduced that higher interest rates will increase savings and reduce borrowing and that the resulting drop in consumer spending and business investment will cause prices to fall.

In the actual world of international money markets, higher interest rates attract money from outside, adding to inflationary pressures. In 1978, 15 per cent of Government of Canada bonds had been held abroad; in 1990, 38 per cent were.[67] Meanwhile, in the first five years of the Mulroney government, provincial and municipal governments and Canadian corporations sold bonds totalling C$87 billion to foreigners.[68] The inflationary pressures of these funds flowing in from abroad were most apparent in the mania for mergers and acquisition, in rising real estate and stock values and in the fashion for conspicuous consumption.

Foreign bond-holders did not get all the benefits from high interest rates. In 1990, 60 per cent of Government of Canada bonds were held in Canada. For people with large sums to invest, high interest rates were a windfall. Expensive credit did increase the cost of doing business and squeezed profit margins but, despite neoconservative praise of the entrepreneurial spirit, profits from enterprise were becoming less important to wealthowners. In the 1950s and 1960s income from interest payments were a third of corporate profits. By the middle 1970s, interest income had risen to half and, in the first five years of the Mulroney government, to three quarters the total of corporate profits. In 1990 interest income surpassed corporate profits in Canada for only the third time since the 1920s. (The other two years were 1932, during the depth of the Depression and 1982, the low point of the last recession.)[69]

Corporate oligarchs were not too concerned with economic development in Canada. By removing the remaining restrictions on the movement of capital between Canada and the United

States, Mulroney's trade agreement encouraged Canadian businesses to set up operations in the US. There they could take advantage of lower costs and even supply the Canadian market. The rising value of the Canadian dollar positively encouraged businesses to move to the US. Before Mulroney took office the Canadian dollar had traded at less than 80 US cents. It fell to 72 cents in his second year in office and then began to rise. By 1990, after the trade agreement, it was trading at 85 US cents. The higher Canadian dollar – a result of higher interest rates – negated any industrial benefit from the elimination of tariffs, which had rarely been more than 15 per cent. But, wealthowners did benefit. The higher exchange rate reduced the Canadian dollar price of exclusive vacation homes in the Florida and California sun and made moving plants to the US more profitable. From 1987 – when it became clear that Mulroney's trade deal would pass – to 1989, direct investments abroad by Canadians – mostly in the US – totalled C$21 billion, nearly twice the amount in the previous three years. [70]

Mulroney's neoconservative policies gave the richest Canadians more money to invest abroad, but the savings rate in Canada – as in the US – went down. In 1984, just before Mulroney became prime minister, 15 per cent of personal income was saved. By the late 1980s this had fallen to 10 per cent. [71] In 1991, Canada's goods producing industries were mired in the most serious slump since the 1930s. Declining profits, due to a high dollar, high interest rates and stagnating consumer income, gave business people little reason to invest in Canada. When they did, they introduced labour-saving machinery. The result was more industrial unemployment and even weaker consumer demand. The growing number of Canadians who had no alternative but to work at entry-level service industry jobs were paid less than half the wages in unionised manufacturing. They saved little.

5 Globalism

International Shipping

The globalisation of shipping can be traced to the scuttling of the
Canadian deep sea fleet shortly after World War II. During the
war, nearly 400 freighters had been built in Canadian shipyards.
Half of these flew the Canadian flag. Unlicensed crew members
(all ratings other than officers) were represented by the Canadian
Seamen's Union – a union that was about to be victimised by the
anti-Communist ideology of the Cold War.

The CSU was a militant union with a left-wing leadership. It
had fought to limit the arbitrary authority officers still exercised
over seamen, and had won improvements in accommodation,
provisions, wages and working conditions. Its collective agreements required that ships hire crews through union hiring halls.
Hiring, conducted openly before assembled seamen, was based
on a system of rotary dispatch – crew members being sent to
work in the order in which they had registered for work.
Discrimination based on employer preference, political views,
past union activity, nationality and religion was strictly prohibited. Kickbacks, favouritism and blacklisting were eliminated. In
1946 the CSU fought and won a strike for the eight-hour day,
higher pay and better overtime provisions on the Great Lakes.
Later in the year, similar gains were made in the deep sea fleet.

The Canadian deep sea fleet had already been reduced from
wartime levels, when it was the third largest national fleet, but
plans to rapidly reconstruct western Europe put seamen in what
seemed a strong bargaining position. The CSU looked forward to
taking the lead in post-war campaigns to expand workers' rights.
The government of Canada had other ideas. Acting in the interests of large exporters and in consultation with British shipowners, the Liberal government decided to get rid of the Canadian
fleet. Taking advantage of the anti-Communist hysteria generated
at the beginning of the Cold War, the government agreed with
shipowners that they should not be required to employ 'subver-
sive elements' supplied by the union hiring hall. When shipowners
announced in 1949 that they would hire crews through government employment offices, the CSU went on strike world-wide.

The government responded by decommissioning ships and
selling them to shipowners in other countries, stranding the
striking seamen abroad. The strike was lost and the union

declared illegal. What remained of a Canadian fleet was crewed by scabs from the Seafarers International Union. The SIU was led by Hal Banks, a convicted felon from the US, who was given admission to Canada by the Liberal government with the task of smashing the CSU. In a few years even the scab fleet disappeared. Canadian companies, like the CPR and MacMillan Bloedel, still owned deep sea ships, but these were registered abroad and carried crews from poor countries who worked for a fraction of the wages that would have been paid to Canadians. Although Canada's trade with the rest of the world grew rapidly, the goods Canadians sold and bought abroad were no longer transported in ships crewed by Canadians.

Globalisation spread to other countries. By the 1960s, ships carrying 'flags of convenience' were replacing the ships of major shipping nations like the US, Britain, Norway and Holland. Shipowners set up shell companies in places like the Bahamas and Liechtenstein that denied the public access to business information. The shell companies then registered ships in Panama, Liberia, Cyprus and other countries that had low taxes and few shipping regulations. By 1990, most shipping was carried on flag-of-convenience vessels. The captain and top officers typically came from Greece, Hong Kong, Japan, Norway or Britain; the crews from low-wage countries like the Philippines, Indonesia, Pakistan, Poland, Ukraine, Russia, China or Burma.

The benefits for shipowners were substantial. Taxes were lower, labour laws did not apply and wages were a fraction of the rates in the home country. In 1993, crew members from countries like Canada, the US, Germany, Norway or Japan could cost shipowners $3,000 or more per month. On flag-of-convenience vessels, the International Transport Workers Federation (ITF) minimum was $850. Sometimes shipowners pay less than half the International Labour Organisation (ILO) minimum of $356 a month.

The ITF does what it can to protect the interests of people who work at sea, but crew members are often at the mercy of shipowners. They will have signed 'articles' tying them to the ship for periods ranging from six months to a year and sometimes longer. These may require them to work as many as 200 hours of unpaid overtime a month. While under articles, they may be given only small amounts of spending money and may not be allowed to take leave while in port. Money that is supposed to be sent to families all too frequently turns out to be less than what was promised. Sometimes, the money does not reach families at all. The ships can be infested with vermin, sanitation facilities broken down, water unfit to drink. Food can be of unacceptable quality. It often consists of little more than rice and canned vegetables. Officers, deck, engine room and galley crews may have been deliberately chosen from among hostile ethnic groups to discourage common action.

Crew members who bring their plight to the attention of ITF representatives in ports with a strong union presence usually get moneys owed plus transportation home. They are often replaced by new crews from countries like Burma, China or the Maldives where membership in a union affiliated with the ITF is a criminal offence. Crew members from these countries, driven by poverty and political repression, have little choice but to accept work at any wage. As a condition of employment, they sometimes agree that the shipowner will pay wages to shipping agencies associated with their governments. These agencies then decide how much the crew members will be paid.

Substandard wages and abominable working conditions are not the worst of the problems crew members face. No international body has the power to set minimum safety standards for ships. Ships that are denied certificates of seaworthiness in one country reappear under the flag of another. Crews are hired not because they are proficient but because they are cheap. Sometimes officers are neither accredited nor properly trained. Engine and deck crew may be entirely inexperienced. Crew sizes are kept to a bare minimum. They are typically far less than is needed for the routine maintenance on which continued seaworthiness depends. In the early 1990s, ageing bulk carriers, including oil tankers, have been breaking apart and sinking at the rate of twelve a year with an average annual loss of 100 lives.[1]

Supporters of globalism claim that all this is in the interests of consumers. They claim that decent wages, the enforcement of labour standards, safety regulations tariffs and other protectionist measures raise costs to consumers. Since everyone is a consumer, everyone loses. While it is true that most people are consumers and more aspire to be, consumption for most people depends on income from employment. When income from employment falls, so does consumption.

The adverse impact of globalism and free trade on consumer demand can be seen in Canada. After the 1990–1 recession had supposedly ended in Canada, economists complained of what they called a 'lack of consumer confidence'. Much of this can be explained by the loss of better paying jobs due to Mulroney's 1988 trade agreement with the US. Trade unionists in Canada and the US have good reason to fear the consequences of the greater freedom capital gets through the North American Free Trade Agreement proclaimed in January 1994. Mexicans have more to fear.

Mexico

The North American Free Trade Agreement is not designed to help Mexico. Its intent is to deny present and future governments of the US, Canada and Mexico any authority to place restrictions on capital movement between these countries. Labour will of course still be subject to national restriction. Freedom for capital is not even matched by freedom for commodities. NAFTA and the earlier Canada-US agreement have not stopped campaigns to restrict imports. Canada and the US remain embroiled in trade disputes over beer, peanut products, pork, fresh fruit, softwood lumber, steel, sugar and wheat.

The elimination of restrictions on the movement of capital will result in the relocation of US and Canadian plants to Mexico, but Mexicans will gain little more than the wages paid in the relocated plants. These are typically a seventh of the wages in Canada. In the *maquiladoras* – border zones in which US companies produce goods for the US market – wages are 20 per cent less than wages in comparable Mexican operations. As NAFTA shifts more labour-intensive operations to Mexico, transnational companies, based mainly in the US, will have a vested interest in keeping labour cheap. Workers will learn that if they do succeed in winning better wages, plants will close and relocate elsewhere.

The wages Mexicans get from producing export goods for the US market will probably be more than offset by imports of US agricultural products, packaged foods, clothing and other mass-produced consumer goods. These are bound to increase once Mexican tariffs and import controls are eased. As more US-owned enterprises operate south of the border, Mexico will import more machinery and equipment, semi-finished products and technologies from the US. Many of the best-paid technical, scientific and managerial jobs will be held by Americans. As restrictions on the movement of capital are eliminated, US corporations will swallow more and more Mexican companies. Profits, dividends and service charges will be remitted back to the US.

Mexico has already had a terrible experience with integration into the global market. The dictator Porfirio Diaz, who ruled Mexico from 1876 to 1910, gave control of economic policy to a party of merchants, landlords and intellectuals called *cientificos*. [2] When put in charge of Mexico's economic affairs in 1893, the *cientificos* began a policy of developing export industries based on cheap labour. By 1905, the textile industry employed 31,000 workers in 150 plants. [3] Much of its product was for export. Raw material exports, especially sisal hemp (used for binder twine in grain harvesting), petroleum, silver, copper, lead, tobacco, sugar and beef, grew even faster. [4] Railway mileage expanded to meet the needs of export industries.

Porfirio Diaz was praised by the world press for his progressive policies. And why not? US newspaper tycoon William Randolph Hearst was given more than a million acres of land for cattle ranching. The exploitation of Mexican oil reserves allowed British engineer Weetman Pearson, later Lord Cowdray, to become one of the wealthiest men in the world; his family's fortune grew to include Penguin Books, the *Financial Times* and the *Economist*. Other foreigners were able to purchase land for as little as one cent an acre. Eight foreign landowners, including Hearst, Cowdray, John D. Rockefeller, E. H. Harriman and the Guggenheims, were given title to 55 million acres of land, much of it along the US border. [5]

In *The Making of Modern Mexico*, Frank Brandenburg wrote,

> Besides the powerful hold that they held over rural lands, foreigners dominated mining, utilities, industry and commerce. Americans seized the cement industry. The French monopolised large department stores. The Germans controlled the hardware business. The Spanish took over foodstores and, together with the French, controlled the textile industry. The Canadians, aided by Americans and Englishmen, concentrated on electric power, trolley lines and water companies. The Belgians, Americans and English invested heavily in the railroads. [6]

When Porfirio Diaz was forced to flee the country in 1910, two thirds of all non-agricultural capital was owned outside Mexico. Foreigners owned 98 per cent of mining, 76 per cent of banking, 100 per cent of petroleum and 62 per cent of railways. Most Mexicans were poorer than they had been before Porfirio Diaz came to power. Foreigners held the best-paid jobs in mining, railways and petroleum.[7] The industrial wages received by Mexicans had fallen as manufacturers sought to increase their competitiveness.

The *cientificos*, who directed Porfirio Diaz's economic policy, had no sympathy with workers. Like present-day neoconservatives, they considered themselves to be strictly rational and scientific. They were Social Darwinists who preached the benefits of survival of the fittest, advocated free trade policies and held that the market was the best arbiter of human relations. In response to workers' pleas for 'just compensation', a spokesman for the *cientifico* regime said, 'In political economy nothing is just or unjust as far as remuneration is concerned. Labour is a product like any other, such as corn, wheat, flour, and is subject to the law of supply and demand.'[8] Another leading *cientifico* dismissed a worker's protests by claiming that the 'labour problem' is 'sociological' not 'political' and that only 'eminent thinkers' are qualified to deal with it. [9]

Workers were not particularly grateful for this scientific advice from their betters. Perhaps they would have been if wages and working conditions had not continued to deteriorate. As it was, many workers saw no alternative but to organise unions and go on strike. When they did, the government followed through on its declaration to place 'all its resources, all its political organisation, all its army, all its authority, on the side of even a single worker who wants to work'. [10]

The *cientificos* were not just intellectual representatives of profiteers, they undoubtedly believed they were doing what was necessary to keep Mexico competitive in the international market. To be competitive, Mexico had to keep the cost of export commodities, land and labour low. To keep the price of land low and to produce more goods for export, land was taken from peasants who could not produce written title deeds. Land was seized that had been farmed by families for generations before the Spanish Conquest. It was turned over to foreigners, or more often to the cronies of Porfirio Diaz at little or no cost. The plots of entire villages were transformed into giant *haciendas* owned by capitalist landlords producing for international markets.

In *Mexico in Transition*, Phillip Russell said that by 1910, 1 per cent of the population owned 70 per cent of the land. In *Intellectual Precursors of the Mexican Revolution*, James Cockroft pointed out that in a country in which 80 per cent of the population lived off the land, a mere 840 *haciendas* dominated agricultural production; all of Mexico's agricultural land was owned by less than 4 per cent of the population. The demand for more and more cheap export commodities made the plight of the landless worse and worse. [11]

In *Barbarous Mexico* – written in 1908 not to disparage Mexicans but to censure Porfirio Diaz and the US corporations that backed him – John Turner reported that 80 per cent of the rural population had been reduced to the status of debt peons, forced by their creditor-employers to work off debts that kept growing. One third of all Mexicans were held as chattels. The most brutally exploited were transported to the sisal and tobacco plantations where the food was so inadequate, the conditions so unbearable that organised terror was required to keep people working. In Yucatan's sisal plantations, beatings and malnutrition killed two thirds of the workers in their first year. [12] In the tobacco fields in *Valle Nacional*, 95 per cent

died within eight months. The supply of labourers was kept
replenished by Porfirio Diaz's officers who were paid by the
head for captives delivered.[13]

Jose Limantour, Minister of Finance and a leading *cientifico*,
justified these practices by saying, 'the weak, the unprepared,
those who lack the tools to emerge victorious against evolution,
must perish and leave the struggle to the more powerful'.[14]

By 1911 the Mexican people had had enough. Armed revolution drove Porfirio Diaz from the country. Civil war raged until
1917 and then flared up from time to time until the 1930s.
Armed men fighting for land reform and rights for labour allied
with, fought against and then succumbed to forces determined to
impose rule by a nationalist capitalist class. Where the peasant
movements were strongest, the pre-conquest *ejido* system of land
ownership was restored. In this system the land is owned by the
village. Plots are assigned to individual families, can be passed on
to heirs, but can neither be bought nor sold. *Ejido* lands were
formally protected in the constitution passed during the presidency of Lazaro Cardenas (1934–40). During this period the oil
industry was nationalised. Foreign control of other industries was
restricted. Industry was redirected toward the domestic market.
Progressive labour laws were passed and land was distributed to
peasants. Despite these gains, Mexico's economic and political
development remained in the hands of *hacienda*-owning generals
and politicians from the ruling Party of Institutionalised Revolution.

For a generation after Cardenas, Mexico did reasonably well
when compared to other former colonial countries. Industrialisation proceeded at a steady pace. Then, in the 1970s, rising oil
prices gave the country a revenue boost and an enviable credit
rating. Western banks stood in line to lend Mexico money. The
country's political and business leaders happily borrowed billions. When oil prices fell and interest rates rose, Mexico was
left with a crushing debt burden. Funds stopped flowing to
Mexico; private businesses failed; government employment was
cut; food subsidies were reduced and eliminated. All available
funds were diverted to pay debt service charges. In 1988, living
standards were lower than they had been in 1970. Mexico had
a foreign debt of $78 billion. Wealthy Mexicans held assets of
$84 billion abroad.[15]

The governing PRI decided to reverse course and return to the
export-driven policies of Porfirio Diaz's *cientificos*. The historic
compromises it had made with peasant village communities and
local markets were abandoned. To prepare for the NAFTA and to
give North American capital freedom to invest in Mexican land,
the government of President Salinas removed provisions in the

Mexican constitution prohibiting the sale of *ejido* lands. The subsequent eviction of peasants from traditional communal lands coupled with the elimination of price supports and the threat of competition from cheaper US produce provoked an armed uprising on 1 January 1994, the day NAFTA formally came into effect. Peasants who supported the Zapatistas believe NAFTA will make their lives worse. Competition from US producers lowers the price farmers get for corn, beans and other crops. Farmers who do not have the capital to compete with transnationals will lose their livelihood. Land will fall into the hands of transnationals. As more Mexican produce is sold abroad, less will be available for consumption at home.

US banks will be the most immediate beneficiaries of an export-driven economy. Increased production for export will provide Mexico with more dollars to pay the debt owed to US and other foreign financial institutions. Mexican wealthowners will benefit as well. Some may even bring money back home. As in Porfirio Diaz's days, cheap labour will allow them to share in the profits of export industries.

The IMF and the Myth of Comparative Advantage

The International Monetary Fund and the World Bank are sometimes viewed as agencies of foreign aid. They actually impose the interests of transnational capital on poorer countries. Both are controlled by private US financial interests. The World Bank favours projects that increase transnational trade. The IMF acts as a trustee and collection agency. Its role is to see that indebted countries pay their bills. Its power comes from the authority its recommendations of credit-worthiness have with transnational financial institutions. Countries that do not pay their debts do not get credits. Countries denied credit are effectively excluded from the world market, unable to import or export goods.

To win the approval of the IMF, countries must show that they are willing to divert resources to the payment of debt. Countries are told to reduce spending on health, education and housing and to cut subsidies for food and local businesses. To increase export earnings and make more funds available for debt repayment, indebted countries are encouraged to provide subsidised services and tax concessions for export industries. To increase further the money that can be shifted abroad, they are told to allow the repatriation of profits by transnational corporations and to lift other restrictions on capital movements.

IMF policies were enthusiastically adopted by Philippines dictator Ferdinand Marcos soon after he declared martial law in

1972. Export Processing Zones were organised to attract foreign business. Companies setting up in these free trade zones were exempted from import and export duties, minimum wage laws and property taxes. All profits could be repatriated and limits on foreign ownership were lifted. Major US companies, including Texas Instruments, Fairchild and Motorola, transferred assembly plants to the zones. The World Bank was so pleased with Marcos' free market policies that during the next eight years it granted the Philippines loans eight times greater than those it had given in the previous 20 years. [16]

Despite praise from the world press for Marcos's enlightened policies, economic conditions in the Philippines went from bad to hopeless. For Filipino workers, mostly young women, who worked in the free trade zones, job security was non-existent. The pace of work on assembly lines was so demanding that workers rarely stayed in a job for more than a few years. Overtime was compulsory. Unions and strikes were prohibited. Desperate workers who did go on strike were beaten by armed gangs paid for by the government and the companies. By the late 1970s, wages in the Export Processing Zones were an average of 49 cents an hour; wages for comparable work was 85 cents an hour in Taiwan and 95 cents in Singapore. [17] By 1982 – after ten years of free trade zones and an export-driven growth strategy – the IMF itself estimated that the Philippines had the lowest economic growth rate of Asia. [18]

Free trade zones had worsened balance of payments problems and increased the country's debt. As foreign enterprises set up in the zones, imports of machinery, equipment and semi-finished products rose. The Philippines economy got little benefit. The goods assembled were sold in other countries. The profits made were repatriated to the US. The wages workers received – as small as they were – were often spent on imported consumer goods. By 1986, when Marcos fled to Hawaii, the government's annual debt service charges exceeded its revenues. Corruption and theft partly explained the problem. But most of the $26 billion debt was a result of the tax concessions, grants, port facilities, nuclear power plants, roads and other subsidised services provided for transnational businesses operating in the export zones. [19]

The IMF's policies made problems worse, but its authority grew along with Third World debt. As debt grew, more and more countries were placed under effective IMF trusteeship. Despite worsening unemployment, poverty, malnutrition and social polarisation, the IMF persisted in imposing export-oriented policies on indebted countries. The object was plain enough: to increase the flow of debt service charges to western financial institutions. The

IMF was not satisfied with squeezing surplus out of the poorest countries, it insisted that everyone would benefit from increased international trade in the long run. This claim was based on David Ricardo's theory of comparative advantage.

In the early nineteenth century David Ricardo had argued that comparative advantage justified national specialisation in trade goods.[20] To come to this conclusion, he began by assuming that England could produce a quantity of wine for 120 units of labour and a quantity of cloth for 100 units, while Portugal could produce a similar quantity of wine for 80 units and a similar quantity of cloth for 90 units. If that was so, England, by producing cloth and exchanging it for wine, would get wine which would have cost 120 units for an outlay of only 100 units of labour. Portugal, by exchanging wine for cloth, would get cloth which would have cost it 90 units for an outlay of 80 units of labour. It would thus be in England's comparative advantage to specialise in producing cloth and in Portugal's to specialise in wine.

How relevant is this? Ricardo himself cautioned that comparative advantage applies only when capital does not move freely between countries. If capital did move freely, trade would harm England because both wine and textiles would be produced in Portugal where labour costs were lower. This was not much of a concern in Ricardo's time because capital by and large remained confined within the borders of individual countries. Given the undeveloped state of communications, it was not practical for capitalists to maintain regular communications across national boundaries. Besides, governments aggressively defended national interests and capitalists were motivated by national spirit as well as by profits. In Ricardo's words,

> the fancied or real insecurity of capital, when not under the immediate control of its owners, together with the natural disinclination which every man has to quit the country of his birth and connexions, and intrust himself with all his habits fixed, to a strange government and new laws, check the emigration of capital. These feelings which I should be sorry to see weakened, induce most men of property to be satisfied with a low rate of profits in their own country, rather than seek a more advantageous employment for their wealth in foreign nations.[21]

England did get comparative advantage by exporting manufactured goods and importing agricultural products from Portugal. The advantages for Portugal were not so obvious. Perhaps the trade relations between the two countries would have been mutually beneficial if Portugal's resources were fully employed – as free market theory assumes. If that had been the case, the movement of capital and labour from cloth to wine could have increased Portugal's total income. In fact, resources in Portugal – a largely agrarian country – were underdeveloped. Shifting resources to vineyards and wine-making aggravated underemployment in other industries. Because the international demand for Portuguese wine was limited, increasing the supply did not necessarily add much to the country's total revenues.

When Ricardo wrote, he suggested that labour cost about 50 per cent more in England than in Portugal. In 1988, Portugal's per capita Gross Domestic Product was less than one third that of the United Kingdom. When 'purchasing power parity' is factored in, Portugal's per capita GDP in 1988 was still barely more than half that of the UK. After nearly 200 years, comparative advantage had given Portugal no noticeable advantage.

Trade between Portugal and England actually had little to do with comparative advantage. The economic ties between the two countries were a result of the Treaty of Methuen, signed in the early years of the eighteenth century.[22] This treaty compelled Portugal to become an importer of British manufactured goods. Since Britain's manufacturing industries were the most efficient in the world, Portugal had little choice but to be an exporter of agricultural products and raw materials. England, in contrast, did benefit from the treaty it had imposed on Portugal. England provided itself with a secure supply of wine during a time when it was more or less in a chronic state of war with France. More important, the treaty gave England the exclusive right to export manufactured goods to Portugal's colony, Brazil – then the world's leading gold producer. In exchange for the machinery, tools and clothing needed in the mines and plantations of Brazil, England got the lion's share of Brazil's gold – gold which helped England secure and extend her domination of world trade.

Military power and comparative advantage have typically walked hand in hand. The defeat of China in the Opium Wars in the middle of the nineteenth century gave Europeans control of that country's finances and trade. China was forced to find comparative advantage in exporting raw silk and importing European manufactured goods.[23] Unable to defend its ancient handicraft industries, China was rapidly de-industrialised. The country fell into a prolonged decline that was to lead to the victory of Mao Tse-tung's Communists.

The Ottoman Empire had the harsh realities of comparative advantage imposed on it by a succession of treaties in the eighteenth and nineteenth centuries, aptly called 'capitulations'.

In earlier times, the artisans of this Turkish-dominated empire had produced high quality textiles and other prized luxury goods in markets that stretched from Austria to Iraq and from Morocco to Arabia. After the capitulations, the manufactured goods of European countries were given unrestricted access to Ottoman markets. Domestic handicraft industries, unable to compete, decayed. As imports chronically exceeded exports, the Ottoman empire sank into a condition of permanent indebtedness to European banks. Egypt, an autonomous region of the empire, was encouraged by Britain to pay its debts by growing cotton for Britain's textile mills. As cotton production increased, food production declined. Egypt's food imports grew; its balance of payments got worse. To compensate itself for unpaid debts, Britain imposed direct rule over Egypt in 1882.[24]

The results of comparative advantage remain much the same. A decade before the neoconservative reaction took hold in more prosperous countries, corporate oligarchs in charge of the International Monetary Fund, the World Bank and the Organisation of Economic Cooperation and Development were urging governments of poor countries to adopt *laissez faire* policies so that they could gain from comparative advantage in the world market. Zambia, Morocco, Jamaica and Brazil all followed their advice.

Zambia, formerly called Northern Rhodesia, is rich in mineral resources. It has fertile soil and more than enough hydroelectric potential to meet its own and regional needs. Copper once provided 80 per cent of its export earnings. When the price of copper fell in the 1970s government revenues fell as well. Zambia agreed to IMF advice. It agreed to cut government spending, to give priority to meeting international financial obligations and to lift restrictions on market forces. By 1993 government spending in real terms was one third of what it had been in 1981. Spending on healthcare was reduced by a quarter, spending on education by a half. Total spending by the government on wages and salaries was half of what was spent on servicing the international debt. Meanwhile, the dismantling of agricultural marketing boards and the subsequent fall in producer prices, benefited large commercial farms (usually white-owned) at the expense of the mass of small farmers who have less access to credits, transportation and markets outside the country. Living standards dropped dramatically. In 1993 one third of households could no longer meet half their basic nutritional requirements.[25]

In the mid-1960s, Morocco agreed to concentrate investment in citrus fruits and fresh vegetables for export. Land that had provided food for the local population was converted to citrus and other crops for the European market. A quarter of all public investments and two thirds of all agricultural investment went to pay for irrigation works for export crops. Meanwhile, other countries, also on the advice of the IMF, expanded their citrus production. As the growth in world supply exceeded demand, prices fell. Moroccans, who had been told they would be better off producing cash crops for export and importing cheaper foreign foods, now found that export earnings did not pay for imports of the food they no longer grew. Malnutrition became endemic in rural and urban areas. During the 1980s, Morocco was wracked by recurring food riots. But its ruling classes, now locked into the IMF-sponsored export policies, could see no alternative.[26]

In Jamaica *laissez faire* policies were adopted after the population had been exhausted by political wars and economic sabotage. Disorders had been provoked by local wealthowners and US business interests violently opposed to the interventionist policies of the social democratic government of Michael Manley, which had been elected in 1972. Once the neoconservative Edward Seaga was installed in office in 1980, Jamaica agreed to follow IMF policies. Restrictions on the movement of capital in and out of the country were lifted. Plans for import substitution were abandoned. The government agreed to concentrate on exports. To make exports more competitive, the Jamaican currency was devalued. This increased the cost of imports, including the machinery and equipment required by farmers. As the price of local produce went up, local farmers lost market share to cheaper US agricultural products. As the purchasing power of farmers dropped, other local businesses declined. Local wealthowners responded by moving their capital out of the country, aggravating the unemployment problem. By the time Michael Manley – chastened and now willing to cooperate with the IMF – was re-elected in 1989, Jamaica was poorer than it had been a decade earlier.[27]

The military governments that came to power in Brazil after the 1964 coup dutifully followed IMF export policies. Money was borrowed for hydroelectric dams, strip mines and for agricultural export industries. Massive hydroelectric projects provided the power needed to mine and transport minerals to export markets. Brazilian agriculture was modernised. As smallholders were bought out and sharecroppers evicted, less corn and beans and fewer chickens were produced for local markets. Land suitable for irrigation produced soya beans for exports. Other formerly subsistence lands were transformed into giant cattle ranches producing beef for export.

As Brazil became more dependent on the export of these

commodities, world prices fell. As its terms of trade worsened, Brazil lost the means to pay for the food imports it now needed. To increase export earnings and to provide for growing numbers of landless peasants, military governments offered lands in Amazonia to ranchers and to settlers. The clearing and slash-burning of rainforests deprived aboriginal people of means of subsistence. Life for the settlers was not much better. Many were driven from their plots by armed gangs hired by ranchers. Those who held on to their plots found that the land was exhausted in a few years.[28] In the 1960s, a third of Brazilians suffered from malnutrition; in the 1980s, after 20 years of IMF-inspired development, two thirds did.[29]

Zambia, Morocco, Jamaica and Brazil were no exceptions. During the 1970s and 1980s, globalisation caused the supply of bananas, bauxite, beef, cocoa, coffee, copper, cotton, iron, oranges, soya beans and sugar to grew faster than demand. As the price of these commodities fell relative to the price of oil and imported manufactured goods, poor countries found themselves unable to pay for the imports they now needed. They borrowed money to meet their daily needs. As their foreign debt and debt service charges escalated, western financial institutions laid claim to more and more of their revenues.

In *A Fate Worse Than Debt*, Susan George documents the drain of funds from poor to rich countries.[30] From 1979 to 1985, Brazil paid $70 billion in interest payments to foreign creditors, yet the country was deeper in debt by the end of this period.[31] From 1980 to 1988, Africa paid more in debt service charges than it received in new loans. For the globe's poorest countries, the net loss from international financial transactions was $300 billion, a sum four times greater than the total of all US Marshall Plan aid to Europe after World War II.[32]

The Case for Protection

Before the neoconservative reaction, most thoughtful free market theorists conceded that government intervention and protectionist measures were justified in some circumstances. John Stuart Mill, Alfred Marshall, John Maynard Keynes and Joseph Schumpeter agreed that countries, especially poor ones, could not develop new industries without protection. In 1956, Gunnar Myrdal presented a rigorous argument for protection and government-led industrial strategies in less developed countries in his *An International Economy – Problems and Prospects*. His argument can be summarised in four points.

First, local industry in less developed countries cannot

compete with the products of more advanced countries. Local markets are stunted by high levels of chronic unemployment. The efficiency of local industry is impaired by a lack of skilled workers and experienced managers and the inadequacy of local transportation, communication, banking and marketing services. Without tariffs and import barriers, local enterprises have little hope of successfully competing even in their local markets with goods from the industrially developed world. But if governments direct investment into import substitution and local industry is protected by tariff barriers, unemployed local labour can be put to work producing goods for the local market. Myrdal conceded that such policies do interfere with market forces, but he held that the expansion in commodity exchange and the growth in money income that results from protectionist policies will have the effect of strengthening market forces.

Secondly, local goods may be of inferior quality and more expensive than imports, but these disadvantages can be outweighed by 'external economies'. As protected industries expand, the demand for skilled workers, engineers and managers will increase. Governments and private interests will be motivated to invest in educational institutions and training centres. Public and private investment in transportation systems and equipment will become more profitable, as will investment in communications, banking and other business services. As the country becomes less dependent on imports, its balance of payments will improve and it will have greater resources available for further industrialisation.

Thirdly, without strict currency and capital controls, efforts to industrialise will likely not succeed. The borrowing of funds from abroad for rapid industrialisation increases the foreign-currency purchasing power of citizens. Without controls on the movement of funds in and out of the country, money will flow out of the country to pay for consumer imports, especially luxuries. If that is allowed to happen, the balance of payments will worsen, making it more difficult to get future financing for industrialisation. However, if a country controls currency and protects domestic industry, expanded consumer demand can be directed to local products. As the markets for local industries grow, more revenues will be available for investment in the machinery and equipment from abroad to increase industrial efficiency and improve the quality of local products.

Fourthly, if less industrialised countries do not regulate the internal movements of capital, investment will flow away from manufacturing to agriculture and materials extraction. Profits are higher in materials extraction because labour is plentiful, skilled and cheap. Investments need not be made in the costly infrastructure and imported machinery and equipment needed for profitable manufacturing. If governments allow market forces alone to determine the utilisation of capital, money will flow to where profits are highest. Industry will be left undeveloped. Governments will in effect be accepting that their people remain hewers of wood and drawers of water.[33]

Myrdal did not reject competitive markets. He was a former professor of Political Economy at the University of Stockholm, specialising in free market theory and went on to become Minister of Commerce in Sweden, a country dependent on foreign trade for its prosperity. When he published his work on the problems of the international economy, he was executive secretary of the United Nations Economic Commission for Europe. He had no doubt that international trade played a critical role in reducing costs and increasing the availability of goods – at least for those who benefited from existing market relations. But unlike Friedrich Hayek – with whom he shared the 1974 Nobel Prize for Economics – Myrdal had a pragmatic, not a dogmatic, view of the market. His knowledge of international exchange relations had convinced Myrdal that market forces, when accompanied by great disparities in access to wealth, perpetuated and worsened inequalities. He concluded that unless governments acted to intervene, the gap between rich and poor would widen, excluding the world's poor from the benefits of the market. Although Myrdal was honoured with a Nobel Prize, his conclusions were ignored by the men who commanded transnational capital. They were unwavering in their commitment to market forces. They agreed with Hayek that government intervention should be rejected out of hand.

If the validity of a theory depends on its success in predicting results, Gunnar Myrdal's interventionist proposals pass the test and neoconservative market theories do not. Myrdal said that without protectionist measures, the industries of poor countries could not compete with goods from the industrialised world even in their own home markets. He was right. Myrdal said that without exchange and import controls, capital would flow out of less developed countries. He was right. Myrdal said that without internal capital controls, investments would flow to agriculture and materials extraction at the expense of manufacturing industry. He was right. Myrdal said that without comprehensive strategies for industrial development, poor countries would get poorer. In 1960, the most prosperous 20 per cent of the world's people got 70 per cent of global gross product. By 1989, they got 83 per cent. The poorest 60 per cent got less than 6 per cent of global GDP.[34]

Neoconservatives who argue that free markets are the road

to prosperity point to a few countries – notably Singapore, South Korea and Taiwan – which have gone through periods of rapid economic growth. Leaders of these countries pay homage to free markets when it is in their interests to do so, but each has relied on high tariffs, import prohibitions, strict currency controls and government-initiated industrial strategies. None of these economies allowed foreign-owned transnationals to take control of its industries, resources or trade. Each adopted the Japanese practice of developing national capital by building close ties between government and favoured conglomerates. In South Korea in 1990, four conglomerates (Hyundai, Samsung, Lucky-Goldstar and Daewoo) accounted for half of gross national product.[35] When it set out to build an automobile industry, South Korea banned automobile imports. Military governments decreed the death sentence for the unauthorised movement of capital out of the country.

In the early 1990s, China's exports and GDP grew at annual rates of 10 per cent and more. The 'Chinese miracle' has been fuelled by foreign investment in factories with export contracts. Young men and women and children migrating from impoverished agricultural regions provide new industries with a limitless supply of cheap labour. Workers toil long hours in conditions that can be compared to those of Europe during the first stages of industrialisation. However, economic growth in China is not based on free markets. Although the power of the central government seems to be eroding, a conservative Communist Party remains in power. Party and state officials at the central, regional and local levels control development and use their positions to favour some, exclude others and enrich themselves. They are transforming themselves into capitalist oligarchs. Transnational corporations are enthusiastic participants in a social transformation that Karl Marx could have called 'primitive accumulation'.[36]

China's neighbours are suffering the consequences of the economic miracle next door. In 1994, the economies of Burma, Laos and Vietnam were being flooded with cheap Chinese manufactured goods: processed foods, textiles, bicycles, small engines and mass produced machines.[37] Local factories were closing down because they could not profitably match the low prices of Chinese imports. According to the rules of the global marketplace, these governments were expected to stand idly by while their already poor countries lose what little industry they have.

In the 1980s, globalism created a buyers' market for agricultural products and raw materials. Exporters of these commodities were made to compete against each other to supply transnationals with these commodities at the lowest possible prices. Supply grew faster than demand. As it did, the revenues earned by exporting countries fell. In 1980 poorer countries – mostly materials exporters – accounted for close to 30 per cent of world trade. By 1990 they accounted for less than 20 per cent.[38] Globalism in the 1990s is doing the same for manufactured goods. As countries compete to supply the cheapest labour, the profits of transnationals will rise while wages, working conditions and the bargaining power of workers deteriorate.

Free market economists are able to ignore the damage done by globalism because they do not see beyond the numbers in national accounts.[39] They point to growth in global gross domestic product. GDP did grow in most countries in the 1980s, but what did this mean? GDP by definition ignores the flow of funds out of poor countries. Until the 1980s the United Nations used gross national product to compare economies and measure growth. Because GNP was constructed to measure income available to a country's residents, income produced in the country but going to non-residents was subtracted from GNP. By the late 1970s the flow of interest payments, dividends and service charges out of poor countries was so high that in many cases GNP was actually declining.[40] Changes had to be made. The UN's 'development decade' was about to begin. Change came swiftly: gross national product was replaced with gross domestic product. (Why one is called 'national' and the other 'domestic' is anyone's guess.) The significant difference was that GDP measured all revenues produced within a country. Income flowing out of countries to non-residents was included as domestic income.[41]

The substitution of GDP for GNP swept a problem under a rug, but no matter which total is used, national accounts do no more than measure revenues and expenditures from a bookkeeping or business perspective. Expenditures by repressive regimes for armoured personnel carriers, security forces and prisons make life worse for people. Yet these are added to expenditures for food, housing, health and education in national accounts. When ranchers in Brazil spend more on burning rainforests and Malaysian logging companies speed the liquidation of hardwood forest, their countries' national accounts will register growth even as the means of livelihood for the people in the area disappears.

Rising GNP or GDP are accompanied by worsening poverty whenever rising export earnings come at the expense of the direct economy. In poor countries, the direct economy provides people with a half and more of the goods they consume. It provides them with food, water, fuel, dwellings and transportation. Surpluses from subsistence activities provide commodities for exchange in markets. When lands that had been used for

direct subsistence are taken over by exporters, some people will
get higher money incomes but many more will be left without
means of livelihood. Production for export, by the logic of
international competitiveness, will provide employment for only
a fraction of the people who had subsisted on the land. The
better paid jobs will require specialist training and will usually
go to outsiders. [42]

Neoconservatives are not troubled that export-driven policies
eliminate means to independent subsistence. Like mercantilists
in the days of Locke and Mandeville, they see the activities and
interests of people who are not employed making profits for
capital as irrelevant, wasted, not worth considering. They sing
the praises of consumerism but they follow policies designed to
push wages down. They expect worsening social polarisation to
be dealt with as a question of law and order. They support
increased expenditure for police and prisons because they
accept that the winners in the capitalist marketplace have to
keep losers under control. They are not worried by the environmentally destructive practices and ethnic rivalries unleashed by
economic desperation. They are confident that wealthowners will
find new ways to profit from human suffering.

A Note on New Zealand

New Zealand, like Canada, officially adopted neoconservative
policies in 1984. In New Zealand it was the Labour Party that
decided that wealthowners' interests should be given precedence.
New Zealand's economy had been in trouble since 1973 when the
UK joined the European Economic Community and New Zealand
lost privileged access to its primary market for lamb and wool. In
an attempt to diversify, the outgoing National Party government
had borrowed billions of dollars to develop a steel industry.
Unfortunately the megaproject was not generating enough revenues to pay its debts. Meanwhile, declining world prices for
coarser wool and the near-total liquidation of the country's natural forests impeded revenues from traditional exports. [43]

The newly elected Labour government was told in 1984 that
its foreign exchange reserves were perilously low, equivalent to
little more than the cost of one month's imports. Sir Roger
Douglas, the Finance Minister, responded by announcing plans to
drastically cut government spending. The age for pension eligibil-
ity was raised from 60 to 65. Farm subsidies were cut and then
eliminated, as were subsidies and grants to domestic manufacturing. Exchange controls were lifted. A massive programme of
privatisation was launched. In 1986 the tax system was radically

reformed. Income and company taxes were cut. A Goods and Services Tax of 12.5 per cent was applied to virtually all transactions.

In the 1987 general election the Labour Party was re-elected. New Zealanders knew their economy was sick. Many retained their faith in a Labour Party that had earlier constructed one of the most comprehensive social security systems in the world. Pensions were generous, minimum wages high. Health care was universally available and publicly funded. Free education and grants to students meant that more than a third of New Zealanders had post-secondary education. Subsidies, tariffs and import quotas allowed a diversified manufacturing industry to flourish despite New Zealand's small population. Until the 1970s unemployment was minuscule. Perhaps the electorate expected that the bitter medicine administered by Labour would help bring back good times.

This hope was soon dashed. Privatisation and the deregulation of the financial industry provoked a speculative stock exchange and real estate boom. The value of shares on the New Zealand stock exchange tripled between August 1984 and September 1987. After the market crashed, criminal investigators discovered that financial pyramiding and phoney real estate transactions had artificially driven prices up. Fraud squads were still uncovering scandals and laying criminal charges in the early 1990s. The drop in real estate prices that accompanied the stock market crash caused a collapse in building and construction activity that continued through the early 1990s. Laws were passed to reregulate financial markets, but the losses for middle-class investors had been so great that venture capital remained difficult to find in New Zealand.

Nonetheless, neoconservatives outside the country continued to applaud the Labour Party's turn to the right. In New Zealand there was less enthusiasm. Prime Minister David Lange, facing a loss of traditional support, fired Roger Douglas from the cabinet. In 1989 opposition within the party forced the prime minister himself to resign. Labour lost the 1990 elections. The National Party – the traditional right-wing party – had campaigned against the harshness of labour policies and promised a softer, more caring approach. Once in office, they launched a new assault on the welfare state. Public spending was cut further. Health care was partially privatised. Schools were required to compete against each other for funding, grants for students were replaced by loans and students' fees were introduced. Changes to labour laws making union membership 'voluntary' severely undermined the ability of workers to maintain wages and working conditions through collective bargaining.

Neoconservatives claim positive results for these policies. They point out that rising exports of apples, barley, kiwi fruit, pears and venison have made the country less dependent on lamb and wool. They point to new markets for beef in eastern Europe, Canada and the US and for fish and shellfish in Japan and other Pacific countries. They add that plantations of radiata pine (publicly planted but since privatised) are maturing and will provide more and more fibre for pulp and paper exports. They fail to explain how this diversification required an assault on the social rights of New Zealanders.

Sir Roger Douglas, who in 1993 continued to travel the world speaking to right-wing groups, insisted that the shift to free market policies was necessary. He said that had he not acted when he did, international creditors would have called in New Zealand's loans pushing the country into bankruptcy. Would they? Countries with far worse finances have continued to get loans. It is probably true that worsening balance of payments in 1984 would have pushed creditors to lower New Zealand's credit rating and to demand higher interest rates. They did that anyway. Interest paid on New Zealand government bonds exceeded 12 per cent throughout the 1980s. Despite draconian neoconservative policies, New Zealand's external debt has continued to grow. In 1984 the country's external debt was equivalent to 47 per cent of GDP; by 1993 it had risen to 90 per cent.

Were there any positive results from free market policies? After privatisation of the national telephone company, rates dropped 20 per cent. The US-based consortium that bought the company cut staff by 200. Its profits rose by 29 per cent. The privatised electrical utility cut rates by 11 per cent and cut employment by 20 per cent. The privatised coal company cut employment by half. The privatised Forestry Corporation cut employment by two thirds. The privatised New Zealand merchant fleet sacked crew members and hired foreigners. New Zealanders – who had set world standards in wages and working conditions – lost their jobs to the lowest-paid crew members privatised companies could find. The corporate press points to these as successes. For whom?

Just before the Labour Party's turn to the right in 1984, unemployment had risen to 80,000, or 5 per cent of the work force. Government cutbacks and layoffs following privatisation doubled that figure. In 1993, nearly a decade after the shock treatment, more than 10 per cent remained unemployed. Those who had jobs were faced with declining real wages. From 1985 to 1990 wages rose at an annual average of 8.5 per cent, but the consumer price index rose by an average of 10.6 per cent.

Compensation of employees, which had accounted for 56 per cent of national disposal income in 1986, fell to less than 52 per cent in 1992.

According to neoconservative theory, lower real wages and higher unemployment is supposed to stimulate economic activity. By the usual measures, there was no evidence of this. The New Zealand economy stagnated in the second half of the 1980s when the global economy was expanding. It lagged behind other economies in the region during the global recession that began at the end of the decade. From 1988 to 1993, employment in manufacturing fell from 286,000 to 247,000. Employment in building and construction fell from 98,000 to 78,000. Employment in agriculture, hunting and forestry, in mining and quarrying, in electricity, gas and water and in transport, storage and communications also fell. Only wholesale and retail trade and community services registered significant employment gains. Despite net emigration of people out of New Zealand, those who remained faced declining economic opportunities. In 1984 slightly more than 66 per cent of adults were economically active. In the early 1990s less than 64 per cent were.

Neoconservatives claim that economic conditions are improving. They point out that more goods have been exported than imported every year since 1988, that the government has budgeted for a surplus in 1993 and that total government external debt fell from NZ$30 billion in 1989 to NZ$27 billion in 1992. This is only part of the story. Exports have exceeded imports partly because New Zealanders have less money to spend on goods from abroad. The government cut its deficits and debt by selling off public assets. As privatised companies looked abroad for capital, private external debt rose from NZ$22 billion in 1989 to NZ$40 billion in 1992. Meanwhile, an ever growing portion of profits, dividends and service charges are flowing out of the country. The annual net loss in investments, interest payments, dividends and service charges grew from NZ$5 billion in 1988 to nearly NZ$7 billion in 1992, 25 per cent of the country's export revenue. This annual drain is equivalent to NZ$2,000 for every man, woman and child in the country. The expansion of foreign ownership after privatisation means that these external obligations will become an increasing burden.

Globalisation has made New Zealand poorer. In the 1970s New Zealand had the world's second highest national per capita income. Ten years after the country placed its fate in the hands of global money markets and on *laissez faire* policies, it had fallen to twenty-second place. The consequences are not anomalous. Globalism gives capital freedom to scour the globe looking for the cheapest and most compliant labour. Working people, in contrast, are constrained by the national licensing of skills, citizenship, immigration laws, domicile and family responsibilities. If they do not accept the wages and conditions capital offers, they get no work. In more prosperous countries, freedom for capital means rising unemployment and declining wages. In poor countries, it means that rising expectations are held in check by the threat of competition from workers in even poorer countries.

Epilogue

Did Keynesianism Fail?

Neoconservatives claim that Keynesian policies failed because the demands of trade unions, visible minorities, women and other interest groups encouraged governments to increase spending until taxpayers could no longer bear the burden of mounting government debt. In fact government debt was not a problem as long as Keynesian policies were actually followed.

In Canada, during the 28 years from 1947 to 1974 the federal budget was in deficit for only 11 years. The combined surplus during the other 17 years was more than double the combined deficit for the period. [1] The net federal debt, which had been greater than the annual gross national product immediately after World War II, fell to a half of GNP in 1952 and then to 15 per cent in 1975, [2] when federal debt service charges represented less than 1 per cent of GDP. In 1990, after 15 years of neoconservative policies, federal debt service charges had increased to more than 4 per cent of GDP. [3]

Debt began to rise in the middle 1970s after Trudeau and his finance minister, Jean Chretien, bowed to business pressure and lowered taxes for corporations and upper-income Canadians. In the same years, the post-war fixed exchange rate system was abandoned. Canada, like other countries, lost control of exchange levels and interest rates. [4] The revenue loss from the wealthowners' tax revolt made governments more dependent on international money markets. Interest rates rose. As more and more revenue went to wealthowners as debt service charges, governments looked for ways to cut social services. They allowed infrastructure to decay and claimed there was nothing they could do about rising chronic unemployment.

Keynesian full employment policies had been accepted by wealthowners only because World War II and its aftermath had convinced them that government intervention was in their class interests. German offensives in the first years of the war had given Hitler control of nearly all the resources of Europe. The Allied response was based on a massive redirection of resources by governments. At a time when soldiers and civilians were being asked to make great sacrifices, wealthowners could not plausibly complain about the high tax levels required to finance the war, especially when the war opened opportunities to make great profits. In any case, government regulation of economic activity in wartime was not new.

For western governments peace was as big a challenge as war. Memories of the social upheavals that followed World War I were still fresh. In February 1917, Russian soldiers refused to fire on women factory workers who were protesting against starvation wages. As the soldiers' rebellion spread, the Czar abdicated and fled. Soldiers' councils took control of the armed forces; workers' councils took control of factories and railways; peasants' councils took control of land and distributed it among villagers. In October, a Bolshevik uprising led to the proclamation of a government of workers' and peasants' councils. In Germany, the armed forces collapsed when soldiers refused to obey orders. Workers' councils were organised to take charge of factories in major industrial centres. Between 1918 and 1921 workers' councils took control of factories in Milan, Turin and other European cities. In France, Britain, Canada and the US, workers and demobilised soldiers responded to inflation and unemployment by organising general strikes and proclaiming their sympathies with workers' council movements.

Social relations after World War II, from a wealthowners' perspective, looked worse. Soviet armies had occupied eastern Europe, penetrating past Berlin. Nominally anti-capitalist parties appeared to be about to win majority support in elections in Britain, Canada, France and Italy. Anti-colonial movements were poised to take power in India, Indonesia and Vietnam. Communist armies controlled much of China. In North America and the UK millions of soldiers, inspired by the democratic ideals of a victorious anti-fascist war, were about to be demobilised into an already militant workforce. In the US and Canada, new unions in steel, automobiles, rubber, electrical goods and chemicals had made wage gains during the war, but rationing and aggressive government campaigns to sell savings bonds held down demand. Consumer goods production had been deliberately kept to a minimum. Investment had been directed toward the war effort. By the end of the war, working people had substantial savings which they wanted to spend.

How could workers' aspirations be met and jobs found for soldiers while inflation was held in check? Governments had little room to manoeuvre. Even though wartime profits were heavily taxed and the top marginal income tax rates were 90 per cent and 100 per cent, government debt exceeded gross annual product.[5]

Governments were not deterred by the fiscal problems. They took responsibility for conversion to peacetime production. Taxes were kept high. Interest rates were pushed down.[6] In Canada, ten-year government bonds paid 3 per cent.[7] The prime rate for private borrowers was fixed at 4.5 per cent in 1946, where it remained until 1955. Low interest rates reduced the cost of servicing the debt and encouraged private investment. Economic growth reduced the weight of the debt. The real value of the debt was further reduced by double digit inflation in three years – 10 per cent in 1947, 14 per cent in 1948 and 11 per cent in 1951. Otherwise, inflation was kept under control. Prices rose by more than 3 per cent in only one other year, 1949, and by less than 1 per cent between 1953 and 1955.[8]

Canada could keep interest rates low because the 1944 Bretton Woods agreement meant that other countries were doing the same. Bretton Woods had been a compromise between British and US negotiators. John Maynard Keynes, representing the UK, urged policies that promoted full employment and eased the burdens faced by debtors.[9] US negotiators, pressured by US bankers, were more concerned with protecting creditors' interests. They insisted that the focus should be on currency stability. Both parties agreed on the importance of international trade. The US negotiators, while impressed with Keynes's arguments, basically got their way. The final agreement established a system of fixed exchange rates with convertibility of US dollars to gold. The result, for the participants, was satisfactory. Governments kept interest rates low and stable currencies encouraged trade.

The Bretton Woods system collapsed in the 1970s.[10] In 1971 Richard Nixon announced that the US had unilaterally abandoned its commitment to convert dollars to gold. The immediate aim was to stop the flow of gold reserves out of the country. Deficit financing of the war in Vietnam had greatly increased the volume of US dollars held abroad. In 1973 major western governments announced the end of the Bretton Woods exchange rate system. Floating exchange rates quickly made currency speculation a trillion dollar a year business. In 1974 Nixon repealed the Interest Equalisation Tax. Capital could now go abroad in search of the highest interest rates without tax penalties. The repeal of the Commerce Department's Foreign Direct Investment Controls in the same year effectively ended government regulation of capital flows in and out of the US.

In 1979 the newly elected Thatcher government removed the remaining foreign exchange controls in Britain. Japan and other countries did the same. International money markets would now set exchange and interest rates. If governments attempted to devalue their currency in order to spur industrial development, trade or employment, they would be faced with higher interest rates. If they tried to lower interest rates for the same purpose they would face a flight of capital abroad. Monetary policy would once again be directed by great creditors in their own interests, as it had been before the Keynesian reformation.

During Keynesian times monetary and fiscal policies were government responsibilities, but wealthowners had certainly not been victimised. Governments were committed to leaving most economic activity in the hands of private capital. After the war, factories financed by governments for war production were transferred to private businesses at nominal cost. Private enterprise built the homes and manufactured the cars, refrigerators, washing machines, radios, record players and television sets that sustained the long Keynesian growth phase. Government acted as an executive committee for private capital. It borrowed the massive sums for housing and social infrastructure that provided jobs for demobilised soldiers. Private capital was allowed to take credit for sustained growth, but before millions of families could move into new homes, billions of tax dollars had to be spent on roads, sewers, sidewalks and schools in the suburbs. Before the automobile could become the vehicle of mass transportation, billions more had to be spent on highways, bridges and interchanges.

In the US, politicians at first justified the vast sums spent on highways by claiming that road networks were needed for military mobility during the Cold War. It quickly became obvious that such a justification was unnecessary. Massive government spending on streets and highways, electrification, sewers and waterworks made mass consumer society practical. Private business was booming.

In western Europe, the threat to capitalism was far greater. Extensive damage had been done to homes, roads, bridges, factories and equipment. A large, battle-hardened Soviet army had pushed its way deep into Europe. Governments and wealthowners did not wait for the invisible hand of market forces. European reconstruction was financed by the US government. Under the Marshall Plan, western Europe got consumer goods, machinery and equipment. Industries in the United States and Canada profited from supplying these goods. After post-war reconstruction was completed, governments continued to take responsibility for economic wellbeing. Spending on education, health care, unemployment insurance and pensions kept aggregate demand growing.

Governments had little trouble balancing budgets, but fiscal responsibility was not their preoccupation. Their concern was steady growth in aggregate demand and employment. With this in mind, they followed counter-cyclical policies. During boom times government surpluses dampened demand. During slumps deficits stimulated demand. From 1958 to 1974 industrial production grew at annual rates of 13 per cent in Japan; 7.5 per cent in Italy; 6 per cent in Canada, France and Germany; 4.5 per cent in the US and 3 per cent in the UK.[11] During most of that time, unemployment was less than 5 per cent in Canada, somewhat lower in the US and around 6 per cent in the UK. In Japan and Germany unemployment was usually less than 2 per cent.[12]

During that now reviled Keynesian time, college graduates found work in occupations they had trained for. Young men and women who left school early were able to find jobs at decent pay. Once they accumulated a few years of seniority, they rarely lost their jobs. If they did, they were able to find other work at comparable pay. Few able-bodied, middle-aged men and women were left without means of livelihood. Cities were not flooded with homeless people living in subways or abandoned buildings, on the streets or under bridges.

Ironically, it was success that undermined Keynesianism. Wealthowners accepted government intervention so long as they believed that meeting some of the aspirations of the people reduced threats to capitalist property relations. The improvement in working-class living standards in capitalist countries, contrasted with the relative stagnation of Communist countries, convinced wealthowners that the threat to capitalism was greatly exaggerated. By the 1970s they no longer saw any need to placate the masses.

The deconstruction of Keynesian policies began with the writings of A. W. Phillips, a British Keynesian. In an article published in 1958, Phillips questioned the compatibility of the twin pillars of post-war economic policy – full employment and monetary stability. In what came to be known as the Phillips Curve, he presented charts to show that declining unemployment levels led to higher inflation rates.[13] Phillips began by ignoring the impact of oligopoly, of rising profits and of interest rates on prices. He simply assumed that inflation was caused by rising wages. Having speculated that low rates of unemployment increase workers' bargaining power, he concluded that inflation is caused by rising employment. The statistical correlation that Phillips included to confirm this proposition proved little. The graphs did not show whether wage increases preceded or followed price increases. Other economists soon provided examples of times and places where Phillips's correlation was absent. Nonetheless, the Phillips Curve encouraged economists who blamed wages for inflation to speculate about a 'natural rate of unemployment' – a rate at which there is neither downward nor upward pressure on wages.

What is the natural rate of unemployment? In the 1950s unemployment of 2.5 per cent was considered effective full employment in Canada. (This seemed reasonable: even with full employment some people will be between jobs.) In the early 1960s, the rate was 3.5 per cent; in the late 1960s, 4.5 per cent. In the early 1970s, rates of 5 to 6 per cent were typical. By the late 1970s, unemployment rates had risen to 8 per cent. [14] If the Phillips Curve held, inflation should have dropped dramatically. In fact it was higher than at any time in the post-war period. Nonetheless, neoconservatives continued to insist that the fight against inflation required that governments abandon the commitment to full employment.

The reaction against full employment policies had been anticipated by Michal Kalecki. Kalecki, a Polish economist, had independently formulated a theory of counter-cyclical intervention. After reading Keynes's *General Theory* he moved to England to work in Cambridge. In his 1943 essay, 'Political Aspects of Full Employment', Kalecki noted that business leaders may support government measures to create employment during a depression when markets are stagnating and many businesses are going bankrupt, but if governments borrow money or raise taxes

> to maintain the high level of employment ... in the subsequent boom, a strong opposition of 'business leaders' is likely to be encountered ... Lasting full employment is not at all to their liking. The workers would 'get out of hand' and the 'captains of industry' would be anxious 'to teach them a lesson'. [15]

Kalecki's prediction of a wealthowners' reaction was not remarkable. During World War II, wealthowners had grumbled about rising wages and the growing power of unions. After the war, they used anti-Communist laws to weaken the more militant unions. They mobilised against steeply-graduated income taxes and social spending, claiming that these were a form of confiscation of private property. In the 1970s, when wealthowners had concluded that capitalist property relations were not threatened, they set out to discredit Keynesian full employment policies. In the writings of Friedrich Hayek and Milton Friedman, this was couched as opposition to inflation, taxes and government tyranny.

By the early 1980s, some neoconservatives had become confident enough openly to advocate higher unemployment. Michael Walker, director of the Fraser Institute, argued that unemployment was not a problem at all, 'it has become a way of life for many ... People displaced by the cyclical downturn will eventually be re-employed.'[16] Michael Goldberg, Dean of Commerce at the University of British Columbia, said, 'Without the wrenching difficulties of the depressed economy, we never would have re-evaluated what we are doing ... Unemployment gives us an opportunity to tap that frustration and creativity and vent it in newer ways.' [17] Ernest Isley, the Minister of Manpower in the Conservative government of Alberta, said, 'From an economic point of view, if you define full employment as everyone having a job, that's not a healthy thing.' [18]

More often, opposition to full employment continued to be disguised as campaigns against inflation and high taxes. In Canada, the fight against inflation was led by John Crowe, governor of the Bank of Canada. To keep inflation in check (more precisely to teach workers a lesson) real interest rates were kept 3 and 4 percentage points higher than in the US. The result was unemployment levels of more than 10 per cent and dramatically increased government deficits. Pierre Fortin, writing in the journal *Canadian Business Economics*, estimated that Crowe's attempts to reduce the inflation rate from 2 per cent to 0.5 per cent during the late 1980s and early 1990s – during a serious recession – had cost the Canadian economy $Can105 billion in lost jobs and production – equivalent to nearly 20 per cent of GDP. [19] Despite this, business leaders supported Crowe's policy. High interest rates meant higher returns for capital and they welcomed the sobering effect of unemployment on working people.

The Chretien government has followed Mulroney's lead in claiming that governments can do little about employment because taxes are already too high. Why do such governments get elected? Of course, during the election campaign Chretien claimed that job creation would be his number one priority. Some people were fooled, others grudgingly accepted the argument that taxpayers can no longer afford the people. The persistent exaggeration by the corporate media of the importance of private consumption has made public spending seem less important. Even working people think that lower taxes would leave them more money for personal consumption. That, however, is not the intention. For neoconservatives 'taxpayers' is code for 'private wealthowner'. The taxes they are concerned with are marginal rates on the highest incomes, estate taxes and capital gains. They happily make up for lost revenues, by raising payroll deductions and consumption and sales taxes.

The tax revolt is a neoconservative campaign to turn the clock back to a time when Adam Smith observed, 'Civil government, so far as it is instituted for the security of property, is in reality instituted for the defence of the rich against the poor, or of those who have some property against those who have none at all.' [20]

Was opposition to the neoconservative reaction blunted by growing environmental consciousness? The Keynesian focus on rising aggregate demand in the most prosperous countries did clash with the realisation that industrial pollution, the depletion of non-renewable resources and the widening gap between prosperous and poor countries were pushing humankind to global crises. Consumerism was becoming problematic, but transnational corporate oligarchs were not proposing solutions to global problems. Their goals were more modest: they aimed to increase their income at the expense of everyone else.

Is there an Alternative?

If Keynesianism failed, it failed because it did not go far enough. Governments that accepted responsibility for full employment and aggregate demand had implicitly expanded social rights to include access to means of livelihood and to a share of the social product. However, most levers of economic power remained in the hands of wealthowning minorities. Once it was in their interests to do so, they scuttled the Keynesian social contract. In the name of free global markets, transnational corporations are disregarding the interests of the people of all countries. In opposition to government control and in the name of competitive individualism, wealthowning minorities are increasing their control over economic life. More and more people – the unemployed, the unskilled, the young – are denied access to means of livelihood.

Governments do not have too much power. The problem is that the elected representatives of the people have conceded control over most economic activity to wealthowners. If governments were committed to the interests of all their citizens, they would make living standards and employment the priorities of economic policy. Access to decent housing, health care and education would be made rights of citizenship. Minimum wages would give people the means to live above poverty levels. Unemployment benefits would be high enough so that people would not be compelled to work for wages that keep them in poverty. Collective bargaining would be made a social right. When working people cannot democratically participate in setting the terms and conditions of employment, capital has free rein to pursue its own interests at their expense.

Chronic unemployment could be reduced if the legal working week was shortened and compulsory overtime was prohibited. New jobs would be created if governments increased spending on public works that improve the quality of life. Many people could be employed making affordable and decent housing available to everyone, providing pre-school child care for all, building and operating fast and comfortable public transit systems and constructing facilities to reduce and eliminate air and water pollution. The expense could be covered by diverting funds from capital flight and extravagant living. Tax loopholes that favour the wealthy could be eliminated. Marginal rates on upper incomes could be increased. Capital gains could be taxed like any other income. Private trusts could be taxed. Corporation taxes could be raised to 1960s levels.

Full employment would be far easier to achieve if governments encouraged and protected domestic industry. Tariffs and import quotas make it possible for domestic enterprises to survive and prosper. When goods that would otherwise be imported are produced internally, employment and aggregate demand rise. The market for the products of other domestic industries expands. In these times of chronic government deficits, tariffs should not be ignored as a important source of revenue. Tariffs, as John Maynard Keynes said, are the only taxes that 'positively cheer people up'.[21]

Protectionism need not be motivated by beggar-your-neighbour attitudes. It can be inspired by the principle that people in all countries and regions have the right – and the responsibility – to produce most of the goods and services they consume. In any case, protectionism does not mean opposition to trade. It means regulated trade. Unrestricted trade in goods is generally beneficial where technologies and labour standards are comparable. Even where conditions of production are not equal, regulated trade increases prosperity. More prosperous importing countries gain by being able to shift labour to more socially useful purposes. Poorer exporting countries gain much needed revenues. In this neoconservative age, bilateral and multilateral trade agreements usually favour capital at the expense of labour.[22] This need not be the case. Trade agreements could be designed to protect living standards in more prosperous countries and to speed industrial development in poorer countries.

If governments were committed to global economic development, they would take measures to stop the drain of funds from poor countries. How can poor countries industrialise when the surpluses generated by their own economic activity flow abroad? The flow of profits, dividends, interest payments and business service charges out of poor countries could be blocked by tax policies and criminal sanctions. Governments of more prosperous countries could give more positive aid by directing a minimum of 2 per cent of GNP into an international development fund. If moneys loaned by the fund were repaid to the fund itself and reinvested in industrial development, debt service charges would not result in a future flow of surplus out of poor countries. Governments committed to rapid development would make technologies available to poor countries. Patent laws that now give corporations exclusive possession of the most advanced technologies reinforce monopolies, discourage competition and worsen disparities between rich and poor countries.

Friedrich Hayek was right to say that trade is the most important form of communication among people.[23] But if trade is communication, capitalist trade is extortion. The capitalist exchange relation – capital for commodities and then commodities for capital – will not normally be consummated unless capital at the end is greater than at the beginning. Based on private appropriation of the products of social labour and control of the links between producers and consumers by middlemen, its aim is to get a greater value than is given. Capitalist exchange is especially prominent in global trade. During the 1970s, internal transactions between branches, subsidiaries or affiliates of transnationals accounted for a quarter of world trade. In the early 1990s, a third was administered by transnationals.[24]

Many poor countries are more than eager to attract transnational investment. In a world dominated by capital, they have little choice. If governments in more prosperous countries were committed to narrowing global disparities as well as to the economic interests of their own people, they would support campaigns to break up transnationals. Where the production of goods and services must be synchronised internationally, this can be done by cooperating national, regional and local units. If all countries controlled their own domestic industry and trade, transnational corporate oligarchs could no longer enrich themselves by driving down wage rates or by redirecting the resources of poor countries to more prosperous markets.

Global realities cannot be denied. A transportation revolution has dramatically reduced the cost of shipping goods. Ships of 80,000 tons and more carry a dozen crew members or less. Containerisation has eliminated nearly all cargo handling. The total labour time required in transshipment has been reduced to a tenth or less of what it was just 40 years ago. A communications revolution has made it practical for corporate managers to maintain direct and immediate contact with nearly any place on the globe.

Supporters of transnational capital claim that governments can no longer regulate capital movements. It is true that financial claims can be transferred from country to country with greater speed and ease than ever before, but advances in electronic technologies also make it practical for governments to monitor all transactions from inside their borders. Governments could apply punitive taxes and criminal sanctions against corporations or individuals who move money out of the country to avoid taxes, evade environmental regulations or to undermine labour standards. All that is lacking is the political will.

Regulation of capital movements would allow governments to regain control of interest rates. If real interest rates in Canada were lowered from 6 per cent or more to 3 or 2 per cent, the cost of servicing the public debt would fall dramatically. Cheaper credit would spur investment in domestic industries. Government revenues would rise, making full employment easier to achieve. Adam Smith himself said that interest rates are too important to the wellbeing of nations to be left to bankers, creditors or the vagaries of money markets. He advocated government intervention to keep interest rates low, writing, 'Where the legal rate of interest ... is fixed but a very little above the lowest market rate, sober people are universally preferred, as borrowers, to prodigals and projectors.'[25]

No government on its own – with the possible exception of the US or the European Union – can successfully challenge the transnational corporate oligarchy. Those that try face a loss of credit, rising interest rates and a flight of capital. But countries are not alone. We have good reasons to act together. Canadians, Americans, Mexicans, Europeans, South Americans, Africans and Asians have all felt the adverse effects of globalism. In this epoch of instant global communications, common approaches to common problems could be quickly formulated and effectively sustained.

Public ownership could reduce the power of wealthowners to set the political agenda. Public ownership by national, regional and local governments would give the majority a democratic voice in the priorities of social labour. Despite the success of campaigns for privatisation, arguments for public ownership remain valid. Capitalist ownership of forests, mineral deposits and petroleum resources places long-term human wellbeing in the hands of people who are preoccupied with short-term profits. Capitalist ownership of social monopolies – railways, electrical utilities and telephone companies – merely adds the short-sightedness of wealthowners' self-interest to the arrogance of centralised bureaucracies. Capitalist ownership of major financial institutions allows wealthowning minorities to direct socially produced wealth in their narrow class interest. Capitalist ownership of newspaper chains and television networks allows corporate oligarchs to monopolise public discourse.

Privatisation has had the nearly unanimous endorsement of the corporate media, but who has benefited? Top managers of privatised companies have gained larger incomes and some shareholders have made enviable returns. Meanwhile, workers have lost their jobs or have had their wages cut. Customers have had to cope with price rises and deteriorating services. Some privatised companies have gone bankrupt; others have required government assistance to survive. So why do even Labour and Social Democratic governments support privatisation?

Relentless neoconservative campaigns against public ownership are not the full explanation. Public ownership had not inspired much active support. It was often a last resort to save jobs or to rescue communities after private enterprise failed. Because public ownership was not motivated by campaigns for democratic control of economic life, it became a form of private ownership in which government was the sole shareholder. Companies owned by governments take pride in acting in a 'business-like' manner. They have adopted the self-serving and secretive managerial structures of corporate capitalism.

If the goal was to give people democratic control of economic life, boards of directors of publicly owned companies would be elected by communities, workers and users. Workers' representatives would be elected to management committees and workers would be given the right to participate in formulating management polices. If management deliberations and records were open to public scrutiny, communities and user groups could also participate in the direction of public assets. Why should secrecy in publicly owned companies be any more acceptable than secrecy in legislative deliberations?

Business secrecy is a wealthowners' privilege that should have no place in a democracy. The right to privacy is justified when it is meant to allow individuals to control their own lives and to enjoy their time and personal possessions without interference from others. When corporate oligarchs are allowed to obscure, conceal and expand their control of economic activity, privacy laws help wealthowning minorities impose their class interests on others.

Neoconservatives insist that democratic control of economic life is dictatorship. This Orwellian claim has an appeal. Control of economic life by wealthowning minorities is taken for granted. The myth of the individual in the market makes it seem that society is divided between the people on one side and governments on the other. In these neoconservative times, governments do little to gain the confidence of people. When running for office, politicians claim they will act in the interests of all. Once in office, they insist that they have no alternative but to act in the narrow interests of wealthowners. Governments often deserve contempt, but private business is no realm of freedom, honesty or high-mindedness. It is just as bureaucratic as government and more self-serving, wasteful and tyrannical.

Top corporate executives spend as much time as government

bureaucrats in meetings and more time playing golf or otherwise entertaining themselves. Politicians and top civil servants would happily exchange their well-publicised pensions for the golden handshakes and golden parachutes given to corporate executives when they retire or are pushed out of office. The corporate media delight in reporting cavalier, stupid and wasteful government practices. They rarely point out that the deplorable growth of self-serving practices in public life represents the adoption by government of business ethics. [26]

Corporate executives are routinely provided with low-interest or no-interest loans to purchase homes in exclusive neighbourhoods, are given company-paid memberships in the most expensive clubs and often have the use of company airplanes and yachts. Their offices and furnishings are more lavish than those of their counterparts in government. The hiring of friends and relatives and the promotion of protégés are viewed as rights of management. Private deals that disregard competitive conditions are routinely accepted as ways of building corporate 'good will'.

The average income of top corporate executives is ten times higher than that received by top government officials. The self-righteous greed unleashed by the neoconservative reaction has created a climate in which top executives are encouraged to grab what they can for themselves. In 1960, when US business was at its height, corporate chief executives were paid an average of 40 times the pay of factory workers. In 1990, with US business in decline, they were paid 85 times more. [27] In 1988, the CEOs of the largest corporations in the US were paid an average of $2 million a year. In 1990, Steven Ross, chief executive officer of entertainment and publishing conglomerate Time-Warner, was paid $78 million. This was more than twice the combined wages and salaries of the 605 publishing division employees laid-off the following year as a cost-cutting measure. [28]

The staggering waste associated with capitalist ownership is documented in *The New Bureaucracy – Waste and Folly in the Private Sector*, by Herschel Hardin. On top of extravagant executive salaries, enterprises are required to pay billions in dividends to shareholders and billions more interest to creditors. To arrange and rearrange payments to wealthowners, the stock exchange system in the US employed 450,000 people in 1987. This massive paper-chasing bureaucracy supported the lavish personal spending of stockbrokers, investment bankers, arbitragists, financial analysts, accountants, pension fund advisers and legions of lawyers – none of whom made any practical contribution to goods and services production.

Supporters of the system claim that stock exchanges mobilise funds for business. Do they? When people buy and sell shares, 'no investment goes into company treasuries ... Shares simply change hands for cash, in endless repetition.'[29] Company treasuries get funds only from new equity issues. These accounted for an average of a mere 0.5 per cent of shares trading in the US during the 1980s.[30] In the second half of the 1980s, share prices were driven up by mergers and acquisitions, leveraged buyouts and hostile takeovers. Spectacular personal fortunes were made on capital gains, on stock options and on transaction fees. One stock exchange manipulator, Michael Milkin, was paid an income of $600 million in 1987.[31]

Meanwhile, inflated share prices forced corporations to increase dividend payments. Bonds floated to pay for mergers and acquisitions dramatically increased corporate debt. The net effect of stock and bond transactions was that non-financial business in the US was drained of $100 billion annually in the second half of the 1980s.[32] As wasteful, unproductive expenditure this was exceeded only by military spending. It was paid for by consumers as higher prices and by workers as lower wages and lost jobs.

There is an important difference between government and capitalist business. Government officials who abuse positions of power can be dismissed by the elected representatives of the people. Governing parties can be removed by the electorate. People have no such control over corporate oligarchs. Chief executives can hire, fire, promote and demote who they please. They can tell their subordinates how to dress and how to vote in elections. They can make people work involuntary overtime. If they have the controlling shares, they can squander company assets on conspicuous consumption or remove them to other countries. The people who depend on these socially produced assets may grumble, but so long as capitalist property relations prevail, corporate dictators will do as they please.

Economic Democracy

The claim that public ownership and democratic control are unwarranted intrusions by government in civil society can be traced to John Locke. According to Locke, every wealthowner has an inviolable right to use and enjoy his property as he pleases. The king is one property owner among many. A king who interferes with the property rights of others is a tyrant. Locke's position reflected a society in which political rights were derived from property ownership. Civil society was confined to wealthowners and the relations they formed with each other and their servants. Government was in the hands of the Crown.

Once political rights were extended to all adults, the separation between government and civil society became problematic. Why would government be viewed as a grasping despot threatening the properties of the many, when – in theory at least – it represented the democratic organisation of all citizens? The distinction between government and civil society as it came from Locke may not have survived universal suffrage. Locke was too obviously a partisan of wealthowners' interests. Adam Smith's theory was brought to its rescue.

If the activities of individuals in civil society are regulated by market forces, why would governments intervene? Indeed, in the late nineteenth century – outside of England – independent individuals producing for the market were still close to a majority. Wealthowners' control over economic life was increasing, but during the first period of universal suffrage independent producers in most countries, mainly farmers, elected majorities or held the political balance of power. This remained so for close to 100 years. At the beginning of World War II, independent producers still accounted for 43 per cent of the population in France; 25 per cent in Canada and 19 per cent in the US. It was the decline of the family farm that pushed independent producers to the fringes of economic life. By 1990 independent producers represented 10 per cent and less of the economically active population in most prosperous countries. (The number is somewhat higher in France and Japan where governments dependent on the farm vote have regulated agriculture to protect smallholdings.)[33]

The choice is not now between competitive individualism and government control. Human populations and wants have grown far beyond the productive capacities of individuals. The choice is between the regulation of economic affairs by corporate oligarchs in the interests of wealthowning minorities and democratic regulation in the interests of the overwhelming majority.

In economic democracies, social means of livelihood would be socially owned. Enterprises producing for local markets could be owned by neighbourhoods, towns and cities. Larger enterprises could be owned by provinces, states, regions, nations and, perhaps, international agencies. Socially owned enterprises would be subject to dual democratic control. Owning communities would appoint managers, control assets and revenues and set the tasks and priorities of social labour. Workers would democratically regulate their labour time through workplace assemblies and elected workers' councils.

Capitalism exalts the individual at the expense of the social. Economic democracies would have little reason to do the reverse. Individual enterprise would be encouraged. Whenever individuals or freely associated groups on their own produced goods or services that others want, communities would be saved the responsibility of organising that activity. Farms, corner stores, repair shops, home builders and personal and business services could operate as partnerships or as individually owned businesses. Restaurants and retail stores could be organised as worker cooperatives. Writing, painting, sculpting would usually be individual. Where teamwork is required, as it is in most music, dance, drama and spectator sports, performers could set up partnerships, form cooperatives or be employed by communities.

Individual initiative could also be encouraged within community-owned enterprises. Engineers, production workers, or administrators who devise techniques that conserve materials or energy or reduce the labour time required in production could be rewarded with a portion of the costs saved or the values produced. Buyers or salespeople could be rewarded with a portion of the revenues their individual efforts generated. Inventors who patent products, machinery or processes would be paid royalties. If the product could be produced with individual labour, an inventor could set up his or her own business. If cooperative labour was required, inventors could approach socially owned financial institutions or local governments with plans to set up new enterprises. If a plan was accepted, the innovator could receive a portion of the enterprise's revenue as royalties and would perhaps be hired as a technical specialist or manager. Such enterprises would be socially owned.

Social ownership would not give workers exclusive ownership of their means of livelihood. Under capitalism worker ownership has merits as a response to plant closures. It can save jobs and give workers experience in the democratic direction of enterprises. Still, worker ownership is a form of private ownership. If generalised, it would lead to new divisions between haves and have-nots, between more and less favourably situated workers. Why should those engaged in only part of an economic process have control of the assets or the values produced?

The interdependence of social labour can be illustrated with the example of a pulp mill. The labour of workers in the mill is critical to the production of the final exchange values, but without the storing and allocation of funds by people employed in the finance industry, money would not have been available for investment in the mill. Without the design and construction of the mill, the plant and equipment would not be there. Without loggers, there would be no logs to pulp. Without roads, railways and docks, the pulp could not be transported to the market. Without the work of housebuilders, municipal workers, health care workers and others in services and the retail trade, mill workers would not be able or willing to live in the town. Without child care, without teachers and instructors, pulp mill workers would not have acquired the skills needed in their jobs. All of these people and more have added their labour to the value of the product of the pulp mill. All have a claim on the social wealth produced. With social ownership, everyone would have a voice and a vote in the disposition of social assets and everyone would have a claim to a share of the social product.

With social ownership it would be obvious that economic wellbeing is a function of the quality, effectiveness, depth and extent of social labour. The quality of social labour depends on the training, education, skills and discipline of labour – on the effort, science, ingenuity and organisation used to transport, alter, fashion and combine the resources and forces of nature into means of production and consumer goods. The effectiveness of social labour depends on the availability of machinery, equipment, technologies and surpluses – on the accumulated products of the past labour of construction, industrial and administrative workers, of engineers and inventors. The depth of social labour depends on the economic diversity and cooperation within communities, on the availability of raw materials and semi-finished goods and on access to communications, transportation networks and financial and other business services. The extent of social labour depends on the cooperation among communities, on the access communities have to the markets, products and surpluses of other communities.

Capitalist property relations make it appear that economic wellbeing depends on capital, but what does capital actually do? Capital is a social relation. It is the right to profit from the labour of others – the right to a kind of private taxation. It is the right to claim ownership of social assets and the right to exclude others from means of livelihood. So long as capitalist property relations prevail, wealthowners will decide who prospers and who does not, but the wealth they control was not created by capital. Individual capitalists may play a role as planners, managers or innovators, but capitalists as capitalists play no necessary role in economic wellbeing. Social labour transforms natural resources into materials for production, manufactures machines and equipment, transports and distributes goods and produces the surpluses invested in new means of production.

Capital is not essential for prosperity, but it is at the root of environmentally destructive accumulation. To maximise profits, enterprises pass the costs of industrial pollution and unsustainable levels of resource extraction to local communities, health care systems, taxpayers, future generations and other species. If capitalist enterprises attempted to absorb such costs, profits would be lower and they would lose the race to their more irresponsible arrivals.

With social ownership, costs could not be so easily externalised. Local communities would not be inclined to pollute their own living space or undermine the livelihood of their own offspring. Broader communities – countries and the international community – would have the legislative authority and the motivation to prevent smaller communities from passing costs elsewhere. Engineers and scientists would be put to work serving communities instead of wealthowners. Human knowledge would be applied to designing technologies and systems that permit the satisfaction of wants without damage to the ecosystems on which human wellbeing depends. Although respect for labour time would encourage efforts to utilise labour most efficiently, owning communities would not be pressured to give marginal returns on investment precedence over human wellbeing.

Capital is also the source of chronic unemployment and disequilibrium. So long as privately owned corporations have exclusive possession of technologies, innovations introduced in one place cause the obsolescence of means of livelihood in other places. With social ownership, innovation would be far less destructive. Longer-term disparities would be minimised by open access to all technologies. Technologies would be available to any individual or community enterprise that paid an agreed royalty to innovators. Short-term disruptions could be eased with financial aid to affected communities from regional and national governments. Funds for such aid could perhaps come from a special tax on additional surpluses earned by innovating communities. Enough of the surplus could remain in communities to encourage innovation.

Economic democracy would have no need to divide people into winners and losers. It would be structured to take everyone's interests into account. Owning communities, composed of working people, would not be likely to withdraw investments from their own workplaces in pursuit of higher returns from cheaper labour elsewhere. People who do lose their jobs to changing wants or changing technologies would remain members of their communities. With a voice and vote in the disposition of social assets, they would be able to defend their interests in ways that are now not possible.

As human energy and ingenuity made it possible for fewer people to produce more goods, communities and governments could respond by raising real wages. If markets were saturated with commodities, people could be put to work in public services that improve the quality of life. If all useful work was already being done, people would relax and enjoy themselves. Hours of work could be reduced with no loss in pay.

Workplace democracy would end the alienation and humiliation inherent in capitalist master–servant relationships. Shorter hours would remove much of the remaining travail from labour. In economic democracies leisure would be as important as consumption. The system would not be driven to invent new wants. Some people would undoubtedly remain preoccupied with accumulating possessions and with consuming as much as they could as quickly as possible, but they would not dominate economic life. Most people would be more concerned with experiencing life, with developing their personal skills and with participating in social labour and community affairs.

From the time of the ancient Greeks, philosophers have taught that only those free from toil have the time to develop as free and responsible citizens. In ancient times, freedom for the few meant extra burdens for the many. Modern technological aids to labour, if accompanied by universal access to means of livelihood, would mean that employment, material comforts and leisure could be available for all.

Beyond Capitalism

Does democracy require capitalism, as supporters of the system claim? It is true that democratic rights have gradually increased under capitalism, but these were won in struggles against wealthowners. Capitalist property rights have from their inception clashed with human rights. Capitalism laid its foundations on the rubble of the democratic village communes that it destroyed. Working people won the campaigns for freedom of association, freedom of assembly, freedom of the press and the right to vote.

In France, during the revolutions of 1789, 1830, 1849 and 1871, the urban poor – artisans, small shopkeepers, shopgirls, women clothing workers and the unemployed – rallied for universal political rights. Capitalists supported kings and emperors. In Britain, working men and women were injured and killed in Peterloo field in 1819 because they chose to defy a ban on unauthorised meetings imposed by a wealthowners' parliament. Before and after that bloody attack, wage workers defied the Criminal Conspiracy Acts to win freedom of association. In the 1820s and 1830s labour clubs fought the Stamp Acts designed to muzzle the radical press. In the 1840s working-class Chartists initiated the mass movement for equal political rights. From the 1850s to the 1890s trade unions campaigned to abolish property qualifications for the vote.

In the early twentieth century, women's suffrage groups in Britain, supported by the Labour Party and many trade unions, won the vote for women. Suffrage leaders were often the educated daughters of the well-off, but it was women's trade unionism in World War I that gave British feminism the support needed finally to win the vote. In Canada and the United States, women won the vote after women factory workers joined farm women in the campaign. (In largely agrarian New Zealand and Australia, women had won the vote in 1893 and 1902.)

After the Bolshevik seizure of power in October 1917, wealthowners supported and funded an anti-Communist, anti-union and anti-democratic reaction. In Italy, Germany and Spain, wealthowners allied with fascists to overthrow democracy. In France, England and the US, wealthowners openly expressed their sympathies with fascism. During the Cold War, after fascism was defeated, wealthowners claimed to support democracy. This did not stop transnational corporations from collaborating with local oligarchs and military leaders to overthrow democratic governments. Capital supported brutal military dictatorships in Africa, Asia, Europe, Latin America and the Middle East. In more prosperous countries, wealthowners for a time grudgingly accepted the Keynesian social contract. When they had the opportunity, they launched the neoconservative reaction to once again give wealthowners' rights precedence over social rights.

Why would democracy need capitalism? Capitalism is a system of private autocracies. Its dominant institutions – transnational corporations – are vast, centralised bureaucracies run by and in the interests of wealthowning minorities. It is true that capitalism is not monolithic, but far greater pluralism would result from social ownership by national, regional and local communities. Plural social ownership and workplace democracy would build checks and balances into basic social structures. Dialogue about long-term and short-term goals, about the general and particular interests would be the rule, not the exception.

Direct democracy would flourish. Workers would meet to direct labour in their occupations and workplaces. Town meetings open to every man and woman in the community would set policy for locally owned enterprises. Representative democracy would no longer be distorted or corrupted by the power of private wealth. Once everyone had a voice and vote in the priorities of economic policy and in the disposition of their communities' assets, elected officials would have little reason not to represent the majority interest.

Freedom of association, freedom of opinion, freedom of speech would no longer be privileges. Means of communication would be democratically controlled. Radio stations, magazines and television channels could be owned as cooperatives. Local communities, regional and national governments and perhaps international agencies would own most daily newspapers and television channels. Wherever communication in an area is controlled by a few enterprises, these would be socially owned. Boards of directors could be structured to represent the diversity of community interests. Journalists, directors, producers, artists, actors, technicians and administrators – just like workers in other occupations – would have the right to take part in democratically regulating their work.

The right to be included in social life would rank along with the right to exclude others from personal spaces and possessions. People who are excluded from means of livelihood are effectively denied the right to participate in social life. People who do not have the right to take part in directing social labour are not full citizens. People who must subordinate their interests to those of wealthowning minorities are not free. People denied a fair share of the products of social labour are denied common humanity.

In economic democracies personal decisions would be made privately, social decisions would be made democratically. With numerous owning communities along with individual enterprise, market forces would regulate much of economic life. The continuation of market forces would make social planning easier and more effective. The market would free economic democracies from the overwhelming – if not impossible – task of deciding the supply levels and prices of all goods. Because communities could compare their plans with those of other communities, a plurality of plans would be self-correcting in ways that monolithic plans cannot be.

Despite a tradition of socialist opposition to market forces, it is capitalist property relations that are responsible for the inequities of the system. Market forces do no more than reflect existing social conditions. They can be benign or malignant. Benign competition improves quality, conserves materials and reduces the labour time needed to produce goods and services. Malignant competition jeopardises health and safety, damages the environment, lowers living standards and destroys means of livelihood.

Most of the malignant effects of market forces result from the capitalist transformation of means of livelihood and labour into commodities. In economic democracies, means of livelihood belonging to communities of working people would not be viewed as capital. Machines and equipment would be produced for sale and replaced when necessary, but as means of livelihood their function would be to provide employment for com-

munities. Employment would not be left to the vagaries of
market forces. Owning communities and workers' organisations
would regulate wages, hours and working conditions. Society
would take responsibility for the meeting of basic needs.

Beyond basic needs, most people will prefer to choose what
they consume. Choices are most easily made when goods are
bought and sold in the market. Where goods are produced by
numerous community-owned and individual enterprises and
where wage rates and access to materials, technologies and
credits are more or less equal, supply levels and prices would
usually be left to market forces. Where goods are produced by
community-owned monopolies and oligopolies, supply and price
levels would be democratically regulated. Public access to all
economic information would make such regulation practical.

Under capitalism, business secrecy is a form of exclusive
possession that reinforces the power of monopolies and oligopolies to profit at the expense of consumers, workers and other
producers. Democratic community ownership and workplace
democracy would make freedom of information a basic right.
Electronic data-gathering would allow people immediately to
access information on production levels, technologies, costs,
market conditions and the plans of all communities and enterprises. Communities and individuals will be able to make the
well-informed decisions that economists assumed were made by
homo economicus.

With economic democracy, market forces will come to the
aid of economic men and women. The invisible hand will be
freed to play the beneficial role assumed by the theory.

Sources and Further Reading

Introduction

1 George Gilder, *Wealth & Poverty*, Bantam, New York, 1981, pp. 30 and 288.
2 Ibid., p. 289.

Chapter 1: The Origins of Competitive Market Theory

1 Bernard Mandeville, *The Fable of the Bees*, Penguin, London, 1989. Biographical material in the introduction by Phillip Harth.
2 Ibid., p. 64.
3 Isaac Ilyich Rubin, *A History of Economic Thought*, Ink Links, London, 1979, p. 22.
4 Manderville, *Fable of the Bees*, introduction, p. 13.
5 Adam Smith, *The Theory of Moral Sentiments*, Dugald Stewart, London, 1880, pp. 449–60.
6 Rational deism is discussed by Christopher Hill in *The Century of Revolution*, Cardinal, London, 1975, pp. 250–68.
7 Adam Smith, *The Wealth of Nations*, Modern Library, New York, 1937, p. 14.
8 Ibid., p. 69.
9 Fernand Braudel, *Civilization & Capitalism*, Vol. 2, 'The Wheels of Commerce', Fontana Press, London, 1985, pp. 223–9.
10 Ibid., pp. 416–21, Vol. 2, pp. 428–33; Vol. 3, 'The Perspective of the World', pp. 190–3.
11 Smith, *Wealth*, p. 606.
12 Ibid., p. 129.
13 Ibid., p. 713.
14 John Locke, *Treatise of Civil Government and A Letter Concerning Toleration*, Irvington Publishers, New York, 1937, p. 100.
15 Christopher Hill, *The Century of Revolution 1603–1714*, Cardinal, London, 1975, p. 253
16 Harry A. Miskimin, *The Economy of Early Renaissance Europe 1300–1460*, Cambridge University Press, London, 1975, pp. 165–6.
17 Locke, *Treatise*, p. 19.
18 Ibid., p. 93.
19 R. H. Tawney, *The Agrarian Problem in the Sixteenth Century*, Longmans, London, 1912, p. 400.

20 Miskimin, *Early Renaissance Europe*, pp. 2–3.
21 Frances and Joseph Gies, *Women in the Middle Ages*, Barnes & Noble, New York, 1978, pp. 148–9.
22 C. B. MacPherson, *The Political Theory of Possessive Individualism*, Oxford University Press, London, 1962, p. 223.
23 Ibid., p. 222.
24 Gustavus Myers, *History of Canadian Wealth*, Vol. 1, Kerr, Chicago, 1914, pp. 38–47; Jack Weatherford, *Indian Givers*, Crown, New York, 1988, pp. 25–6; H. A. Innis, *The Fur Trade In Canada*, University of Toronto, 1956, p. 135.
25 MacPherson, *Possessive Individualism*, p. 253.
26 Tawney, *Agrarian Problem*, pp. 92–3, 102, 159–60. Additional material on communal democracy for an earlier period, in M. M. Postan, *The Medieval Economy & Society*, Penguin, London, 1975. See especially pp. 61, 82–3, 123–5, 129–33, 169.
27 Tawney, *Agrarian Problem*, p. 99.
28 Ibid., p. 100.
29 Ibid.
30 Ibid., pp. 150–2; Brian Manning, *The English People and the English Revolution*, Penguin, London, 1978.
31 Tawney, *Agrarian Problem*, pp. 177–312.
32 Carolyn Merchant, *The Death of Nature: Women, Ecology and the Scientific Revolution*, Harper & Row, San Francisco, 1983, p. 61.
33 Tawney, *Agrarian Problem*, p. 179.
34 From *Utopia*, quoted in A. L. Morton, *A People's History of England*, International Publishers, New York, 1968, p. 167. See also Miskimin, *Renaissance Europe*, Cambridge University Press, London, 1975, p. 34.
35 Rubin, *A History of Economic Thought*, p. 24.
36 Andre Gunder Frank, *World Accumulation: 1492–1789*, Monthly Review, New York, 1978, p. 177.
37 Michel Foucault, *Discipline and Punish*, translated by Alan Sheridan, Vintage Books, New York, 1979, p. 143.
38 Ibid., pp. 200–8.
39 *The Fontana Economic History of Europe*, edited by Carlo M. Cipolla. *Vol. 3 The Industrial Revolution*, Samuel Lilley, 'Technological Progress', pp. 192–213. *Vol. 4(1) The Emergence of Industrial Societies*, Phylis Deane, 'Great Britain,' pp. 174, 184. Fontana, Glasgow, 1973.
40 Ramkrishna Mukherjee, *The Rise and Fall of the East India Company*, Monthly Review Press, New York and London, 1974, pp. 343–51; J. F. C. Fuller, *The Decisive Battles of the Western World*, Vol. 2, London, 1970, editor's note, pp. 15–17.
41 G. D. H. Cole, *The British Common People*, Methuen, London, 1961; Brian Inglis, *Poverty in the Industrial Revolution*,

Panther, London, 1971; A. L. Morton, *A People's History of England*.

42 Smith, *Wealth*, pp. 78–9.

43 Braudel, *Civilization & Capitalism*, 'The Perspective of the World', Vol. 3, p. 409.

44 Smith, *Wealth*, p. 250.

45 Ibid., pp. 66–7.

46 Destutt de Tracy, quoted in Karl Marx, *Capital*, Vol. I, Vintage Books, New York, 1977, p. 802.

47 Rubin, *A History of Economic Thought*, pp. 231–4.

48 David Ricardo, 'On the Principles of Political Economy and Taxation', *The Works and Correspondence of David Ricardo*, Vol. 1, edited by Piero Sraffa, Cambridge University Press, Cambridge, 1981.

49 Ibid., p. 388.

50 Cipolla (ed.), *The Fontana Economic History of Europe*, 'The Industrial Revolution', Vol. 3, pp. 15–16; Brian Inglis, *Poverty and the Industrial Revolution*, pp. 114–19, 231–2, 419–25; Henry Pelling, *A History of British Trade Unionism*, Penguin, London, 1971.

51 Frank, *World Accumulation*, Paul Kennedy, *The Rise and Fall of the Great Powers*, Fontana, London, 1988.

52 J. A. Hobson, *Imperialism*, University of Michigan, 1965, pp. 252–72; Basil Davidson, *The African Slave Trade*, Atlantic Monthly, Boston, 1961; Walter Rodney, *How Europe Underdeveloped Africa*, Tanzania Publishing House, Dar-es-Salaam, 1972.

53 Jack Weatherford, *Indian Givers*, Crown Publishers, New York, 1988; Ronald Wright, *Stolen Continents*, Penguin, London, 1993.

54 Paul Kennedy, *The Rise and Fall of the Great Powers*, Fontana, London, pp. 190–2.

55 Ramkrishna Mukerjee, *The Rise and Fall of the East India Company*, Monthly Review, London, 1974; Michael Barratt Brown, *After Imperialism*, Heinemann, London, 1963.

56 Victor Nee and James Peck, *China's Uninterrupted Revolution*, Pantheon, New York, 1975; Frans Schurmann and Orville Schell, *Imperial China*, Vintage, New York, 1967.

57 John Locke, *Treatise*, p. 27.

58 Smith, *Wealth of Nations*, p. 33.

59 John Stuart Mill, *Principles of Political Economy*, Longmans, London, 1871, pp. 277 and 63.

60 Frank Jellinek, *The Paris Commune of 1871*, Grosset, New York, 1965.

61 'Address of the General Council of the International Working Men's Association on the Civil War in France, 1871', in

Civil War in France: The Paris Commune, by Karl Marx and
V. I. Lenin, International Publishers, New York, 1968, p. 61.
62 Otto Kahn-Freund, *Labour and the Law*, Stevens, London,
1977, pp. 163–6 and 228–9.
63 Joseph Schumpeter, *History of Economic Analysis*, Oxford University Press, New York, 1954; Lord Robbins, *The Evolution of
Modern Economic Thought*, Adline, Chicago, 1970; William
Stanley Jevons, *The Theory of Political Economy*, edited by R. D.
Collison Black, Penguin, London, 1970; Alfred Marshall, *Principles of Economics*, Ninth Edition, Macmillan, London, 1961.
64 Jevons, *Theory*, p. 13.
65 Schumpeter, *Economic Analysis*, p. 923; see also Jevons,
Theory, pp. 188–216.
66 John Maynard Keynes, *The General Theory of Employment,
Interest, and Money*, Harvest, New York, 1964, see especially
pp. 27–34 and 99–108; D. E. Moggridge, *Maynard Keynes*,
Routledge, London, 1992, especially pp. 557–70.
67 Moggridge, *Keynes*, p. 611.
68 Ibid., p. 96.
69 John Maynard Keynes, *The Economic Consequences of the
Peace*, Harcourt, New York, 1920.

Chapter 2: Corporate Oligopoly

1 *The Big Business Reader*, edited by Mark Green, Pilgrim
Press, New York, 1983, Jim Hightower, 'Food Monopoly',
pp. 3–11; Dan Morgan, *Merchants of Grain*, Penguin, 1980.
2 *Yearbook of Labour Statistics*, International Labour Organisation, Geneva, 1945–89 and 1945–91 editions, Table 2B,
relevant countries.
3 Martin Mittelstaedt, 'Builders Exploit Loophole in tax law',
Globe and Mail, 17 May 1994.
4 Alfred D. Chandler, Jr., *The Visible Hand. The Managerial
Revolution in American Business*, Harvard University Press,
Cambridge, Mass., 1980, p. 4.
5 Ibid., pp. 6–7.
6 Ibid., emphasis added.
7 Chandler, *The Visible Hand*, pp. 79–187.
8 Ferdinand Lundberg, *The Rich and the Super-Rich*, Bantam,
New York, 1969, p. 682.
9 Ron Chernow, *The House of Morgan*, Touchstone, New York,
1990, p. 67.
10 Ibid., p. 82.
11 Ibid., p. 56.
12 David Noble, *America By Design. Science, Technology, and
the Rise of Corporate Capitalism*, Knopf, New York, 1977.

13 Ibid., pp. 6–10, 93–5.
14 Ibid., pp. 89–90.
15 Ibid., p. 16.
16 Ibid., pp. 16–17.
17 Ibid., pp. 116, 120, 122–3.
18 Ibid., pp. 118.
19 Ibid., p. 87.
20 Axel Madsen, *Private Power*, Morrow, New York, 1980, pp. 24–5; *Trilateralism: Trilateralism and Elite Planning for World Management*, edited by Holly Sklar, South End, Boston, 1980, 'Economic Nationalists *v*. Multinational Corporations', pp. 441–5.
21 *Business Week*, 17 July 1989, 'The Global 1000 – The Leaders', p. 139.
22 *World Investment Report 1994*, published by the United Nations Conference on Trade and Development, reported in *Globe and Mail*, 31 August 1994.
23 Michael Tanzer and Stephen Zorn, *Energy Update: Oil in the Late Twentieth Century*, Monthly Review, New York, 1985, pp. 29–30.
24 Anthony Sampson, *The Seven Sisters*, Bantam, New York, 1976, pp. 52–134.
25 Robert Sherrill, 'The Case Against Oil Companies', in *Big Business Reader*, Pilgrim, New York, 1983, pp. 12–17.
26 Exxon and BP company annual reports, 1980 and 1981.
27 Marshall B. Clinard and Peter C. Yeager, *Corporate Crime*, Free Press, New York, 1980.
28 Size and profits of largest companies derived by comparing figures from 'The Fortune 500', *Fortune*, 23 April 1990 with national account figures from *Survey of Current Business*, US Dept. of Commerce.
29 'The Top 1000', *The Globe and Mail Report on Business Magazine*, July 1992.
30 Russell Kelly, *Pattison: Portrait of a Capitalist Superstar*, New Star, Vancouver, 1986.
31 Karel van Wolferen, *The Enigma of Japanese Power*, Vintage, New York, 1990, p. 397.
32 Ibid., pp. 46–7; Clyde Prestowitz, Jr., *Trading Places: How We are Giving Our Future to Japan and How to Reclaim It*, Basic Books, New York, 1989, pp. 300–2.
33 Wolferen, *The Enigma*, pp. 385–6.
34 Roy Thomas, *Japan: The Blighted Blossom*, New Star, Vancouver, 1989, pp. 24–6; see also Prestowitz, *Trading Places*, pp. 8–11, 131, 138–47, 231–3 and Wolferen, pp. 44–6.
35 Bill Emmott, *The Sun Also Sets*, Touchstone, New York, 1991, pp. 105–6; Wolferen, pp. 124–6.

36 Wolferen, *The Enigma*, pp. 61–5.

37 Thomas, *Japan*, pp. 27–9.

38 Ibid., pp. 29–59; Wolferen, *The Enigma*, pp. 117–18, 132–6, 141–3.

39 Endymion Wilkinson, *Japan Versus the West: Images and Reality*, Penguin, London, 1990, p. 161.

40 Shigeto Tsuru, *Essays on Japanese Economy*, Kinokuniya Bookstore, Tokyo, 1977; see also Thomas, *Japan*, pp. 1–21; Prestowitz, *Trading Places*, pp. 293–7; Wolferen, *The Enigma*, pp. 380–5.

41 Ernest van Helvoort, *The Japanese Working Man*, University of British Columbia Press, Vancouver, 1979, pp. 24–5; Thomas, *Japan*, pp. 14–15.

42 Emmott, *The Sun*, p. 21.

43 *Economic Statistics Annual 1990*, Research and Statistics, The Bank of Japan, pp. 331–3.

44 Wilkinson, *Japan Versus the West*, p. 189.

45 Prestowitz, *Trading Places*, pp. 144–7, 307–8.

46 Paul Samuelson, *Economics, An Introductory Analysis*, McGraw Hill, New York, 1951, p. 40.

47 Herschel Hardin, *The New Bureaucracy: Waste and Folly in the Private Sector*, McClelland & Stewart, Toronto, 1991, p. 238.

48 Herb Hammond, *Seeing the Forest Among the Trees – The Case for Wholistic Forest Use*, Polestar, Vancouver, 1992, p. 79; Ian Mahood and Ken Drushka, *Three Men and a Forester*, Harbour, Medeira Park, 1990, p. 224.

49 Hammond, *Seeing*, p. 75.

50 *Employment, Earnings and Hours, 1993*, Statistics Canada, Ottawa, Cat. No. 72–002, Table 7, pp. 57–9; see also Daphne Bramham, 'B.C. Still primary-industry driven', Vancouver *Sun*, 8 June 1994.

51 Hammond, *Seeing*, pp. 62–7; *Jobs, Trees & Us*, Pulp, Paper and Woodworkers of Canada, January, Vancouver, 1993; David Susuki, talk at 'Clayoquot's last stand', Vogue Theatre, Vancouver, 24 June 1993; Joe Garner, *Never Under the Table*, Cinnabar Press, Nanaimo, 1991; Chris Maser, *The Redesigned Forest*, R. & E. Miles, San Pedro, 1988; Orville Camp, *The Forest Farmer's Handbook – A Guide To Natural Selection Forest Management*, Sky River Press, Ashland, Oregon, 1984.

Chapter 3: Corporate Hierarchy

1 Aristotle, *Politics*, The Modern Library, New York, 1943, pp. 140–1.

2 *Globe and Mail*, 'Report on Business'; Dan Westell, 'Big chunk of business in hands of a few', 25 August 1984; Paul Goldstein, '2nd Bronfman empire expands', 21 July 1984.

3 Diane Francis, *Controlling Interest: Who Owns Canada?*, Macmillan, Toronto, 1986.
4 *Taxation Statistics 1982 Edition*, Revenue Canada, Ottawa, Table 2, p. 57 and Table 2A, p. 79. (In totalling income, figures for capital gains were doubled because 50 per cent of capital gains was taxed at the time.)
5 Congressional Joint Economic Committee, reported in *Globe and Mail*, 27 July 1986; *Forbes*, 22 October 1990.
6 G. William Domhoff, *Who Rules America Now?*, Prentice Hall, Englewood Cliffs, N.J., 1983, pp. 36, 43.
7 Clinard and Yeager, *Corporate Crime*, p. 31.
8 Peter F. Drucker, *Concept of the Corporation*, Mentor, New York, 1983, pp. 34, 36.
9 Ibid., pp. 35–6.
10 Ibid., p. 49n.
11 Chandler, *The Visible Hand*, pp. 72–5.
12 Noble, *Design*, p. 24.
13 Ibid., p. 35.
14 Ibid., pp. 264–77.
15 Harry Braverman, *Labor and Monopoly Capital: the Degradation of Work in the Twentieth Century*, Monthly Review, New York, 1974, pp. 112, 113 and 115.
16 Noble, *Design*, pp. 274–7, 280–1, 287–302.
17 'Free Speech Within the Corporation', in *The Big Business Reader*, pp. 302–3.
18 Ibid., p. 294.
19 David F. Noble, *Forces of Production: A Social History of Industrial Automation*, Knopf, New York, 1984.
20 Thomas, *The Blighted Blossum*, p. 136.
21 Ibid., p. 165.
22 Ibid., p. 163.
23 Ibid., p. 164.
24 Ibid., pp. 166–7.
25 A. A. Berle and G. C. Means, *The Modern Corporation and Private Property*, Macmillan, New York, 1933; J. Burnham, *The Managerial Revolution*, Pelican, London, 1945; J. K. Galbraith, *American Capitalism*, Houghton Mifflin, New York, 1952.
26 Domhoff, *Who rules America Now?*, pp. 17–37 and 67.
27 Talcott Parsons, *The Social System*, The Free Press, Glencoe, Illinois, 1951.
28 Vilfredo Pareto, 'Elites, Force and Government', in C. Wright Mills, *Images of Man*, George Braziller, New York, 1960, pp. 262–91.
29 Robert Michels, *Political Parties: A Sociological Study of the Oligarchical Tendencies of Modern Democracy*, Free Press, New York, 1962.

30 Wolferen, *The Enigma*, pp. 111–12.
31 Ibid., pp. 111–12, 120–30.
32 Thomas, *The Blighted Blossum*, pp. 93–120; Wolferen, *The Enigma*, pp. 83–93.
33 Thomas, *The Blighted Blossom*, pp. 69–84.
34 Wolferen, *The Enigma*, pp. 176–81.
35 *Forbes*, 5 October 1987.
36 Thomas, *The Blighted Blossom*, pp. 30–63; Wolferen, *The Enigma*, pp. 127–38.
37 Friedrich A. Hayek, *Law, Legislation and Liberty*, Vol. II, 'The Mirage of Social Justice', Routledge, London, 1976, p. 138.
38 Hayek, *Law, Legislation and Liberty*, Vol. I, 'Rules and Order', Routledge, London, 1973, pp. 50–2.
39 Michael H. Brown, 'Love Canal and the Poisoning of America', *The Big Business Reader*, Pilgrim, New York, 1983, pp. 121–33.
40 'Pinto Madness,' ibid., pp. 32–45.
41 'Bhopal probe discloses horrors', *The Province*, Vancouver, 28 January 1985.
42 Clinard and Yeager, *Corporate Crime*, pp. 116, 119.
43 Ibid., p. 44.
44 Ibid., p. 80.
45 Daniel M. Berman, *Death on the Job: Occupational Health and Safety Struggles in the United States*, Monthly Review, New York, 1978, pp. 39, 43–4, 46.
46 Author's own files. (I represented CBRT & GW, Local 400, Seamen's Section in Federal and British Columbia hearings into the causes of the grounding.)
47 *The World Almanac and Book of Facts 1982*, Newspaper Enterprise Association, Inc., New York, relevant countries.
48 'Salvador death squads threaten leftist leaders', *Globe and Mail*, 14 January 1991.
49 Andre Gunder Frank, *Capitalism and Underdevelopment in Latin America*, Monthly Review, New York, 1969, and *Dependent Accumulation and Underdevelopment*, Monthly Review, New York, 1978.
50 James Connolly, 'Labour in Irish History', in *Labour In Ireland*, Colm O Lochlainn, Dublin, 1922, see especially, pp. 127–37; P. Berresford Ellis, *A History of the Irish Working Class*, Braziller, New York, 1973, see pp. 37–69, 96–121.
51 Sampson, *The Seven Sisters*, pp. 59–69, 70–1, 78–82; Gerard Chaliand (ed.), *People Without a Country: The Kurds and Kurdistan*, translated by Michael Pallis, Zed, London, 1980.
52 H. Montgomery Hyde, *British Air Policy Between the Wars 1918–1939*, Heinemann, London, 1976, p. 92.
53 Ibid., pp. 122–3.

54 Peter Sluglett, *Britain in Iraq 1914–1932*, The Middle East Centre, St. Antony's College, Oxford, 1976, p. 266.
55 Ibid., p. 264.
56 Noam Chomsky, *The Fateful Triangle: the United States, Israel, and the Palestinians*, South End Press, Boston, 1983.
57 R. T. Naylor, 'Faith, Hope and Tax-Exempt Charity: Congress's Deep Pockets and Israel's Long Reach', in *Bankers, Bagmen, and Bandits*, Black Rose, Montreal, 1990, pp. 156–7.
58 Gordon Adams, 'The Iron Triangle: Inside the Weapons Elite', in *Big Business Reader*, pp. 241–7.
59 Smith, *Wealth*, p. 328.
60 'Statement from UNCTAD VI', in *Banking On Poverty*, edited by Jill Torrie, Between the Lines, Toronto, 1983, p. 321.

Chapter 4: The Political Power of the Oligarchy

1 Smith, *Wealth*, p. 250.
2 G. William Domhoff, *Who Rules America Now?*, Prentice Hall, 1983, pp. 123–4.
3 'The Report to the Chief Electoral Officer', *Vancouver Sun*, 5 July 1985.
4 *Forbes*, 22 October 1990, pp. 122–3.
5 *Financial Post*, 'Company Files', 1990.
6 Domhoff, *Who Rules?*, pp. 103–4.
7 Ibid., pp. 92–5.
8 Holly Sklar (ed.), *Trilateralism*, South End Press, 1980.
9 Ibid., pp. 37–8.
10 Mark Green and Andrew Buchsbaum, 'The Corporate Lobbies: The Two Styles of the Business Roundtable and Chamber of Commerce', in *Big Business Reader*, p. 206.
11 Sklar, *Trilateralism*. p. 37.
12 Green and Buchsbaum, *Big Business Reader*, pp. 204–9.
13 Linda McQuaig, *Behind Closed Doors: How the Rich Control Canada's Tax System*, Viking, Toronto, 1987; Linda McQuaig, *The Quick and the Dead: Brian Mulroney, Big Business and the Seduction of Canada*, Viking, Toronto, 1991.
14 Walter Block, *Defending the Undefendable*, Fleet Press, New York, 1976, p. 29.
15 Smith, *Wealth*, p. 321.
16 John Stuart Mill, *Principles*, p. 43.
17 George Gilder, *Wealth and Poverty*, pp. 107–8.
18 Friedrich A. Hayek, *The Road to Serfdom: A classic warning against the dangers to freedom inherent in social planning*, University of Chicago Press, Chicago, 1976.
19 Ibid., p. 75.
20 Friedrich A. Hayek, *Law, Legislation and Liberty*, Vol. I, 1973;

Vol. II, 'The Mirage of Social Justice', Routledge, London, 1976; Vol. III, 'The Political Order of a Free People', University of Chicago Press, Chicago, 1979.

21 Hayak, *Law*, Vol. II, p. 40.
22 Hayek, *Law*, Vol. III, pp. 73–4.
23 Ibid., p. 144.
24 Ibid., pp. 31–2.
25 Hayek, *Serfdom*, p. ix.
26 Hayek, *Law*, Vol. III, p. 12.
27 Milton and Rose Friedman, *Free to Choose*, Avon, New York, 1979, p. 57.
28 Milton and Rose Friedman, *Tyranny of the Status Quo*, Harcourt, New York, 1984, pp. 6–7.
29 Paul Wachtel, *The Poverty of Affluence*, New Society, Philadelphia, Santa Cruz, 1989.
30 Friedman, *Free To Choose*, p. 222.
31 Ibid., pp. 221 and 224.
32 Ibid., p. 224.
33 Milton Friedman, *Capitalism and Freedom*, University of Chicago Press, Chicago, 1962, p. 123.
34 Joseph A. Schumpeter, *Business Cycles: A Theoretical and Statistical Analysis of the Capitalist Process*, Two Volumes, Porcupine Press, Philadelphia, 1982 (reprint of 1939 edition). For a summary of the concept of creative destruction see pp. 87–102
35 Smith, *Wealth*, p. 250.
36 Keynes, *General Theory*, p. 374.
37 *United Kingdom National Accounts*, Government Statistical Service, 1989 edition, Table 1.3.
38 Martin Loney, *The Politics of Greed: the New Right and the Welfare State*, Pluto, London, 1986, p. viii.
39 Mintel Agency, 1994 British Lifestyles, reported in the *Globe and Mail*, 1 February 1994.
40 Smith, *Wealth*, p. 98.
41 *UK National Accounts*, 1989, Table 3.1.
42 Ibid., Table 17.1.
43 Ibid., Table 1.7.
44 'Book of Vital World Statistics 1990', *The Economist*, pp. 40 and 70.
45 Robert Lekachman, *Greed is Not Enough, Reaganomics*, Pantheon, New York, 1982, pp. 44–56; see also Frank Ackerman, *Reaganomics: Rhetoric v. Reality*, South End Press, Boston, 1982.
46 Kevin Phillips, *The Politics of Rich and Poor: Wealth and the American Electorate in the Reagan Aftermath*, Random House, New York, 1990, p. 83.

47 Ibid., pp. 16–18.

48 Madelaine Drohan, 'OECD unemployment cure gets Axworthy's endorsement', *Globe and Mail* 'Report on Business', 8 June 1994.

49 Phillips, *Rich and Poor*, p. 11.

50 Ibid., p. xi, and Appendix B, p. 241.

51 *Statistical Abstract of the United States*, 1990, US Dept. of Commerce, Table 497.

52 Phillips, *Rich and Poor*, p. 79.

53 *Statistical Abstract*, 1990, Table 694.

54 Herchel Hardin, *The New Bureaucracy*, McLelland and Stewart, Toronto, 1992.

55 Stephen Pizzo, Mary Fricker and Paul Muolo, *IN$IDE JOB: The Looting of America's Savings & Loans*, Harper, New York, 1989, pp. 109–64. Figures quoted from p. 162.

56 Ibid., p. 463.

57 Ibid., p. 486.

58 Ibid., p. 390.

59 Ibid., pp. 486–7.

60 *Canadian Economic Observer*, 'Feature Article: the Growth of Federal Debt', Statistics Canada, June 1991, p. 3.6 and *Canadian Economic Observer*, 'Historical Statistical Supplement 1990–91', Table 1.9, p. 18.

61 *OECD Economic Outlook*, 31 July 1982, OECD, Paris, Tables R9, R3, R2 and R1.

62 *Taxation Statistics 1982 Edition*, Revenue Canada Taxation, Table 2, pp. 56–7. (Income from capital gains was doubled to correct for only a half being assessed for tax purposes.)

63 Ibid., Summary Table 2, p. 30; *1992 Edition*, Summary Table 2, p. 88.

64 *Taxation Statistics, 1982 Edition*, Table 2A, p. 141.

65 Linda McQuaig, *The Wealthy Banker's Wife: the Assault on Equality in Canada*, Penguin Books, Toronto, 1993, p. 150.

66 *Quarterly Economic Review*, 'Annual Reference Tables', June 1990, Table 91, p. 139.

67 'Feature Article: Foreign Investment in the Canadian Bond Market, 1978 to 1990', *Canadian Economic Observer*, June 1991, Statistics Canada, pp. 3.19 and 3.27.

68 'Historical Statistical Supplement 1990–91', *Canadian Economic Observer*, Table 1.21, p. 31.

69 Ibid., Table 1.1, p. 2.

70 Ibid., Table 1.21, p. 31.

71 Ibid., Table 1.5, p. 11.

Chapter 5: Globalism

1 CBC documentary, 'Scandal at Sea', Prime Time News, 9 July, 1993. This material also based on conversations with ITF representatives Tom McGrath, Gerry McCullough, Mike James and Peter Lahay.

2 Rodney D. Anderson, *Outcasts in their Own Land – Mexican Industrial Workers 1906–1911*, University of Illinois, 1976, pp. 34–7; James D. Cockroft, *Intellectual Precursors of the Mexican Revolution, 1900–1913*, University of Texas, 1976. pp. 36, 56–7.

3 Anderson, *Outcasts*, p. 100.

4 John Kenneth Turner, *Barbarous Mexico*, University of Texas (reprint), 1969, pp. 1–67.

5 Turner, *Barbarous Mexico*, pp. 106–8; Sampson, *The Seven Sisters*, pp. 100–1; Frank Brandenburg, in *Revolution in Mexico 1910–1940*, edited by James W. Wilkie and Albert L. Michaels, Knopf, New York, 1969, p. 18; Phillip Russell, *Mexico in Transition*, Colorado Rivers Press, Austin, Texas, 1977, pp. 62–75; L. Gutierrez de Lara and Edgcum Pinchon, *The Mexican People – Their Struggle for Freedom*, Doubleday, Garden City, New York, 1914, pp. 277–8, 315–21.

6 Quoted in Brandenburg, in *Revolution in Mexico*, p. 20.

7 Russell, *Mexico in Transition*, p. 62.

8 Anderson, *Outcasts*, pp. 36–7.

9 Ibid., p. 126.

10 Ibid., p. 127.

11 Russell, *Mexico in Transition*, p. 73; Cockroft, *Intellectual Precursors*, p. 29; Turner, *Barbarous Mexico*, pp. 90, 93.

12 Turner, *Barbarous Mexico*, pp. 49–50.

13 Ibid., pp. 54–67.

14 Anderson, *Outcasts*, p. 34.

15 Roy C. Smith, *The Global Bankers*, Truman Talley Books, New York, 1989, pp. 115 and 144.

16 Elaine Elinson, 'The Philippines: the Failure of Bank Strategy', and Sister Mary Soledad Perpinian, 'The Philippines: Collision Course', both in *Banking on Poverty: the Global Impact of the IMF and World Bank*, edited by Jill Torrie, Between the Lines, Toronto, 1983.

17 Elinson, in *Banking on Poverty*, p. 165.

18 Ibid., p. 167.

19 Susan George, *A Fate Worse Than Debt*, Penguin, London, 1989, p. 18.

20 Ricardo, *Principles*, pp. 128–49.

21 Ibid., pp. 136–7; an argument against comparative advantage

can be found in Herman E. Daly and John B. Cobb, Jr., *For the Common Good – Redirecting the Economy Toward Community, the Environment and a Sustainable Future*, Beacon Press, Boston, 1989, pp. 209–18.

22 Smith, *Wealth*, pp. 511–22; Frank, *World Accumulation*, pp. 76, 116–20.

23 *Imperial China*, edited by Franz Schurmann and Orville Schell, Vintage Books, New York, 1967, especially, Tsiang Ting-Fu, 'The English and the Opium Trade', pp. 132–45; Lt. Col. G. J. Wolseley, 'From *War With China*', pp. 155–9; John K. Fairbank, 'The Western Impact', pp. 161–4.

24 Stanford J. Shaw and Ezel Kural Shaw, *History of the Otto-man Empire and Modern Turkey*, Vol. II, 'Reform, Revolution and the Republic', Cambridge University Press, New York, 1977, pp. 122–3, 145–6, 193–5; Maxime Rodinson, *Islam and Capitalism*, translated by Brian Pearce, University of Texas, 1978, pp. 121–3; Bernard Lewis, *The Muslim Discovery of Europe*, W. W. Norton, New York, 1982, pp. 48–9.

25 John Stackhouse, 'Zambians feeling just pain, little gain', *Globe and Mail*, 27 August, 1994.

26 George, *Fate*, pp. 77–85.

27 Richard L. Bernal, 'Jamaica: Democratic Socialism Meets the IMF', and Kari Polanyi Levitt, 'Jamaica: Manley's Defeat – Whose Responsibility?' in *Banking on Poverty*, edited by Jill Torrie, pp. 217–60; George, *Fate*, pp. 178–88.

28 Cheryl Payer, *The Debt Trap: the IMF and the Third World*, Penguin, London, 1974, pp. 143–65; Teresa Hayter, *Aid As Imperialism*, Penguin, London, 1971, pp. 135–42; George, *Fate*, pp. 145–7.

29 George, *Fate*, pp. 137–8.

30 Ibid., p. 236.

31 Ibid., p. 46.

32 Ibid., p. 86.

33 Gunnar Myrdal, *An International Economy: Problems and Prospects*, Harper, New York, 1956, see Chapter XIII, especially pp. 253–4, 275–8, 288–9.

34 United Nations Human Development Report 1992, New York.

35 Michael Bociurkiw, 'Conglomerates dominate day-to-day life', *Globe and Mail*, Report on South Korea, 8 October 1991.

36 Karl Marx, *Capital*, Vol. 1, pp. 873–941.

37 'Flood of cheap Chinese goods hurting neighbors', *Globe and Mail*, 4 July 1994.

38 George, *Fate*, p. 73.

39 'Apocalypse Deferred', *Globe and Mail*, 9 April 1994.

40 R. T. Naylor, *Hot Money and the Politics of Debt*, McLelland and Stewart, Toronto, 1987, especially pp. 327–46.

41 Marilyn Waring, *If Women Counted*, Harper, San Francisco, 1990, pp. 56–7 and 71.

42 Ibid., pp. 235–6 and 278–9.

43 *New Zealand*, 'Country Reports', *The Economist Intelligence Unit*, London, 1993; Julia I. Lane and Peter A. Lane, 'What Price "Free" Markets?', in *Challenge*, September–October1991.

Epilogue

1 *Economic Review*, April 1980, Department of Finance, Canada, Reference Table 62, p. 224.

2 Ibid., Reference Table 63, p. 225.

3 'Annual Reference Tables', *Quarterly Economic Review*, June 1990, Department of Finance, Ottawa, Table 11, p. 21; 'Historical Statistical Supplement 1990–91', *Canadian Economic Observer*, Table 54, p. 93.

4 'The Growth of Federal Debt', *Canadian Economic Observer*, June 1991, pp. 3.1–3.17.

5 *National Accounts, Income and Expenditure 1926–1956*, Dominion Bureau of Statistics, Ottawa, 1958, Table 1, p. 33 and Table 53, p. 96.

6 CANSIM, BI4020.

7 CANSIM, BI4013.

8 *The Consumer Price Index*, May 1993, Statistics Canada, Cat. No. 62–001, Table A, p. 50.

9 Moggeridge, *Keynes*.

10 Michael Moffitt, *The World's Money – International Banking from Bretton Woods to the Brink of Insolvency*, Simon & Schuster, New York, 1983; Roy C. Smith, *The Global Bankers*, Truman Talley, New York, 1990.

11 *Main Economic Indicators*, OECD, Paris, December 1976, pp. 10–11.

12 *Second Annual Review*, Economic Council of Canada, December 1965, Ottawa, Chart 2.2, p. 14; *Main Economic Indicators*, OECD, p. 12.

13 Robert Lekachman, *Economists at Bay: Why the Experts Will Never Solve Your Problems*, McGraw-Hill, New York, 1976, pp. 44–57.

14 *Economic Review April 1980*, Department of Finance, Ottawa, Reference Table 40, p. 202.

15 Michal Kalecki, in *The Last Phase in the Transformation of Capitalism*, Monthly Review, New York, 1972, p. 82.

16 *The Sun*, Vancouver, 8 October 1983.

17 Ibid.

18 Ibid., 10 July 1984.

19 Ibid., 6 July 1993.

20 Smith, *Wealth*, p. 674.

21 Moggridge, *Keynes*, p. 513.

22 See Ravi Batra, *The Myth of Free Trade*, Charles Scribner, New York, 1993.

23 Hayek, *The Political Order of a Free People*, University of Chicago, 1979, p. 68.

24 Axel Madsen, *Private Power*, p. 24; *1994 World Investment Report*, United Nations Conference on Trade and Development, quoted in *Globe and Mail*, 31 August and 5 September 1994.

25 Smith, *Wealth*, p. 340.

26 Herschel Hardin, *The New Bureaucracy*, McLelland and Stewart, Toronto, 1991.

27 Ibid., p. 18.

28 Ibid. and *Globe and Mail*, 26 September 1991.

29 Hardin, *The New Bureaucracy*, p. 151.

30 Ibid., p. 153.

31 Ibid., p. 78.

32 Ibid., p. 162.

33 *Yearbook of Labour Statistics*, International Labour Office, 1945–89 and 1991, Table 2B, relevant countries.

FURTHER READING

On John Locke:
Locke, *Treatise of Civil Government and A Letter Concerning Toleration*, Irvington Publishers, New York, 1937, introduction, pp. vii–x.

Christopher Hill, *The Century of Revolution 1603–1714*, Cardinal, London, 1975.

Christopher Hill, *Reformation to Industrial Revolution*, Penguin, London, 1969.

On the Levellers:
Christopher Hill, *God's Englishman*, Penguin, London, 1970.

Christopher Hill, *The World Turned Upside Down*, Penguin, Harmondsworth, 1975.

Brian Manning, *The English People and the English Revolution*, Penguin, London, 1978.

On the Meiji Restoration and the Building of a Modern Industrial State:
Jon Halliday, *A Political History of Japanese Capitalism*, Monthly Review, New York, 1975.

John Whitney Hall, *Japan from Prehistory to Modern Times*, Dell, New York, 1970.

Richard Story, *A History of Modern Japan*, Penguin, London, 1960.

On the Theory of Oligopolies:
Joan Robinson, *Economic Heresies: Some Old-Fashioned Questions in Economic Theory*, Basic Books, New York, 1971.
Michal Kalecki, *Theory of Economic Dynamics*, Modern Reader, New York, 1965.

On Japan:
Ernest van Helvoort, *The Japanese Working Man*, University of British Columbia Press, Vancouver, 1979.

On the Destruction of the Canadian Merchant Fleet:
Jim Green, *Against the Tide*, Progress Books, Toronto, 1986.
John Stanton, *Life and Death of the Canadian Seamen's Union*, Steel Rail Educational Publishing, Toronto, 1978.

On Early Capitalist Master–Servant Relations in Shipping:
Marcus Rediker, *Between the Devil and the Deep Blue Sea: Merchant Seamen, Pirates, and the Anglo-American Maritime World 1700–1750,* Cambridge University Press, New York, 1987.

On the Treatment of Seafarers on Flag of Convenience Ships:
ITF News, International Transport Workers' Federation, issues 1988 to 1993.

On Freedom and Rights Beyond Capitalism:
C. B. MacPherson, *Property*, University of Toronto, 1978.

On the Struggle Against Capitalism for Democracy in Britain:
Winstanley, *The Law of Freedom and Other Writings*, edited by Christopher Hill, Penguin, London, 1973.
G. D. H. Cole and Raymond Postgate, *The British Common People 1746–1946,* Methuen, London, 1961.
Joyce Marlow, *The Peterloo Massacre*, Granada, London, 1971.
Joyce Marlow, *The Tolpuddle Martyrs*, Granada, London, 1974.

On Capital as a Function of Property Relations:
Michael A. Lebowitz, *Beyond Capital: Marx's Political Economy of the Working Class*, Macmillan, London, 1992.

On Post-capitalist Society:
Karl Marx, *Economic and Philosophical Manuscripts (1844)*, in *Karl Marx, Early Writings*, edited by Quintin Hoare, Vintage, New York, 1975, pp. 279–400.

Index